Ego Psychology
and
Dynamic Casework

Ego Psychology
and
Dynamic Casework

**Papers from the Smith College
School for Social Work**

Edited by Howard J. Parad

FAMILY SERVICE ASSOCIATION OF AMERICA
215 Fourth Avenue   New York 3

48296

Library of Congress Catalog Number: 58–9724

Printed in the U.S.A.   *Price: $4.50*

To

Florence R. Day
July 21, 1898–August 18, 1957

and

Annette Garrett
June 7, 1898–November 16, 1957

*Two great women of courage and distinction who exemplified
in their lives the highest ideals of professional service*

Contributors

Lucille N. Austin, Professor of Social Work at the New York School of Social Work, Columbia University, and member of the graduate seminar faculty, Smith College School for Social Work

Elizabeth Barry, District Agent of the Berkshire County Office, Massachusetts Society for the Prevention of Cruelty to Children

Cornelia T. Biddle, School Social Worker in the Marion County School System, Bryn Mawr, Pennsylvania

Sophie T. Cambria, Professor of Sociology and Anthropology at the Louis N. Rabinowitz School of Social Work, Hunter College, New York

Yonata Feldman, District Supervisor of the Bronx Office of the Jewish Board of Guardians, New York, and faculty member of the Smith College School for Social Work

George E. Gardner, Head of the Department of Psychiatry, Children's Medical Center, and Director, Judge Baker Guidance Center, Boston

Annette Garrett, from 1935 until her death in 1957, Associate Director of the Smith College for Social Work

Gordon Hamilton, recently retired as Professor of Social Work, New York School of Social Work, Columbia University

Florence Hollis, Professor of Social Work, New York School of Social Work, Columbia University, and member of the graduate seminar faculty, Smith College School for Social Work

Flora Hunt, District Director of the Somerville-Arlington-Belmont Office of the Family Service Association of Greater Boston

Irving Kaufman, Staff Psychiatrist of the Judge Baker Guidance Center, Boston, and Lecturer at Smith College School for Social Work

Ner Littner, Psychiatric Consultant to the Illinois Children's Home and Aid Society, Chicago

Grace Nicholls, Assistant Supervisor, Psychiatric Clinic, Massachusetts General Hospital, Boston, and Field Work Supervisor, Smith College School for Social Work

Sylvia Perry, Chief of Social Service, James Jackson Putnam Children's Center in Boston

Norman A. Polansky, Associate Professor of Social Work and Psychology, Western Reserve University, and faculty member of the Smith College School for Social Work

Herman D. Stein, Director of Curriculum Study at the New York School of Social Work, Columbia University, and private consultant to industry

Jerome Weinberger, Staff Psychiatrist of the Massachusetts General Hospital, Department of Child Psychiatry, Boston

Contents

Page

Introduction   1
   Howard J. Parad

Part I—EGO PSYCHOLOGY AND CASEWORK THEORY

1. A Theory of Personality: Freud's Contribution to Social
     Work 11
     Gordon Hamilton, L.H.D., LL.D.

2. Modern Casework: The Contributions of Ego Psychology   38
     Annette Garrett

3. The Worker-Client Relationship 53
     Annette Garrett

4. The Impact of the Client's Unconscious on the Case-
     worker's Reactions 73
     Ner Littner, M.D.

5. Personality Diagnosis in Casework 83
     Florence Hollis, Ph.D.

Part II—SELECTED APPLICATIONS IN CASEWORK PRACTICE

6. Therapeutic Considerations of the Borderline Personality
     Structure 99
     Irving Kaufman, M.D.

7. Basic Concepts in Diagnosis and Treatment of Borderline
     States 111
     Jerome L. Weinberger, M.D.

8. Treatment of a Disturbed Mother-Child Relationship: A
     Case Presentation 117
     Grace Nicholls

CONTENTS

Page

9. Some Problems in Protective Casework Technique: A Case
   Presentation 126
   Elizabeth Barry

10. Dynamics and Treatment of the Client with Anxiety
    Hysteria 137
    Lucille N. Austin

11. The Balanced Expression of Oedipal Remnants 159
    George E. Gardner, Ph.D., M.D.

12. The Conscious Use of Relationship with the Neurotic
    Client 164
    Sylvia Perry

13. Initial Treatment of the Client with Anxiety Hysteria: A
    Case Presentation 174
    Flora Hunt

14. Casework Intervention in a School 183
    Cornelia T. Biddle

Part III—TOWARD NEW KNOWLEDGE FOR PRACTICE

15. Learning Through Recorded Material 203
    Yonata Feldman

16. The Responsibility of School and Agency in Student
    Research 216
    Sophie T. Cambria, Ph.D.

17. Social Science in Social Work Practice and Education 226
    Herman D. Stein

18. Clinical Research in a Child Psychiatry Setting 241
    George E. Gardner, Ph.D., M.D.

19. Getting Down to Cases in Casework Research 254
    Norman A. Polansky, Ph.D.

    Index 276

Introduction

OURS IS a practice-oriented profession. New theories and new methods derive from professional experience and are in turn tested by practice. In recent years, caseworkers have shown intense interest in the structure and functioning of the ego and the ways in which the understanding of ego phenomena can be effectively applied in helping relationships. In recognition of this interest, the Smith College School for Social Work has stimulated the preparation of a number of papers dealing with subjects from the broad range of casework practice—practice that has been illuminated by and has reflected light back to the field of ego psychology. This volume contains a collection of these papers.

The reader will find in these pages a series of interrelated inquiries into the dynamics of personality and the technical problems of casework treatment. Problems are inevitable in a profession that has developed as rapidly as has social work during the past few decades. It is neither essential nor desirable that there be agreement about the extent or solution of these problems. For example, differences of opinion are apparent on a number of issues, such as the extent to which the worker can understand and deal with unconscious derivatives in the interview situation, and the validity of initiating discussion of sexual problems with the neurotic client. A number of other technical questions are discussed: Is the sex of the worker of importance in the treatment of certain cases? How much self-awareness is demanded of the student by the supervisor? How can research of casework problems best move forward?

This volume is perhaps best used as a book of readings, since these contributions do not pretend to offer a definitive or summary statement of social casework theory. Rather they represent explorations into the subtleties of diagnosis and treatment.

1

For purposes of organization, the papers have been divided into three parts: (1) Ego Psychology and Casework Theory, (2) Selected Applications in Casework Practice, and (3) Toward New Knowledge for Practice. Of necessity, some overlap is involved in any such division. For example, some of the papers in Part II deal with theoretical considerations as well as applications to practice. It seemed best to include them in this section, because they are mainly concerned with the translation of ego theory into casework theory and the application of treatment principles to specific types of psychosocial dysfunctioning.

Part I begins with a paper that appraises the influence of psychoanalysis on casework and points to the fact that ego psychology serves as a connecting link between early and present-day casework practice. This paper traces the dramatic evolution of casework, from the pioneer formulations of Mary Richmond to our contemporary emphasis on the psychosocial concept, depicting clearly the impact of Freud and the theory of personality which has evolved from his great discoveries. Other papers in this section analyze the anatomy of the worker-client relationship, the nature of transference phenomena in the interview situation, the components of personality diagnosis, and the way these various factors mold the casework treatment plan. A basic ego-centered approach to treatment classification is also presented.

Two main questions emerge from the papers in this section. In what specific way has ego psychology contributed to casework theory? What new treatment techniques has it made available to caseworkers?

Ego psychology provides us with a comprehensive approach to understanding how the human personality deals with the complicated network of forces and counterforces from instinct, conscience, and the larger sociocultural environment. It affords penetrating insights into the ego's patterns of adaptation and its way of coping with, and mastering, ordinary demands and extraordinary stresses, both internal and external. It provides us with an understanding of ego defenses against various kinds of anxiety and the part they play in everyday social functioning. At the same time, it makes clear that it is an empty gesture merely to label defenses, for to be of real help to a client we must know not only the "what" of his

2

defenses but also the "how" and "why"—how they are used and with what specific effects for him as a unique person. For example, it enables us to differentiate the healthy adaptive features of repression and denial from the maladaptive ones.

By emphasizing proper appraisal of the ego's integrative capacities, ego psychology gives us a view of the total person so that our diagnostic formulations assume depth and breadth. It sheds light on the causative factors in personal and interpersonal breakdown and makes possible a dynamic implementation of the "person-in-situation" approach. This is far more effective than our former static and stiff categorization of assets and liabilities that generalized more than it specified what was true for *the* human being who required our help. As our diagnostic understanding became more precise, it was possible to develop differential techniques and to focus treatment in a way that brought better results. In consequence, casework resources have been deployed in a more purposeful manner. Making the most effective use of casework time is, of course, no academic matter in this era of rapidly expanding social services.

In brief, then, our increased understanding of the ego has led to the weaving of dynamic psychology into the fabric of casework theory and practice. Ego psychology is a total, not a partial, concept. It includes at once the interconnections between unconscious libidinal factors, conscious adaptive patterns of behavior, and the elements of support, stimulation, or hindrance in the interpersonal sphere in which the client and his family live.

Part II introduces selected applications of insights stimulated by ego psychology. In work with neurotic clients whose ego capacities are intact, we are reasonably sure of our efficacy as remedial agents. In dealing with clients who have serious ego deviations, however, we have much to learn about underlying dynamics and successful ways of interrupting lifelong patterns of impulsiveness, neglect, and antisocial behavior. The effects of unintegrated ego functioning in these clients are seen in their poor reality perception, failure to learn from experience, unsatisfactory object relations, and primitive aggressive behavior. The contributors to this section believe that, despite such serious problems, many of these disturbed clients can be reached and helped as a result of our increasing diagnostic acumen.

The papers on clients with anxiety hysteria indicate how the caseworker can help such persons to a much fuller life through freeing the ego capacities that have been bound by neurotic conflict. The authors also point to the collaborative roles of the psychiatrist and the caseworker and make some useful suggestions for deciding between casework and psychiatry as the treatment of choice.

This section also includes a paper that applies ego psychology principles to the child's problem in learning and in adapting to a school setting. The author shows how the school experience fosters in the child the attainment of the social, motor, and intellectual skills that are so important to the ego in dealing with developmental tasks. A clear example is offered of how the caseworker uses this understanding for therapeutic intervention when normal growth and healthy adaptation are threatened.

The papers in this section suggest that the formulations of ego theory, although still in process of development and refinement, will continue to have far-reaching implications for our future direction in practice. They should help to open new avenues for productive collaboration between caseworkers and persons in related disciplines.

The articles in Part III consider some of the factors involved in the profession's thrust for new knowledge. The first paper demonstrates how the supervisor can pace the teaching of new material to the student or practitioner through use of recorded material. Basing teaching method on an appreciation of how new knowledge can be mastered, the supervisor helps the student gradually bring his intuitive ability under the service of the ego. The aim is to avoid cleavage between the student's feelings and conscious use of casework techniques.

Mindful that today's social work student will be tomorrow's research designer, data gatherer, or informed practitioner, we have included in this section a concise statement of the goal, method, and challenge of student research. Often, the worker's orientation to research has been crystallized during the period of graduate preparation. In this process, thesis adviser, field supervisor, and *all* faculty members act as culture-bearers. They determine whether positive and knowledgeable or negative and deprecatory attitudes toward research will be transmitted.

4

Ways of furthering productive use of social science materials in social work, as well as the importance of fostering new patterns of interprofessional collaboration, are discussed. There are pitfalls to be avoided in these co-operative activities, such as the magical expectation that social science will make our discoveries for us. The other pitfalls are remarkably similar to the ones we have already experienced in our use of the psychiatric consultant in agency practice.

In this section the research advantages of the intramural, clinic, team approach will be noted. Yet one should not overlook the resourceful use of extramural teams, as exemplified in those agencies that are constructively utilizing in their research outside assistance from both psychiatric and social science consultants. Nor should we minimize the value of imaginative case study or "wisdom research" which can be profitably undertaken by social workers themselves.

This section concludes with an invigorating paper that challenges the profession to convert its current platitudes about extending the frontiers of knowledge into palpable realities. Various types of research activity are discussed which offer guidelines for the present and may yield rich dividends for future practice. Concrete suggestions are made concerning the direction that casework research should take if it is to make discoveries that will maximize the number of therapeutic successes and minimize the number of failures.

The articles in this section all stress the need for scientific motivation and personal investment in advancing knowledge if research is to produce the desired results. There must be leadership in both schools and agencies, to engage the practitioner's zeal and mobilize those qualities of steadfastness necessary for the tasks at hand. Broadly speaking, these tasks are twofold: To discover urgently needed new knowledge of the causative factors in maladaptation; and to find ways of increasing the benefits of our therapeutic intervention in those situations still inaccessible to casework.

It is hoped that the reader—whether student, practitioner, or educator—will be rewarded by gaining a new perspective on areas of controversy within the profession. These areas are often befogged by the use of illusory labels and the creation of deceptive dichotomies. A partial and cursory listing of these dichotomies might include:

1. *The unconscious versus the conscious.* The attempt to limit the area of competence or of interest of social work to conscious phenomena negates the fact that we work with human beings. Since our interest is in people and their adaptations, unconscious phenomena cannot be ruled out as irrelevant. We have a professional responsibility to understand and deal appropriately with such phenomena and in doing so we are not, as one of our contributors points out, poaching on another profession's territory.

2. *The individual versus the environment.* This schism is an old skeleton that reappears in our family closet whenever we think we have dispatched it for good. The articles in this volume all subscribe to the view that the "individual-in-culture" or the "person-in-situation" constitutes the only sensible social work approach.

3. *Research versus practice.* The papers in this volume make it abundantly clear that research and practice must come together in the interest of the clients we serve. Our contributors make a plea for *research-oriented practice* and *practice-oriented research,* and we hope this plea will not be ignored.

4. *Generic versus specific.* The case material in this volume reflects a generic orientation to social work knowledge and method. The techniques discussed, such as ego support and the differential use of the relationship, are relevant to current practice in all social work settings.

5. *Treatment versus prevention.* Although there are qualitative differences between certain services, some being more clearly preventive and others more clearly restorative, the demarcation between the two cannot be sharply drawn. Treatment that results in improvement in a client's functioning usually prevents further deterioration and has the added advantage of preventing disturbances in other family members. The case presentations exemplify the preventive aspects of effective casework treatment.

Ego psychology has given us a firmer grasp of the fundamentals of human motivation and behavior, enabling us to be much more skilful in helping people to mobilize and fulfil their capacities. Although we have much to learn, social work is moving into an era that promises new understanding and new techniques for dealing with old problems. It will be an era of rich fulfilment of the traditional humanistic ideals of social work, so that human energies and talents will be increasingly released for creative and productive living.

Acknowledgments

The impetus for preparing this book came largely from the many requests that the Smith College School for Social Work received for copies of the papers presented at various lecture series sponsored by the Alumnae Association. It therefore seemed desirable to publish them together and to supplement them with a few other published papers that were no longer available.

I should like to express appreciation to the chapters of the Alumnae Association which have sponsored the professional forums at which these papers were presented. Our greatest debt of gratitude, of course, is to the contributing authors.

Where space permitted, a few shorter papers presented as discussions at these meetings have been included. These shorter papers, in general, elaborate points made by the major contributors. As part of the editorial plan, we have also included a variety of case illustrations. We hope that these cases will serve as an aid to the reader in relating theory to practice; they should also help him draw his own conclusions about the pertinence and value of the theoretical formulations. Although no effort at complete representation of setting has been made, the cases were chosen to demonstrate the scope of practice which has drawn on the findings of ego psychology.

We extend our thanks to the American Orthopsychiatric Association for permission to reprint "The Worker-Client Relationship" by Annette Garrett (which has been in great demand) and "Clinical Research in a Child Psychiatry Setting" by Dr. George E. Gardner, both of which appeared in the *American Journal of Orthopsychiatry*. The original sources of publication of all reprinted articles are given in footnotes to the chapters.

I am indebted to the members of the Smith College School for Social Work faculty who read articles and manuscripts and who made suggestions about the contents of this volume. Of this group,

Esther H. Clemence, Norman A. Polansky, and Nancy Staver have been especially generous with their time.

Special thanks are also due to Cora Kasius and Shirley M. Martin of the Family Service Association of America for their valuable assistance in the preparation of this volume.

Finally, I want to record a word of appreciation to my wife, Libbie Parad, for her help with the index.

HOWARD J. PARAD, *Director*
Smith College School for Social Work

Northampton, Massachusetts
March, 1958

Part I

Ego Psychology and
Casework Theory

1. A Theory of Personality: Freud's Contribution to Social Work *

Gordon Hamilton

ALTHOUGH I HAVE ASSIGNED myself this extraordinarily difficult task, I have not the presumption to restate what is already so familiar—those great hypotheses of Freud which not only "troubled the sleep of the world," but changed fundamentally man's most significant perceptions into the inner world of the human being. I shall attempt to discuss here only how Freud's theory of personality, his psychoanalytic therapy, the illumination thus cast upon anxiety, child development, the family, and the professional use of relationship, made casework not only what it is today, but what it may become. Freud not only radically changed social work practice, but fundamentally affected professional education. In this paper I shall restrict myself to Freud's effect on casework, but it is obvious that a theory of personality, if true at all, is fundamental in all social work processes and for all interpersonal relationships. The contemporary revolution in group work, in which treatment goals and means are also substantially influenced by the same theory, is momentous, but I do not have the experience or the data to do justice to these trends and adaptations in group processes.

Freud was born in 1856 and, as everyone knows, outlined his preliminary views in 1895 in a work written with Joseph Breuer.

* Presented at a meeting sponsored by the Chicago Chapter of the Smith College School for Social Work Alumnae Association, Chicago, May 6, 1957.

In this article the reference numbers refer to the bibliography at the end.

11

Between this time and his death in 1939, his new psychology slowly penetrated everywhere. Psychoanalysis as an evolving body of theory is today more complicated than when, in various direct and indirect ways, it began to transform the social casework of my generation. It will continue to be difficult to comprehend and, as is true of every scientific theory, some concepts will be modified and some replaced by new discoveries. Meanwhile we may recount with humility and awe how, within the professional life of some of us, the influence of Freud and the Freudians changed a social process into a psychosocial process, changed the casework social history, through the new psychogenetic approach, into a theory of growth and development, revolutionized diagnosis, and gave social work its first glimpse of the possibility of treatment in other than environmental terms.

The Pre-Freudian Period

Let us ask the question: What did Freud's theory of personality, his therapeutic principles and method, do to social casework? As one who entered social work before its Freudian period (although psychiatric social work had been building, chiefly in Boston, with some Freudian emphases, for more than a decade), I lived through a mind- and life-shaking revolution. Freud's creative genius did for the human spirit what political revolutions sometimes aim to do and sometimes partially succeed in doing—free the mind and actions of the common man for further self-realization and self-development. Although we were often chided with determinism, those of us who found Freud found a new liberty, a power to choose, hitherto circumscribed by ignorance and our own neuroses.

I shall first describe how most of us practiced family social work in the East in the early twenties. *Social Diagnosis,* published in 1917, was a scientific and logical approach to social investigation. Mary Richmond had always intended to follow this book by a volume on treatment, but it is my personal conviction that she was, in part, blocked from doing this by the new psychoanalytic psychiatry, which she found disturbing, if not alarming. I cannot document this observation, but in my contacts with Mary Richmond she always spoke with immense distaste of Freud, although she was interested in Jung, who seemed to her to be "moral." She also admired

12

greatly the work of Adolf Meyer at Johns Hopkins. Looking back, one sees that the early volumes of *The Family* and of the *Charity Organization Bulletin* dealt with social issues, agency structure, and fervid appeals for casework methods of study. What actually was treated was the *problem*—desertion, alcoholism, poverty, or illegitimacy—rather than the person. There were few articles in any social work publication which dealt with treatment as process or, indeed, treatment in any therapeutic sense.

A common formula in family casework for the deserted family was to put the children in a day nursery and have the woman go to work. It was thought by social workers, boards of agencies, volunteers, and society in general, that desertion, like other "bad" behavior, should be punished, and that if self-help failed, the family must acquiesce in the economic and other burdens laid upon it. We should be less than knowledgeable if we imagined that this represented hard-heartedness on the part of social workers and philanthropists. There were always those who worked hard to improve social conditions and block the downward path. The truth was simply that the causes of behavior were little understood and the culture imposed its morals and values on social work, as on all the humanistic professions. It would not be true to say that the casework of Richmond was narrowly social, since she called attention to insights as well as to services, or actions, and underlined the importance of the worker-client relationship.[12] However, there were then, and indeed there still are, attempts to restrict casework to those operations that involve social services and to split off counseling and psychotherapy from the unity of casework treatment. It goes without saying that in the early days of casework, and even in its "dark ages," there were always individual leaders full of compassion and intuitively gifted in helping others. It was a long time, however, before the phrase "not alms but a friend" comprised the idea of giving services and counseling as a friend or through the use of relationship.

Casework prior to World War I had a socio-economic, rather than a psychosocial, center. Stability was highly prized. The family was not only the unit of work, but the repository of all goodness. Workers' goals for family and individual adjustment were not characterized by uncertainty. Indeed, there was a well-known worker who approached all unmarried mothers with a pocketful of wedding rings! In social work, however, a liberal philosophy of welfare was beginning to surge forward. Trade unions were forming. Teachers like Edward T. Devine and Edith and Grace Abbott were enlarging men's vision in the sphere of economics—on such topics as minimum wage, social legislation for children, adequate standards of assistance, prevention and relief of unemployment. Julia Lathrop and Jane Addams were preaching and demonstrating social action. The piecemeal remedies of the old Poor Laws were giving place to new concepts of assistance and insurance, but in the realm of personality, concepts remained relatively static, and the gain in therapeutic skill minimal. Into this era of moral conformity Freud's theory of personality burst like the atom, and the "fall out" from that explosion proved extremely frightening to many people both in and out of the profession. The tremendous consequences, however, which flowed from Freud's dedication of his discoveries *to the science of healing* can never be adequately expressed. He taught not only a new way of thinking about people, but an entirely new way of helping them.

Investigation, Diagnosis, and Treatment

Annette Garrett tells us that when she entered casework at the end of the Richmond period and the beginning of the psychoanalytic emphasis, the history-gathering aspect of casework was dominant. Psychiatrists in child guidance clinics were teaching the importance of facts and were helping social workers toward selectivity of relevant facts. Still, many of us labored under the delusion that if we had enough facts we would know what to do. Early history had been largely sociological but, with the advent of Freud, history became psychogenetic, that is, "psychosocial" and "dynamic."

The early child guidance movement had taught social workers to gather history so as to observe life patterns. Knowledge and understanding of the child's bio-psychological growth process, especially in infancy, the nursery years, and in the struggle to solve the problem of the "parents as a couple," * revolutionized ideas of family

* A phrase used by Dr. J. H. W. van Ophuijsen, indicating their not belonging to the child exclusively, as he wishes, but to each other; in short, the oedipal situation.

relationship and of interaction. The component parts of the personality—ego, superego, and id—became not merely usable in understanding behavior, but essential in focusing treatment. All of us came to realize, as Freud himself insisted, that the assimilated facts of personality make-up, like the facts of bodily make-up, "must be a long time practiced clinically" before psychiatry could become art as well as science. Those who had told us that social insurance would decrease the intake of social agencies by 75 per cent were thinking only in terms of economic dependence, rather than personality adjustment. Who knew better than caseworkers that when all untoward things had been prevented or abolished—unless they prevented or abolished people—social work would still have a job? Caseworkers now began the slow uphill climb to practice clinically, with therapeutic aims and tools that were to change the profile of social work.

It was a new approach to incorporate into histories the growth and development of children, the effects of gratification and frustration, fixation, and regression. Among other influences, Dr. David Levy's "attitude therapy" had encouraged the social worker to work with parents as persons.[23] This inevitably brought the social worker into a treatment (therapeutic) relationship with the adults in the child guidance clinic, a role that would have been useless had it not been for the light thrown on *all* family relationships through Freud's theory of personality.

Many social workers trained in child guidance clinics had begun to assume leadership positions in family and children's agencies; understanding parent-child relationships genetically, they could now, with the help of analytic consultants, be concerned with the affective aspects of family relationships with which the ego could not cope. Social workers came to see how anxiety can be a useful danger signal or a crippling force; how too much repression may lead to neurosis; how too little repression and integration of love and aggression may lead to "acting out." In the uncared-for infant, known to both family and children's agencies long before his parents might bring him into a child guidance clinic, one could observe fear of desertion and of loss of love, normal and abnormal types of anxiety, the survival of fears, repression, and sometimes, happily, the resolution of conflict. Social workers viewing behavior

15

in this context could not disregard the signs of psychopathology, even though they only supported ego strengths and family balance; such support was supposed to be the sole appropriate focus for their attention. They could not help but understand what they already knew empirically, that is, that many marital relationships are established to escape anxiety; that the marital partner or the children may serve the purpose of saving the individual from neurotic or psychotic breakdown; that the family as a whole may serve as a bastion against strains and so uphold the weak ego of one of its members; or that there may be too much unconscious compliance with family patterns. Perhaps the most important thing they learned from the consultants was to recognize certain differentials in treatment, not only among clinical diagnoses, such as psychoneuroses, psychoses, and character disorders, but between methods appropriate for adults and for children.

Dr. Karl Menninger [27] is my authority for saying that there was almost no "sex" in early American psychiatry. I remember that, when I was engaged on a research project at Presbyterian Hospital in New York to incorporate social diagnosis into the medical record, I was cautioned to be careful not to mention sex because "the doctors didn't like it." Also, there was little sex in early group work, even when acted out in plain view, and almost none described in Gesell's early observations and by many nursery schools. As Lucille Austin notes, the child "had to pretend innocence in order to keep the parent from knowing how much he knew about sexual matters and how intense was his sexual life." * One thing that psychoanalysis did for social work, as for psychiatry and education, was to help everyone to understand the inner life of the client and the significance of family interaction, hitherto approached as a moral problem.

Since medical psychiatry was individualistic, the new child guidance concept of family interaction was carried out through "the team." The first emphasis was on manipulation of the parents for the child's good, with a later trend toward psychological treatment of the parent as "patient." The position taken by child-guidance oriented analysts, however, that one must *treat* parents if one wants to help children, began to shift the approach from manipulative

* See p. 144 of this volume.

16

guidance to therapy. The age of the child became important in differential techniques for both the child and his parents. A child in latency or puberty was considered to have his distinctive problems. The parent-child relationship was no longer viewed merely in culturally traditional terms, but as a variant of the unresolved oedipal situation, with problems of rivalry, of choice of love objects, and of identifications. In short, it became clear that the parental role cannot be understood without an understanding of the motivations and drives of parents and that children are often the focus, or extension, of parental frustrations and anxieties, serving as a channel through which unconscious drives and hostilities are acted out. In fact, parental hostility, for a long time, was thought to be an almost universal ingredient in child guidance cases, and workers tried to coax it forth in the interview.

The work of the neo-Freudians, such as Sullivan, Horney, Fromm, and others, supplied an important cultural orientation.[28] Most social workers of the period considered culture to be internalized largely through the family and perceived few of the other sources of acculturation. The libido theory, in general, was renounced by the "revisionists." How one can understand culture without Freud's libido formulations remains a mystery to me.

What, indeed, can one say about the staggering theory of the unconscious? For obvious reasons this is hard to pin down. Many workers familiar with the concept that behavior is purposive did not at all understand the unconscious determinants of behavior. Many workers who slid easily into the notion that they were parental surrogates in the parent-child situation knew little of transference as expressed within the interview situation. A few workers, analyzed early, thought they could get close to the infantile neurosis through techniques modeled as closely as possible on their own analyses. It was a long time before experience in practicing clinically and the hard realities of analytic psychology taught us how to work with derivatives of the unconscious, and particularly with the defenses. Understanding these derivatives and what the wisest, best-taught, and most humble learned about defenses, transference, and countertransference, radically changed the whole basis and techniques of interviewing, including play interviews with children. Taught earlier to be "objective," the worker now had to learn to

17

manage the transference situation and not to exploit the transference neurosis, to refrain more often than not from the alluring possibility of interpreting phases of relationship and—even more difficult—to recognize and control, if possible, his own reactions. Social workers, typically, confronted with deprived people and demanding transference attitudes, were all too easily precipitated into exaggerated sympathy or "hard-boiled" defenses. Sincere interest had to be constantly balanced by reality testing.

Somewhat arbitrarily I should like to select three aspects of psychoanalytic theory which had the greatest impact on social work and did most to transform casework practice.

1. Even after the client's social history had become a history of growth and development, it was some time before we realized that a very factual-appearing social history cannot be taken literally. Because of the client's defensive structure, there is often distortion. This recognition does not mean that one points out the distortions to the client, then or subsequently, but one must understand that they may be present.

2. Before caseworkers understood psychodynamic theory they realized that much of the client's ingratiating approach or his hostility was not beamed at the worker. This knowledge was the beginning of a long process of understanding the basic positive transference, ambivalence, the necessity to recognize transference reactions whenever they occur, and the rare but important exceptions to the rule of not interpreting the transference.

3. It took years of practicing clinically—and the problem is as yet by no means solved—before we realized that the "insightful" worker must understand how often the parents' complaints against a problem child are a repetition of his own childhood experiences and attitudes (displacement), and have little to do with the reality of the child's problem. Other displacements and defenses are, of course, now familiar to practitioners.*

---

* I am indebted to Mrs. Yonata Feldman for a fragmentary observation which illustrates a common child guidance problem:
The mother, who is very fat, in the initial history and in subsequent interviews complains constantly that her son, who has a number of annoying behavior disorders, insists on eating all the time, raiding the refrigerator against permission, and that his father does the same thing. This is no doubt true. It becomes increasingly evident that denial of love, expressed by food, is the mother's own problem. The worker says, in effect, in one or two

Aichhorn,[1] Glover,[14] and others have insisted that at least with certain delinquents (those with character disorders), as well as with psychotics, the primary concern or therapeutic objective is to *socialize the person*. The social worker of today is rediscovering the unique combination of social and psychological therapies most effective with the acting-out offender. The social worker once again finds that he should make contact with the client on as many levels as possible. He must help the client not only to modify his feelings but also to think more intelligently and rationally. It is not Freud's fault—great scientist and intellectual that he was— that social workers were feeling their way like blind men through the interview, instead of opening their eyes to see, stopping to think, and so helping the clients move away from the office interview into their life situations.

It is important to emphasize again that to practice clinically means to understand not only general considerations about psychoneurotics, but that antisocial behavior in children may stem from responses to unspoken, as well as overt, attitudes and behavior of their parents. Deviations in instinctual development, seduction, and unconscious gratification must be reckoned with. This knowledge reinforces the current emphasis on interpersonal, multiple-patient focus which has always been characteristic of social work. Treatment of the whole family is once more a valid aim with greatly improved techniques.

By the middle thirties, caseworkers had arrived at several important recognitions: the disappearance of symptoms was not considered an evidence of cure; development of differential treatment on the one hand, and the failure of treatment on the other, pointed toward the need for research rather than to a decision to rule out clients as inaccessible to treatment. Although there was steadily more reference to resistance in the Freudian sense and to defenses, social workers, like analysts, had for the most part worked with neurotics—chiefly persons with anxiety hysteria and, particularly

interviews, "Food is good. Is it so bad to eat?", and working along this line gently and patiently brings out the woman's own extreme libidinal deprivation. This understanding and permission reaches into the home in all sorts of ways which cannot be reproduced here, but the net result is that as the eating habits of all three change—within the transference and, with the worker's insight—the home atmosphere becomes less tense. As an unanticipated bonus, the mother herself finds other satisfactions than food and, happily, loses weight.

19

in child guidance clinics, with compulsive parents. Few social workers had the clinical knowledge and experience to meet head-on the naked impulses of the psychotic (although there were many psychotic clients in family agency caseloads); and there were few qualified social workers in the field of corrections, where acting out (impulsivity) in delinquency was the chief mode of behavior. In mental hospitals, the role of the social worker was chiefly allocated to the relatives of the patient. The applicant, not the hard-to-reach person, was the acceptable client. In the referred case social work somehow had lost its interpersonal role, with the spouse-spouse, parent-child, patient and patient group. Behavior disorders were indeed familiar, but in the child guidance clinic the child was usually treated by the psychiatrist, and in the family agency the alcoholic or abusive or deserting spouse was seldom a participating client.

Federn, in relation to the treatment of psychotics, had pointed out that "in manifest and latent psychoses the typical analysis used in neuroses is harmful and must be abandoned, or used only in homeopathic doses—a dosage so small that it does not inhibit any function and provokes only very slow change." [7] His techniques suggested a comparatively new approach to support of the ego which could not even be understood without grasp of the meaning of the defenses and resistance, and which called for an imaginative use of reality opportunities and controls. It took social workers some time to recognize that the release of the id forces, which they had been seeking through various types of cathartic interviews, was constantly blocked by the defensive reactions of the ego. By the late thirties, papers on resistance [3] and on finding and supporting the ego strength [25] of the client were being published, although sometimes written by those who were discounting or ignoring Freud's unique discovery of the phenomenon of resistance. Defenses were too often equated with resistance; the less well-taught worker "lowered the boom" on any defense, much as the worker before the period of ego psychology watched, with excitement, for any manifestation of infantile neurosis.

I shall not take time to review the "diagnostic" and "functional" disparities of the post-Freudian era. Suffice it to say that by 1933 the gap between two methods—the diagnostic (Freudian), directed toward the family and interpersonal relationships, and the functional (Rankian), in which therapy was almost exclusively based on the use of the self in a one-to-one relationship—was widening. As a by-product of the nondirective techniques of this period, sometimes called passivity, there was for the functional group renunciation of any surrogate "parental" role. Pleasure, pain, and responsibility for the self in the relationship were both means and end. There is no doubt that the emphasis on self-determination by the client was good, but obviously this value alone could not equally reach all types of persons or all levels of problems. The shift by both groups from doing things *for* people to helping clients to do things *with* the caseworker and for themselves led, in extremes, to a "client-centered" therapy which often became, for the client, a fruitless recounting of feelings and experiences.

The use of time as a dynamic and control was practiced. Workers, from their own personal analyses, introduced the hour interview, which became conventional with the diagnostic group, and a special control or limit with the functional group. There was a decided swing away from external reality and a preoccupation with the intrapsychic factors. Jessie Taft and others thought that the workers should not be entangled with the client's external reality or concern themselves with his past. What she called "active" attention, by identifying or adapting to whatever came through in the interview, was considered an adequate basis for the treatment itself. Time limits were used to effect short contacts. Diagnostic workers took directly from their personal analyses the "patient" focus, with unhappy detachment of the "patient" not only from other persons but from social reality itself.

Reality, Ego Strength, and Ego Psychology

Let us turn the clock back to the late twenties for a moment. As pursuit of emotional material took workers farther and farther into the deeper realms of the personality, the specter of emotional dependency, even more frightening than the economic dependency to which workers had become unhappily accustomed, aroused new anxieties. Grace Marcus, then in the family field, was one of the first to bring out the extent of emotional need which seemed to her little short of "ominous."

21

Comprehension of dependency in its wider, deeper significance is a recent development not yet become the common currency of casework . . . underlying the financial dependencies are emotional dependencies that may undermine the possibilities of financial rehabilitation and if these emotional dependencies can be handled at all, they must be handled by casework.[26]

When America headed into the bleak depression of the thirties, caseworkers, already preoccupied with the uncertainties, fears, and profound dependency to which they were exposed, carried a grim load. In those terrible winters of barest survival, it was astonishing to see, over and over again, the resilience of the human being. As one managed to face, ashamed and discouraged as one was, not only the clients' needs for all too minimal food and shelter, but the engulfing emotional fear and rage from those who could find no jobs nor look after their families, one again had to come to terms with the hard facts of feelings as well as of jobs. Our thankfulness for the Social Security Act of 1935 perhaps only increased the challenge to work for emotional security as well. Professional education,[16] interacting with professional practice, came to consider the total functioning of the personality in a real world, balanced with self-awareness essential to the controlled use of the self.

When ego psychology began to permeate psychoanalytic theory, caseworkers would no doubt have grasped its importance even if they had not been harrowed in a literal sense by reality stresses of the depression years. The experience of this period helped them to rediscover those inner resources of character to which casework itself had always been attuned. It is part of man's heritage that under the greatest pressures he seems to attain his greatest stature. Perhaps the renewed emphasis on ego strength [7] was a desperate last stand in a world that was crumbling to pieces; perhaps it was part of the vision of man's strength and sturdiness under adversity. (The dignity and courage of Freud bear witness to this.) Certainly casework method was again fundamentally reorganized as new ways, not merely of accrediting but of working with ego strength, were found. Perhaps so long as the personality functions fairly normally and society is stable, one cannot fully sense what Federn calls "the ego feeling." His studies of the functional patterns of the ego led not only psychiatrists and analysts, but social workers, to a fresh orientation in treatment. The groundwork both for defenses and

22

ego psychology was laid by Freud, but it was Anna Freud [9] who pointed most clearly to the new road that psychosocial therapy must take.

It was one of the aberrant features of the attempt to carry psychoanalytic principles and techniques, primarily concerned with the neurotic, into casework that treatment became so preoccupied with the inner life as almost to lose touch with outer reality and the social factors with which social workers were most familiar. It was primarily through the application of ego psychology to persons with mental illness and character disorders that its chief lesson was finally learned, namely, that capacity for social functioning continues to develop of its own accord, or within ordinary experience, if one can succeed in bringing the person back into social reality and to take an active part in it. This has been repeatedly found true with relation to the adolescent, the mentally ill, the aged, the feeble-minded, and many types of delinquents—indeed, just all of us.

I shall not deal extensively with the effects of ego psychology on casework practice, since this has been so admirably treated by Annette Garrett in another paper in this series.* She has shown how ego psychology, beginning with Freud's formulations, has sharpened diagnostic procedures; given caseworkers a healthy respect for the phenomenon of resistance; helped develop differential treatment approaches; and given us new tools to build up strengths in the personality and to support constructive defenses. Caseworkers, in short, stopped digging for "undistorted id impulses" and began to work with the derivatives of the unconscious, with impulses as disguised and modified by ordinary concerns, relationships, activities, attitudes, and behavior. Uncovering techniques are now sparingly used even when the ego is strong enough to permit pointing up and clarification of unconscious motivations. Since clients live out their unconscious impulses through action, this dimension can be effectively used in casework for understanding and treating problems of social functioning.

Social workers had been taught early to regard behavior as purposive, as symptomatic, but it has only been during the last two decades that they have worked with the defenses, as such. The

* See Chapter 2 of this volume.

23

first approach was to try to attack and so "remove" the defense, largely through interpretation. Confronted with a defense, many social workers felt compelled to puncture it, and in this they were astonished to find themselves faced with a new series of defenses, including much hostility. Bit by bit one came to make use of, to elaborate and refine, supportive treatment, with controls of the transference, rather than the exploitation of a full-blown transference neurosis. Awareness of transference phenomena helped the worker to reduce seduction, relinquish authoritative positions, and handle other aspects of countertransference. He learned to point *up*, instead of to point *out;* to grasp what the client was saying about his conscious and preconscious feelings; to release feelings in an atmosphere of warmth and acceptance until tension was released and the time favorable for adjustive learnings. Added to techniques of relating oneself to the reasonable, mature side of the client, so far as possible, was recognition of the eternal truth that healing takes place through the basic positive transference. But even though we learned that security with the therapeutic practitioner reduces the client's defenses, there was still so much to learn of how the unconscious operated, not only through general attitudes and the behavior of the ego, but through the relationship itself.

Use of Self in Relationship and Transference

Mary Richmond had offered a systematic approach to diagnosis which was not fully adopted, partly because it seemed to offer so little toward reaching treatment goals. The Freudian diagnostic revolution stemmed from the concept that intellectual ideas, discussion, counseling, and argument were of little value in changing attitudes; that the emotionally effective component in change in personal pathology lay in the relationship. For the first time then there was clear meaning, although insufficiently clear direction, as to the relationship. Although caseworkers tried valiantly to apply the new insights, they still floundered badly. As Bertha Reynolds has remarked about *A Changing Psychology:* [32] "The startling note of Miss Robinson's book is that this relationship, whatever it is, is the fundamental thing in case treatment." An early variation of the concept of relationship was that the worker was a catalytic agent, or a screen upon which the client projected his feelings and ideas. But this was an academic notion, since the client never really saw any worker in this unemotional way. He had his own personally and culturally determined view of the social worker—his own expectations. The caseworkers were staggered to discover not a beautiful objectivity in themselves but the unruly quality of countertransference.

At first "relationship" had been used in the child guidance clinics and family agencies as a means of securing developmental history. Later, social workers tried to get clients to relive the past, somewhat in the analytic sense, especially if they themselves had been analyzed. The use of relationship as therapy *in itself,* an idea underlined largely by Ferenczi and Rank, led to a type of therapy—promoted particularly by the group of social workers then called Rankian, and later "functional"—in which the focus was almost wholly on the client-worker relationship. "Free association" had not only been introduced in the literature of the period—by James Joyce, for instance—but had been brought forward as a fundamental psychoanalytic technique. Social workers, somewhat naively, dropped their overdirected interviews in favor of so-called free association. It was hoped that this technique would lead to healing by catharsis (and there was no doubt that there was hope, too, that somehow the nuclear neurotic conflict would pop up to the eager gaze!). But free association is difficult, if not impossible, to achieve in the interview unless the basic psychoanalytic rule is imposed and the transference fully developed.

Interviewing, up to the Freudian period, had followed a pattern of social inquiry, usually with a barrage of questions. Social workers, whether in family agencies or child guidance clinics, had been required to produce a full, logical social history. Almost overnight, advanced practitioners who had now been brought under "the influence" learned to listen in a completely new way. Social workers did not use a couch (though a few would have liked to), and it took some time before it was understood that even the techniques of listening would not call unconscious libido from the vasty deep. For in the early days it was "libido," not ego strengths and defenses, to which social workers were attuned, and discipline in securing developmental history only made them eager to follow the Master and uncover the oedipal and early sexual conflicts.

25

By the middle of the late thirties, the early permissive listening and "free association," through which we had hoped we might also get a peek at the infantile neuroses, had been succeeded by attempts on the part of some practitioners to obtain knowledge of the unconscious directly; another group took the position that "obtaining a knowledge of the unconscious from the client is not our function, nor are we equipped for it." [13] Working with the derivatives of the unconscious, that is, the defenses, was to come later. One of the early papers of this period, by Dr. Finlayson,[8] described how psychoanalysis can give social workers insight into psychodynamics, and he discussed reaction formation as a defense. He postulated, as fundamental, the psychosexual development of the individual and outlined the classical stages of psychosexual development. He recognized that the caseworker must have insight into unconscious mechanisms, but warned against applying it directly in casework other than in diagnosis.

With all of casework's aberrations, respect for the integrity of people grew as workers gained greater understanding of personality and began to work, not solely with problems, but with ego strengths. Gradually the grasp of the psychosocial configuration became firm, even though casework had almost been swept out to sea by the impact of the psychoanalytic tide. The elaboration of the psychological, in the long run, led to a surer conviction about the psychosocial.

The interview itself changed as we came to understand that the client, or even the worker, might or might not be objective about his situation; that only the client could tell about his feelings and attitudes, and even these might not be what they seemed. We learned that communication, in the new art of interviewing, takes place in both verbal and nonverbal ways. Blundering, doubting, guessing, and often staggered and staggering, caseworkers then began to wrestle, as Jacob with the Angel, with transference and countertransference.

One positive result of the adventure in "passivity" was that social workers, for the first time, did really begin to listen, and to observe the client's verbal and nonverbal productions. What no one had realized at first was that this method of interviewing could set up an uncontrolled relationship, just as exaggerated pursuit of his-

26

tory had tended to close it off. One inevitably discovered that transference mobilizes not only conscious and preconscious materials, but stirs up the unconscious in unpredictable ways. When the phenomenon of transference as discovered by Freud began to be comprehended, interviewing techniques could be corrected and further developed. Awareness of these interactions—of transference and countertransference—helped caseworkers define both the goal and process of treatment. As they learned about the derivatives of the unconscious, they came to understand, like Ulysses, that they were a part of all that they had met.

It is hard to identify the gradual phases through which the Freudian ideas of transference and resistance were assimilated. The merit of pre-Freudian interviewing, as we have said, was held to lie in its objectivity. From being "catalysts," social workers turned to the new role of being good parent to the client—that is to say, those who had not been analyzed. Those who had been analyzed perceived correctly that it was the client who transferred attributes of childhood figures to the interview. After literal attempts by some workers to elicit transference neuroses, the trend moved toward greater understanding and skill in handling the relationship and in managing the irrational attitudes in the transference and toward the goal of supportive treatment, with utilization of the techniques of clarification and the development of some degree of self-aware-ness and self-dependence. Deep insight, in the analytic sense, was not considered a practicable aim.

Some caseworkers, however, seeking a key to the inner world, still thought insight development to be the only acceptable goal. Neither "attitude therapy," nor the relationship therapy of Rank and the Philadelphia group, sufficed those—a small, heroic, some-times misguided band—who panted after insight. There were all sorts of cults—the analyzed and the unanalyzed, those who were being analyzed by the wrong people, and those who were dedicated to therapy as opposed to analysis. For a time we saw transference in everyone and talked far into the night, like college seniors, about insight. There was little interest in using transference merely toward client improvement, or what was then thought to be the minor role of supporting defenses or of turning a defense into a more acceptable channel. A few daring practitioners longed to get into the deepest areas of infantile conflict through the use of dreams, although dream analysis was regarded as the prerogative of the best trained and, in fact, was more discussed in low tones after hours than actually used in the interview. Still, it was hard for caseworkers to give up the idea of insight development leading, as we were then so sure, toward complete personality change. It had been an alluring thought that guilt and sex could somehow be "fixed up," and oh, how earnestly we tried!

Since medical psychiatry was individualistic, its ultimate responsibility for diagnosis had kept much of its processes out of reach of laymen. Social workers had been correctly taught that whenever they found an acute symptom formation, they should seek the physician, taking also for granted that whenever intensive psychotherapy is undertaken there will have been a medical examination. Freud's theory of personality, however, could not be circumscribed in quite the same way. Social workers, having eaten of the Tree of Knowledge of Good and Evil, found that they were in danger of being ejected from the new psychological Eden. Family and child welfare agencies for years had been handling persons with character disorders—alcoholic spouses, inadequate parents, unmarried mothers, and quarreling couples—without benefit of doctors and without compunction or guilt. The idea of insight development and getting at "pure" unconscious material had fascinated the analyzed and, perhaps still more, the unanalyzed. Many of the analytic consultants were urging social workers to attempt some form of abreaction around specific areas of problems or specific defenses and thus remove, if possible, the pressure at one point. On the other hand, Dr. David Levy and others had called to our attention that, in our work with the child, growth was on our side; that the educational therapeutic process should go with the grain and, in one sense, "the less therapy the better."

The Effect of Personality Theory on Learning

If Freud radically changed casework practice, his ideas even more radically changed professional education. Although there may have been little "sex" in psychiatry before Freud, and perhaps still less in the medical schools, the child guidance clinics, increasingly Freudian, took cognizance of the child's psychosexual development. These clinics, located in various cities, were used by schools of social work as field work centers. The psychiatric information courses at the schools gradually turned into courses on *growth and development* from the psychogenetic Freudian point of view. Before 1920, William James, Josiah Royce, and others had given out the exciting idea that the human mind as well as the body could be the object of scientific study. However, there had been little acceptance of this idea by the professions, nor was it easily assimilated even after Freud brought psychoanalysis to America. Menninger[27] attributes to Lawson Lowrey the multi-discipline idea in the child guidance clinic. Mary Jarrett and Marion Kenworthy certainly outlined and largely sparked the psychiatric social work movement of the early twenties.

Before this time one could say that for social work, as for other professions, the study of personality had not been written down either as science or art. It existed only in life. Dr. Richard Cabot had warned us that diagnosis in casework, as in medicine, would run far ahead of treatment. It was psychoanalytic psychiatry that introduced not only more complete diagnosis, but the beginnings of a therapeutic process that was to be a unique characteristic of casework.

It would not be true to say that casework had had no psychiatric influence before Freud was consciously accepted by the new profession of social work. From James J. Putnam, E. E. Southard, and others, particularly in the Boston Psychopathic Hospital, from which Mary Jarrett went to Smith College and Mary Antoinette Cannon to the New York School of Social Work, social workers gained intimations of this approach to personality. One must accredit the extraordinary role played by the Smith College School for Social Work in furthering this movement. In 1917, as an outgrowth of World War I (when a Mental Hygiene Section of the National Conference had been organized), the first training course for the psychiatric social workers was launched at Smith College. In 1919, at the National Conference of Social Work, in Atlantic City, psychiatry took the place by storm. Although the era of ego psychology had not yet dawned, Mary Jarrett[18] made an enduring contribution by defining the treatment function of social work as the restoration of the capacity for normal living.

The first phase of incorporation of psychoanalytic theory, in the main, was in diagnosis, but in diagnosis pointed toward treatment.

29

Dr. Marion Kenworthy, at the National Conference of 1926, gave a paper stressing cause-and-effect relationships as reflected in the behavior of individuals. She ended her striking paper, which received a great ovation, with the following:

. . . It is through the contribution of the psychoanalytic school to mental hygiene that the understanding of the root beginnings and processes of the neuroses, psychoses, delinquency, criminal careers, and other problems of unadjustment has been made.[21]

Her famous ego-libido method of case analysis, "positive and negative," "constructive and destructive," a schematic method for analyzing cases according to the love and ego experiences of the child, was perhaps the first structured use of psychoanalytic concepts in teaching social workers. Generations of social work students thereafter were taught an orderly way of looking at the inner and outer life of the individual, particularly of the child. Dr. Kenworthy, however, never left her students at the diagnostic point but always insisted that her chart should help us to know what to do in treatment. She called her scheme "purposive diagnosis."

Bertha Reynolds, creative and inspiring teacher, brought important psychoanalytic insights into learning which enabled students to achieve more accurate perceptions of behavior, and taught them to draw inferences from nonverbal as well as from verbal behavior.[31]

I am not sure when Freud's theory of personality became the theory of choice at the Smith School, in the sense that this was taught as basic content, but it seems to me, looking back, as if it was always shining like a beacon light on the campus! Florence Day commented in a letter to the writer on this point, "Dr. Southard's idea in the summer of 1918 was to offer a course which would teach the fundamental principles of human behavior, normal and abnormal, social and antisocial. Thus the training was seen to combine social psychiatry, psychology, and sociology, as well as the 'practical work.'" Dr. LeRoy Maeder, an early member of the Smith faculty, through a basic paper,[24] had an enormous effect on precise formulations. Concerning Dr. Erik H. Erikson,[6] Annette Garrett said to the writer, "I learned child development from him and his children, and he flowed through all my teaching."

I shall not go into the debate on what is psychotherapy, or who should do it. Whoever masters Freud's basic theory of personality inevitably has access to the principles of psychotherapy. Since the twenties casework had incorporated Freudian principles and concepts and derivatives of psychoanalytic technique into its essential process. The question of adequate training to qualify one for practice in any form of psychotherapy is not debatable—persons who meet the standards and requirements of the professional task should be allowed to practice. Much of the argument seems to be a jurisdictional dispute, but Freud himself is our authority for seeing the application of his principles to the understanding of human beings everywhere and in all fields of knowledge. The psychotherapies that derive from psychoanalytic hypotheses include a wide variety and many contributions of therapeutic techniques. The characteristic casework method is interpersonal and combines *both psychological and social therapies.* One rarely sees a case carried in "pure" psychotherapy, although phases of interviewing may not be easily distinguishable from psychotherapy conducted by psychiatrists. We remind ourselves, however, that psychotherapy, no matter how sound, is not *psychoanalysis,* although psychoanalysis lies within psychotherapy.

It was inevitable that social workers, realizing the astounding implications of Freudian psychology in therapy with clients, should, on becoming supervisors, carry these insights directly into the teaching of students. Supervision or, as we now say, field instruction, went through an evolution in which there was at first a preoccupation with attempts to understand the student thoroughly in terms of his early growth and development, his problems and complexes, through the use of relationship as the chief medium of teaching (often in therapeutic terms). There were two main schools of thought in supervision, as there were in practice, one focusing largely on content in the student's learning and goals, and the other on the supervisory relationship in process with learning goals little defined. Under the latter method, the student had to find his own way to whatever learning he wished within the time limits of courses, semesters, and the Master's program as a whole. We now accept that in true education content and process must be interwoven.

During the passivity period, students were encouraged to feel rather than to think, and intellectual efforts in field work were apt to be regarded by supervisors as defenses. Positive educational aspects, however, came out of this period, such as an understanding of the worker-client relationship and the concept of the student as a human being—as a learner, with drives, impulses, and inhibitions. Most students come to school believing that behavior is rational, and are upset by the Freudian explanations of sources of behavior. The recognition of aggression in clients has led to a better understanding of aggression in the professional self.

Even before formal training was begun for psychoanalysts, in New York in 1929, and in Chicago in 1932, social workers in the large family agencies in the East were attending seminars led by outstanding European analysts. Social workers were not so directly affected by Dr. Adolph Meyer as by the translation of some of his works describing his client-centered emphases. Dr. William A. White's textbook, *Outlines of Psychiatry*,[35] was widely used in the psychiatric information courses in schools of social work. The social workers of the late twenties and thirties were influenced by Freudian psychoanalysts coming from Europe who generously gave seminars and became consultants to family and children's agencies.

Students in classes and in field work, especially in the child guidance clinics, were pressed toward more precise diagnosis, but even more toward treatment that was seen to have psychotherapeutic possibilities; the use of relationship became the chief dynamic of treatment. In the New York Charity Organization Society, under the leadership of Anna Kempshall, a number of analysts gave seminars and helped to incorporate clinical thinking and psychodynamics into the whole casework process. Other family societies, such as the Family Society in Philadelphia, under Betsey Libbey, and the Cleveland Family Service, under Helen Hanchette, also moved in the same direction. The Judge Baker Foundation in Boston and the Institute for Juvenile Research in Chicago and elsewhere attracted key analysts as teachers and staff members. At the Jewish Board of Guardians in New York, Dr. J. H. W. van Ophuijsen gave a rigorous discipline in psychoanalytic principles to the staff. The striking fact is that Freudian concepts were worked into casework practice *so fully as to make casework a thera-*

peutic process long before there were acrid debates as to the nature of psychotherapy and who should, or should not, be allowed to practice it. For more than twenty-five years casework has practiced its distinctive forms of psychotherapy, and, at its best, it has continued to make use of all the familiar social services as social therapies.

In field instruction, Freud's contributions to therapeutic insight and motivation have led toward methods of developing self-awareness in the student and of using the relationship to foster learning. In the supervisory conference, the trend has shifted from efforts to release childhood memories in the student to examination of his current behavior in practice. Whatever devices are used, attention to the learning pattern, which itself reflects the life pattern, has become the center of attention in so far as one is dealing with attitudes and behavior in the giving of social services or in other aspects of counseling or guidance. Interpretations to the student of unconscious motivation for his attitudes and behavior have proved to be as ineffectual for learning as premature interpretations in psychotherapy for healing.

Today some of the more important adaptations of Freudian theory are found in the attempt to evaluate selective responses to learning demands which, in turn, reveal the essential personality structure. The approach is from the observation of the student's current behavior in respect to cases or other learning situations. Supervisors who recognize a repetitive pattern will, at the appropriate point, call the student's attention to it—at first without interpretation. A possible pattern shown may be, for instance, that of difficulty with parents as clients. The supervisory approach may, however, remain deliberately supportive. The student may be given opportunity to discuss how a parent-client may have come to be so, and it may well happen that, within the first year, and certainly the second, he will react so far as to say, "Yes, I can see that I have more difficulty with adults, especially parents, than with children."

The normal and not too neurotic student needs release of fears and clarification of his learning difficulties, as well as support. With capacity for self-awareness, some students begin to make specific connections between their unresolved parental conflicts and their

33

work with clients. How far the supervisor will go in clarification of these attitudes will depend on a number of variables: the personality of the learner (the doer, the thinker, the intuitive, the empathic student, or that rarest and most cherished one in which all these qualities are balanced in the learning behavior); the goal set for the semester or year; the presence or absence of stressful situations that stir up unusual anxiety; and factors in his life experience. The essential point is that Freudian personality theory is now adapted for the learning-teaching situation, as well as for practice. Because of greater familiarity with the theory and more skill in its individual application, the same goal is not insisted upon for every learner.

At present there is no agreement as to whether all caseworkers should be analyzed, but Freud, like Socrates, placed emphasis on knowing oneself. His method, which revolutionized practice and field instruction, made it clear that *self-awareness is essential in order to treat another human being,* not only in psychological terms but even, to some extent, in the use of a practical social service.

Freud was optimistic about the ability of human beings to help themselves and to be helped. For a while this belief inspired interminable treatment because the expectations exceeded the tools. Greater knowledge of both social realities and clinical psychopathology has brought casework into better balance. There are certain pitfalls into which students characteristically fall and in regard to which behavior patterns can be clearly delineated; reactions to authority, the uses and abuses of aggression, infantile and dependency reactions are the most common. The supervisor, like the therapist, notices at what point the student first says "No"; [2] that is, at what period in the student's life he has first encountered a situation to which he cannot adapt himself. The experienced supervisor actually observes these first blockings which may be accounted for by common fears, ignorance, or quite normal anxiety, but which, if repeated, suggest a basic conflict that will interfere with learning. Where does he block? Repetitive blockings point to hidden repressions and conflicts.

Critics of Freudian theory often comment that, while the principles may have improved clinical practice, they had an unfortunate effect on professional education, in that the clinical overshadowed

34

the social, at least for a time. It is true that the Freudian contribution emphasized—we might even say "introduced"—subjectivity and motivation into learning theory. No doubt here, as in casework, since practitioners were the teachers, the early therapeutic emphases on relationship, resistance, self-knowledge, and the meaning of attitudes and behavior tended to replace intellectual processes and ideas; the substantive knowledge was usually spoken of as "content." Again, it was not Freud's fault that the pendulum swung too far. The founder of psychoanalysis had a great distrust of emotional enthusiasts. There are still unfortunate applications of the concept that learning is primarily emotional and not rational. Self-awareness may become the end of learning, not the means or the by-product, in which event there is always distortion. However, it is not the first time that teachers have been caught indoctrinating instead of teaching. For every Socrates there will be one hundred who, in the struggle for Truth, demand not learning but acceptance of dogma! Schools of social work today are studying these patterns of learning behavior and appropriate teaching responses. There is now a well-defined Freudian theory of personality from which adaptations and modifications have been made from various sources; sooner or later there will be a comparable theory of society.

In closing, I should like to quote a recently published letter of Freud's[11] written in July, 1936 (after the rise of Hitler).

Dear Sir,

You surely do not believe that I am proud of having been right? I was right as the pessimist against the enthusiast, as the old man against the youngster. It would have been better to have been wrong.

But I know you still will find out what to hold on to.

With warmest wishes,

Yours,

Freud

The practice of social work, including casework, is undergoing profound changes. Social work is in one of its most critical phases of reorganization and assimilation of new materials. In such periods it is not unexpected, although inevitably disturbing, that questions are raised which seem to attack the very foundations of practice. Aware that our special angle of vision should include new

35

aspects of the humanities and social sciences, we shall maintain our steadfast belief in the importance of the psychosocial approach. Those of us who have studied and followed Freud will, I am sure, find out what to hold on to.

Bibliography

1. Aichhorn, August, *Wayward Youth,* Viking Press, New York, 1935.
2. Alexander, Franz, M.D., "Two Forms of Regression and Their Therapeutic Implications," *Psychoanalytic Quarterly,* Vol. XXV, No. 2 (1956), pp. 178–196.
3. Aptekar, Herbert, "The Concept of Resistance," *The Family,* Vol. XVIII, No. 10 (1938), pp. 346–349.
4. Boston Psychoanalytic Society and Institute, "Psychotherapy and Casework," Symposium, *Journal of Social Casework,* Vol. XXX, No. 6 (1949), entire issue.
5. Day, Florence R., "Current Developments in the Graduate Curriculum," *Journal of Social Casework,* Vol. XXIX, No. 9 (1948), pp. 335–342.
6. Erikson, Erik H., *Childhood and Society,* W. W. Norton and Company, New York, 1950.
7. Federn, Paul, *Ego Psychology and the Psychoses,* Basic Books, New York, 1952, pp. 95, 155.
8. Finlayson, Alan D., M.D., "The Diagnostic Process in Continuing Treatment," *The Family,* Vol. XVIII, No. 7 (1937), pp. 228–233.
9. Freud, Anna, *The Ego and the Mechanisms of Defense,* International Universities Press, New York, 1946.
10. Freud, Sigmund, *Basic Writings,* translated and edited by Dr. A. A. Brill, Random House, New York, 1938.
11. —————, "Four Unpublished Letters," *Psychoanalytic Quarterly,* Vol. XXV, No. 2 (1956), p. 150.
12. Garrett, Annette, "Historical Survey of the Evolution of Casework," *Social Casework,* Vol. XXX, No. 6 (1949), pp. 219–230.
13. Gartland, Ruth, "The Child, the Parent, and the Agency," *The Family,* Vol. XVII, No. 3 (1937), p. 76.
14. Glover, Edward, M.D., *The Technique of Psychoanalysis,* International Universities Press, New York, 1955.
15. Green, Sidney, M.D., "Psychoanalytic Contributions to Casework Treatment of Marital Problems," *Social Casework,* Vol. XXV, No. 10 (1954), pp. 419–423.
16. Hamilton, Gordon, "Self-Awareness in Professional Education," *Social Casework,* Vol. XXXV, No. 9 (1954), pp. 371–379.
17. —————, *Psychotherapy in Child Guidance,* Columbia University Press, New York, 1947.
18. Jarrett, Mary C., "The Psychiatric Thread Running through All Social Case Work," *Proceedings of National Conference of Social Work,* 1919, pp. 587–593.
19. Jones, Ernest, M.D., *Life and Work of Sigmund Freud,* Vol. III, Basic Books, New York, 1957.

20. Kasius, Cora (ed.), *Principles and Techniques in Social Casework*, Family Service Association of America, New York, 1950.

21. Kenworthy, Marion E., M.D., "Psychoanalytic Concepts in Mental Hygiene," *The Family*, Vol. VII, No. 7 (1926), p. 223.

22. Krug, Othilda, M.D., "The Dynamic Use of the Ego Functions in Casework Practice," *Social Casework*, Vol. XXXVI, No. 10 (1955), pp. 443–450.

23. Levy, David M., M.D., "Attitude Therapy," *American Journal of Orthopsychiatry*, Vol. VII, No. 1 (1937), pp. 103–113.

24. Maeder, LeRoy M.A., M.D., "Diagnostic Criteria: The Concept of Normal and Abnormal," *The Family*, Vol. XXII, No. 6 (1941), pp. 171–179.

25. Marcus, Grace, "Social Case Work and Mental Health," *The Family*, Vol. XIX, No. 4 (1938), pp. 99–105.

26. ————, *Some Aspects of Relief in Family Casework*, Charity Organization Society, New York, 1929, pp. 57–59.

27. Menninger, Karl A., M.D., "Freud and American Psychiatry," *Journal of the American Psychoanalytic Association*, Vol. IV, No. 4 (1956), pp. 614–625.

28. Munroe, Ruth L., *Schools of Psychoanalytic Thought*, Dryden Press, New York, 1955.

29. Peck, Harris B., M.D., and Bellsmith, Virginia, *Treatment of the Delinquent Adolescent*, Family Service Association of America, New York, 1954.

30. Pollak, Otto, and others, *Social Science and Psychotherapy for Children*, Russell Sage Foundation, New York, 1952.

31. Reynolds, Bertha, *Learning and Teaching in the Practice of Social Work*, Farrar and Rinehart, New York, 1942.

32. Robinson, Virginia, *A Changing Psychology in Social Case Work*, University of North Carolina Press, Chapel Hill, 1934.

33. Ross, Helen, and Johnson, Adelaide M., M.D., "Psychiatric Interpretation of the Growth Process," Parts I and II, *Journal of Social Casework*, Vol. XXX, Nos. 3 and 4 (1949), pp. 87–92, 148–154.

34. Sacks, Patricia, "Establishing the Diagnosis in Marital Problems," *Journal of Social Casework*, Vol. XXX, No. 5 (1949), pp. 181–187.

35. White, William A., M.D., *Outlines of Psychiatry*, Nervous and Mental Disease Publishing Company, Washington, D.C., 1932.

36. Wineman, David, "Group Therapy and Casework with Ego-Disturbed Children," *Journal of Social Casework*, Vol. XXX, No. 3 (1949), pp. 110–113.

2. Modern Casework: The Contributions of Ego Psychology*

Annette Garrett

CASEWORKERS, AS WELL AS automobile advertisers, lay great stress upon being modern. Sometimes they seem as distrustful of any casework ideas or methods that have been floating around for a couple of years as the advertisers have taught us to be of two-year-old cars and television sets.

"Case work's theories, its aims, its best intensive practice, all seem to be converging of late years toward one central idea; namely, toward the development of personality." That old-fashioned quotation is, of course, familiar to all of you. It is from Mary Richmond's *What Is Social Case Work?*, written in 1922.[1]

Before delving into the present, I should like to read a few more excerpts from that period, which is, for many of you, prehistoric.

Success in social case work demands a high degree of sensitiveness to the unique quality in each human being. An instinctive reverence for personality, more especially for the personality least like his own, must be part of a case worker's native endowment. . . . It is the case worker's privilege to discover and release the unduplicated excellence in each individual—to care profoundly for the infinitely varied pattern of humanity and to strive, with an artist's striving, to develop the depth and richness of its color tones.

---

* Presented at a meeting sponsored by the New England Chapter of the Smith College School for Social Work Alumnae Association, Boston, January 14, 1955.

[1] Mary E. Richmond, *What Is Social Case Work?*, Russell Sage Foundation, New York, 1922, p. 90.

38

Miss Richmond continues by saying that success in casework involves "growth in personality for the case worker herself. The service is reciprocal." [2]

And again,

Social case work . . . in addition to its supplementary value in other tasks, has a field all its own. That field is the development of personality through the conscious and comprehensive adjustment of social relationships, and within that field the worker is no more occupied with abnormalities in the individual than in the environment, is no more able to neglect the one than the other. The distinctive approach of the case worker, in fact, is back to the individual by way of his social environment, and wherever adjustment must be effected in this manner, individual by individual, instead of in the mass, there, some form of social case work is and will continue to be needed.[3]

Recurrent Themes

As I reread casework literature, in preparation for discovering where modern practice begins, I noticed four themes running throughout the early twenties, reappearing at intervals—all of them burning issues today. The areas of emphasis in those early days were:

1. *The development of personality*—which we now talk about in terms of therapy and will be discussing primarily today in terms of ego psychology.

2. *The social aspects of casework*—for which the modern phrasing is "putting the social back into social casework."

3. *Self-awareness*—which is certainly modern, and is the title of two companion articles in *Social Casework.*[4]

4. *The generic aspects of casework*—a topic that continues to occupy a great deal of space in printed material.

During those early years, there were innumerable minor themes paralleling today's interests. What is now called aggressive casework was undefensively taken for granted in those days. The following could well be a statement of the modern so-called diagnostic school of thought. "The failure of a case worker to learn his client's

2 *Ibid.,* p. 158.
3 *Ibid.,* p. 98.
4 Gordon Hamilton, "Self-Awareness in Professional Education," and Hyman Grossbard, "Methodology for Developing Self-Awareness," *Social Casework,* Vol. XXXV, No. 9 (1954), pp. 371–379, 380–386.

social and personal background usually means failure to effect any permanent adjustment, but these diagnostic processes interplay with those of treatment and no sharp line can be drawn between them." [5]

I do not propose to pursue all these themes into the present. The first two, however—the development of personality and the importance of the social aspects of casework—are closely interrelated with our current interest in ego psychology. Many of the concepts of ego psychology can be very helpful in deepening the social worker's understanding of the casework situations that confront him, and in organizing his conceptual tools for effective use. When superficially understood and prematurely embalmed in casework practice, these new concepts will but multiply a social worker's dilemmas. More fully grasped in their dynamic implications, they will illuminate many otherwise obscure problems.

It is, indeed, unfortunate that caseworkers, in their eagerness to acquire new skills, have permitted a situation to arise in which social scientists and psychiatrists teach them their own unique heritage. Dr. Irving Kaufman [6] and other psychiatrists have remarked that they often find themselves in the peculiar position of pointing out or asking questions about significant reality factors. Mary Richmond said:

> When we put social in front of the word environment, the environment ceases to be environment in space merely—it widens to the horizon of man's thought, to the boundaries of his capacity for maintaining relationships, and it narrows to the exclusion of all those things which have no real influence upon his emotional, mental, and spiritual life. . . . The art of social case work is the art of discovering and assuring to the individual the best possible social relations.[7]

Thus, modern casework practice cannot be defined in terms of new goals, aims, ideals, philosophy, or even of new methods or techniques. Rather, its modernness is evident in a more subtle depth of understanding and new meanings in familiar words and, at its best, in more precise and differential application of theory

[5] Mary Richmond, *op. cit.*, p. 255.
[6] See Chapter 6 of the present volume.
[7] *Op. cit.*, p. 99.

and skill. Words written or spoken have meaning only as they are sifted through the mind and experience of the reader or listener. We are fortunate to have such a rich inheritance. Those of us sincerely desirous of practicing modern casework will do well to reread, yearly, Mary Richmond's writings and the Milford Conference Report,[8] as well as Anna Freud's *The Ego and the Mechanisms of Defense*.[9] Moreover, our professional development would probably be steadier and less subject to pendulum swings and fads if we were required to reread literature on the subject before proceeding to expound new ideas.

Our profession struggles constantly against an undertow, a tendency to forget or discard old ideas as we take on new, or to herald old ideas as new simply because we as individuals have just discovered them or because they have been presented to us in new terms. There *is* much that is new to be learned, but its full contribution can be utilized only when the old and the new are integrated in proper balance. Repetition reinforces and deepens our understanding and practice, but repetition of old ideas under new names without a recognition of the connecting links with our past confuses and blocks our progress.

One of our difficulties stems from the fact that we often fail to recognize the universal, generic aspects disguised in new problems. Symptoms vary from period to period and reflect the changing external forces. Depressions, wars, and postwar uneasiness influence the manifestations of ageless internal drives.

Concepts of Ego Psychology

The application of ego psychology to casework practice exemplifies one of the most popular modern casework trends. Ego psychology embraces and gives added meaning to much that is familiar to caseworkers. It also involves some of the most complicated psychoanalytic theory, much of it in the process of being developed and refined by the analysts themselves, much of it beyond our comprehension and involving methods that do not

[8] Report of the Milford Conference, *Social Casework: Generic and Specific*, American Association of Social Workers, New York, 1929.

[9] Anna Freud, *The Ego and the Mechanisms of Defense*, International Universities Press, New York, 1946.

41

fall within the area of casework. The term "ego psychology" is subject to many confusions, misunderstandings, and misuses, of which this paper is probably an example. At the risk of over-simplification, I shall try to reduce this very complicated set of theories into some simple concepts that are of use to caseworkers in increasing their understanding of human behavior.

What do we mean by ego psychology? We speak of ego psychology in contrast to what? What other psychology is there? Many of us think of ego psychology in contrast to the psychology we studied in college, sometimes referred to by my students as "rat psychology." To others, Watsonian, McDougal, or Gestalt psychology would come to mind. Among social workers, and occasionally, psychiatrists, it is sometimes used in contrast to libido psychology, but mistakenly as if it were supplanting libido psychology.

It is important to remember that Freud first discovered and studied the libido or instinctual life. His discovery of the role of the ego came later. It is my understanding that, owing to a delay in adequate translation, the United States felt the impact of Freud's revision of his libido theory and the development of his ego theories much later than did Europe. This delay perhaps made his ego theories seem to us more revolutionary than evolutionary.

In any case, one frequent misunderstanding is the assumption that the ego theory negates the libido theory. Some psychoanalytic offshoots are based on this premise. These ignore or deny the importance of the instinctual drives, particularly the sexual drive. Along with this denial there is often a minimizing or discarding of the importance of the past with primary emphasis on the "current reality" or the current interpersonal relationships. All of these variations, of course, take account of only one aspect of Freud's comprehensive ego theory. As we know, one of the ego's most important functions is to handle the instinctual drives.

Another misconception that is frequently found, particularly among social workers, is that ego psychology is somehow simpler, easier, and safer for a social worker to deal with than libido psychology. Again, we shall see that this assumption represents a very limited, superficial view of ego psychology.

42

Perhaps some of these things will become clearer if we pause and ask ourselves just what we do mean by the ego. In any group, there certainly would be a wide range of definitions, including perhaps "the conscious part of the personality." Most of us know, when we stop to think about it, that the ego is not wholly conscious; in fact, the very mechanisms of defense, which give us so much difficulty, must, by their very nature, be unconscious. Yet we frequently behave and talk as if the ego were conscious. That misconception may account for the idea that ego psychology is easier or simpler than other types of psychology. For the purposes of this discussion, I shall define the ego as the sum total of the integrating efforts of the personality or, stated in another way, the sum total of all of the mechanisms of dealing with conflict. We may describe the functions of the ego as "Stop, Look, and Listen!" The ego receives stimuli from the id, from external reality, and from the superego. That is, it faces three ways. The impulses originating from the id are governed by the pleasure principle, "I want what I want when I want it." Thus, from birth onward, the ego develops methods of dealing with chaotic drives, external danger, and superego prohibitions. In brief, the ego: (1) thinks of consequences, (2) anticipates things that haven't happened, and (3) works out solutions. Its guide in working out these solutions is the avoidance of pain.

We hear a great deal about strengthening the ego. What do we mean by a strong ego? Is it an indication of ego strength when a client insists that he wants to work out things for himself and does not need anyone's help? Or, for that matter, when any individual, including a caseworker, professes these sentiments vehemently? Does a child of two have a weak ego if, during his mother's absence, he eats a piece of candy left within reach? Does it make any difference in assessing ego strength whether the person is a child of four, six, or eight years; or a diabetic of seventy? Does the individual who must always have the last word in an argument have a strong ego? The strength of the ego is determined by its capacity to bear frustration, but this frustration or pain must have a purpose.

In the development of the child, frustration is accepted in return for some compensation. At first, the compensation is a substitution on the same level—the mother hands the infant a rubber toy as she

43

removes a sharp knife he has found. There is not much real frustration on this level, but most of us continue to meet a multitude of frustrations through this method of substitution of an almost similar reward. Later, frustration is tolerated because of the compensation afforded by the approval of the parents. And finally, *the height of maturity for which we strive is the compensation of our own approval.* Few of us achieve this high level. When we examine our motives honestly, we usually find that most of the things we do are done primarily in order to gain the good opinion of others. Theoretically, these distinctions are easy to make, but in practice their simplicity evaporates. How, for example, can one determine whether the conscientious objector, who goes to jail rather than fight, is a saint or a crack-pot? I always think of Freud as an example of unusual ego strength in his steadfast search for truth that was so disagreeable to his contemporaries.

The difference, then, between neurosis and ego strength is that the latter represents the ability and the freedom to do various things, without one's being irrationally coerced to do them. It is often difficult to distinguish this mature ego from an overcompensatory ego which displays an apparent independence that is but a semblance of strength. Such a false strength often results from a basic inability to accept frustration. A rebellious acquiescence involving repression does not result in real ego growth. Real ego strength involves an active acceptance that marshals new strength with which to confront a difficult situation.

The various mechanisms of defense are the methods the ego uses to deal with the demands from the three sources mentioned above whenever they are in conflict. Thus, we never see the undistorted id impulse, but rather the id impulse modified by some defense mechanism on the part of the ego, in turn disguised in some ordinary conscious activity or attitude. Thus, "I am clean" may hide not only the anal desire to smear, but also the mechanisms of repression and reaction formation. Likewise, "I am so happy" may hide not only hostility, but the ungratified longing to be cared for which gave rise to the original anger.

Before proceeding further, I should like to recapitulate what has been said. In contrast to the previous interest on the part of social workers in inner pressures, the unconscious, and instinctual drives, ego psychology is often regarded as being concerned exclusively with conscious intellectual processes and rational attempts to deal with outer realities. When applied in this limited sense, ego psychology sometimes gives rise not so much to an enriched and broadened understanding of personality as to a disguised rationalization of punitive casework. The worker then takes advantage of ego psychology to avoid understanding the complexities of causative behavior and emotional drives and to concentrate instead on helping—sometimes forcing—the client to "face" his current reality problem. This is indeed a limited view, for ego psychology does not displace the psychology of instinct and emotion. Rather, it includes it as part of a comprehensive and systematic study of the total personality.

Assessing Ego Strength

The primary function of the ego may be thought of as maintaining a balance within the personality between the demands of inner needs and outer reality. To realize its ends, the ego uses both unconscious mechanisms and conscious methods. It functions smoothly in so far as inner and outer needs are integrated with a minimum of conflict. Its maturation from childhood to adulthood may be measured by its increasing powers for smooth integration. Its strength at any given time is always relative to the person's age and is indicated by his capacity to make difficult choices and to endure the consequent deprivation of desired but renounced alternatives.

Ego strength is not a static or fixed condition but must always be evaluated in relation to the age of the individual and the intensity of pressures. A strong ego of a four-year-old is unable to tolerate the same frustrations and pressures as that of a ten-year-old, sixteen-year-old, or thirty-year-old.

Even this greatly oversimplified statement of basic ego theory introduces more questions than it answers. If much of the ego's operations are unconscious, how can we know the strength of an individual ego, let alone be sure which mechanisms it is using to handle what conflicts? Anna Freud has said:

The strength of the ego-factors when we encounter them—whether in the form of the dream-censorship, or in that of resistance to free associations—has

45

always been impaired and their influence diminished, and often it is extremely difficult for us to picture them in their natural magnitude and vigor. We are all familiar with the accusation not infrequently made against analysts—that they may have a good knowledge of a patient's unconscious, but are bad judges of his ego. There is probably a certain amount of justification in this criticism, for the analyst lacks opportunity of observing the patient's whole ego in action.[10]

Caseworkers have always dealt with the total functioning of the ego, but often with unseeing eyes. It is a paradox that, as analysts are becoming more aware of the significance of the patient's handling of external reality, caseworkers, in spite of their many opportunities to observe the ego in action, have become careless in appreciating what they see. By tradition, and for the most part currently also, caseworkers are familiar with how the individual functions in his social environment. Usually they have used good practical judgment in this area, but they have not always grasped the full import of all that they see and know. A man's work record, a woman's housekeeping, a child's school grade, and similar ego development information, formerly uniformly secured, are sometimes not noted because of the caseworker's absorption in transference manifestations, resistance, or defense mechanisms. Here, indeed, we have new wine in old bottles. The wealth of social information was previously often routinely secured and its full significance not grasped. A full appreciation of ego psychology reveals new meaning as we integrate the concept that the unconscious ego operations are manifested in a myriad of ordinary, day-by-day, characteristic ways of functioning. Putting the social back in social casework does not mean one whit less attention to and need for knowledge of unconscious and instinctual behavior, but it does mean an enriched blending of both as the unconscious significance of the social aspects is increasingly appreciated, and practical manifestations of the unconscious are recognized in familiar, taken-for-granted activities.

Freud has observed that the scientist uses the psychical apparatus to observe and study physical phenomena. He notes that one of the difficulties in studying human behavior is that in this science the object of study is itself the apparatus which we use in making that study. I have, however, been fascinated recently, in reading a book about Einstein, to come across the following quotation which

[10] *Ibid.*, p. 23.

illustrates the parallel problems in the so-called exact sciences and human science.

Einstein has pointed out that common sense is actually nothing more than a deposit of prejudices laid down in the mind prior to the age of eighteen. Every new idea one encounters in later years must combat this accretion of "self-evident" concepts. And it is because of Einstein's unwillingness ever to accept any unproven principle as self-evident that he was able to penetrate closer to the underlying realities of nature than any scientist before him. Why, he asked, is it any more strange to assume that moving clocks slow down and moving rods contract, than to assume that they don't? The reason classical physics took the latter view for granted is that man, in his everyday experience, never encounters velocities great enough to make these changes manifest. In an automobile, an airplane, even in a V-2 rocket, the slowing down of a watch is immeasurable. It is only when velocities approximate that of light that relativistic effects can be detected. . . . Relativity does not therefore contradict classical physics. It simply regards the old concepts as limited cases that apply solely to the familiar experiences of man.[11]

Of the many similarities, I was particularly impressed with the evidence that the quality of genius in either exact science or human science lies in the imaginative ability to distrust the obvious in a never-ending quest for deeper truths.

Understanding Resistance

Ego psychology has sharpened our diagnostic procedures and has enabled us to be more discriminating in our treatment goals. Let us consider now how some of the theory we have learned from ego psychology has enhanced casework understanding of that ubiquitous phenomenon, resistance. As we know from the history of psychoanalysis, Freud gave up hypnosis, which comfortably immobilizes the stubborn interference of the ego, when he became convinced that the ego could not be so casually pushed aside if permanent results were to be achieved. With the substitution of free association, and yet the continued interference from the ego, began Freud's study and development of a comprehensive ego psychology, which included the unconscious drives, the repressed impulses, the superego, as well as the conscious and unconscious ego operations. The analyst's most difficult task is the analysis of the ego, but if

11 Lincoln Barnett, *The Universe and Dr. Einstein,* William Sloane Associates, New York, 1948, p. 52.

this task is neglected, the results obtained through free association are no more permanent than those obtained through hypnosis. Caseworkers, too, need to understand at least some general principles of total ego operation in order to refine their skills and develop appropriate casework methods for dealing with those problem areas responsive to their methods.

Thus, from ego psychology, caseworkers have learned a healthy respect for resistance. They no longer see it as an obstacle that challenges them to overcome it by any and every clever device. They recognize that the strength of the resistance is in direct proportion to the strength of the drives or the objective anxiety the ego is attempting to handle by the best method at its disposal. They recognize that the weak ego, such as one finds in the psychotic, needs help in maintaining its resistances; that the immature ego of the child may need reinforcement to help him consolidate necessary repressions that are normal for various ages. The so-called "uncovering technique" is used discriminately and only when diagnostic evaluation indicates a strong enough ego to tolerate a good deal of anxiety and only when there is evidence that the casework relationship is firmly established so that the individual feels sufficient support to risk recognizing his unacceptable feelings.

Defenses Against Anxiety

Anna Freud states that the ego develops defenses to ward off three kinds of anxiety: (1) superego anxiety; (2) objective anxiety; (3) strength of the instincts anxiety.[12]

Although she is discussing psychoanalytic treatment, her discussion is applicable to casework. It corroborates some of the conclusions we have arrived at and explains the success of certain casework methods as well as the failure of others. She states that superego anxiety is the easiest to relieve. Caseworkers often speak of softening the superego through various techniques such as acceptance and the client's identification with the caseworker's less severe attitude. Relieving this anxiety probably accounts for many of our successes with mothers in child guidance clinics and with certain children.

12 *Op. cit.,* pp. 58–70.

Anna Freud states that objective anxiety is more difficult to treat but still responsive to psychoanalysis. In order to relieve objective anxiety, one must modify the environment or show the patient that the situation he fears really belongs in his past. Applied to casework, her use of "modifying the environment" probably relates to such activities as the caseworker's modification of parental attitudes so that, in effect, the child's environment is modified. Many other casework situations come to mind— modification of a spouse's attitude in marital problems, of teachers' attitudes in certain school cases, and so on. In less severe cases, the caseworker also undoubtedly achieves some success in helping the individual gain insight into the irrational nature of fears that have their origins in situations long past.

The third type of anxiety—anxiety arising from the strength of the instincts—Anna Freud considers to be the most difficult to treat. She warns of the danger of psychosis if the ego cannot be strengthened at exactly the same time as the instincts emerge. Caseworkers have been aware of this danger and have developed various methods of working with psychotics and potential psychotics. Non-psychoanalytic methods, including casework based on psychoanalytic understanding, perhaps offer more hope than does psychoanalysis for many of the clients in this group. Caseworkers in social agencies have long had a vast experience with ambulatory schizophrenics, so-called psychopaths, or "borderline" non-hospitalized cases.[13]

On the other hand, many of our failures have occurred with this group of clients because we do not always distinguish which of these three types of anxiety we are dealing with in helping an individual. Also, we too often make an inappropriate application of a valid concept or we confuse goals with methods. The weak ego of the delinquent or of the client who "acts out" is not strengthened by a direct attempt to soften the superego or by lessening the objective danger of consequences. Neither is it strengthened by prematurely setting up standards for the client, even though these may be included in one's ultimate goal.

Frequently more than one of these three kinds of anxiety are present in the same individual. Casework treatment may be

[13] Discussed in Part II, Chapters 6–9, of the present volume.

49

effective with one kind but may leave the others essentially unchanged.

Dependence and Independence

Another direct application of ego psychology to casework occurs in the treatment of conflicting human needs for dependence and independence. Social workers sometimes fluctuate between the extremes of fostering dependence, and of avoiding dependence at all costs, even to the exclusion of other relevant factors. Inexperienced caseworkers often can see no alternative between either fostering dependence through expressing sympathy with the client's illness or hard lot, or fostering independence by refusing sympathy. Some are motivated exclusively by a desire to help and to compensate for the client's previous suffering while others concentrate on the goal of self-reliance without adequate attention to the development of valid methods for helping the client achieve it. The two extremes are equally destructive for the client.

Much of our casework confusion is due, not to the invalidity of the concepts used but to their misapplication, or to overemphasis on certain concepts to the exclusion of others which need equal recognition in a given situation. We find it difficult to embrace more than one idea, concept, or procedure at a time. For example, the idea that "children need to be loved" is sometimes pursued to the total exclusion of their need to be disciplined. The generalization "overindulgence results in weak ego development" may lead the caseworker to fail to furnish adequate support.

In all fields, casework included, principles must be considered in relation to complementary principles and higher principles. "Independence is good," yet in excess it becomes lack of co-operation when a tubercular patient for whom bed rest has been ordered refuses to submit. In this instance, the capacity to be dependent may connote ego strength since the mature desire to be independent is giving way to the higher motive to get well. Merely because the strength of the ego may be tested by its capacity to bear frustration, one should not thereby infer that frustration will strengthen a weak ego.

Certain misconceptions have crept in to distort obvious truths. All growth is painful. It does not follow that all pain promotes growth. As we have said earlier, the pain of growth is endured because of the compensation it affords. This compensation is experienced first in the approval of parents. With increasing maturity the individual approaches the ideal of self-approval as a sufficient compensation for enduring temporary pain. This ego strength, the capacity to tolerate frustration for the sake of compensation, is developed slowly from birth on. Our understanding and effective use of the casework relationship are enhanced as we gain more appreciation of the complex way in which the support it offers the client may gradually enable him to increase his low tolerance for frustration or anxiety.

The caseworker who recognizes the ubiquity of the drive for independence as well as the need for dependence is not afraid of permitting the client some dependence in the relationship, and is less concerned with instilling independence than in discovering ways and areas in which it can be released. He does not wallow in the issue of dependence versus independence. Rather, he directs his activities toward providing more opportunities for client choice, self-determination, and responsibility. He is content if at first the client needs considerable support and is able to take advantage of only a few of the opportunities the worker offers him in making responsible decisions of his own. He remains flexible and reduces the amount of help he offers the client as he becomes increasingly able to get along without it.

In many instances, a client is in conflict between these two drives. He fears that becoming independent will entail loss of the satisfactions he is deriving from his dependency; and, conversely, he is afraid of becoming overly dependent and of never again being able to call his soul his own. Caseworkers, too, must resolve satisfactorily similar conflicts between dependency and independency drives in their own lives so that their needs will not determine their decisions as to what their clients require.

Conclusion

I have tried to identify only a few of the many rich concepts of ego psychology that are applicable to casework. The effective use of ego psychology in casework requires much more than the easy acceptance of such phrases as "help the client develop his ego strengths" and "work with his assets," or a glib listing of mechanisms of defense. To help the client achieve self-reliance has been a casework aim since the days of Mary Richmond and has held an honored place in the varying emphases developed since then. What ego psychology has done is to give new, deeper, and more vital meaning to this goal and to add to our knowledge of the means necessary for achieving it. Ego psychology, for example, has enriched our understanding of the nature of self-reliance and of the underlying forces tending to promote or inhibit its development. Formerly, we tended to note only one aspect of ego function, its conscious adjustment to the outer environment. Now we recognize that the ego works unconsciously as well as consciously, that it faces inward as well as outward, and that, confronted with the id, the superego, and external reality, it seeks to realize its interests as best it can.

To help restore or strengthen such a complex mechanism as the ego is no simple task. We know now, for example, that it does not necessarily help a client to pat him on the back and assure him, "I know you can do it." A punitive forcing of the client to assume responsibilities or make choices is equally useless. Effective help requires some understanding of the unconscious forces that are causing the predominance of the client's dependency needs, some acquaintance with the perhaps overstrong demands of the superego, some estimate of the strength of the instincts as well as the ego capacity, and an evaluation of all of these in the light of the environmental situation. The growth of our ability to render such aid proceeds slowly. It requires particularly the avoidance of the confusion of the goals to be achieved with the methods of achieving them. As we continue to integrate our theory and practice in this field, our work is becoming increasingly effective.

Casework wisdom includes our original humanitarianism with its warmth and intuitive appreciation of people, our social emphasis, our conscious use of the casework relationship, and, added to all of these but not substituted for them, a more precise clinical approach. Herein is the ideal of modern casework.

3. The Worker-Client Relationship*

Annette Garrett

THE TERM "RELATIONSHIP" as it is used in both casework and analytic literature has a variety of meanings. It sometimes signifies an over-all concept including transference, countertransference, and a conscious reality relationship. In some instances it is used as a synonym for transference, and in others it signifies a reality relationship in contrast with and excluding transference. The shifting phases of the casework relationship are seldom clear-cut or mutually exclusive; normally, now one, now another predominates.

Although in a sense everyone develops gradually, through years of experience, characteristic ways of relating to people, it is helpful to distinguish relationships that are based predominantly on unconscious displacements from early life and those that are primarily reactions to the real attitudes and behavior of the present-day person. A relationship of the latter type, as it occurs between client and caseworker, is based on the client's conscious appreciation of the worker as he really is, and may be called a reality relationship. It differs in many respects from what has come to be known technically as transference—the unconscious projection onto the caseworker of the client's attitudes toward a potent figure of his early childhood.

In cases where the client is relatively mature, his first contacts with the caseworker, if they have been satisfactory, will tend to

* Reprinted, with permission, from the *American Journal of Orthopsychiatry*, Vol. XIX, No. 2 (1949).

develop a rapport between the two; whereas, if they have been irritating, they may lead to an inharmonious relationship. In either case they are apt to be fairly direct results of reality factors in the immediate situation.

In the case of such reality-adjusted behavior, the caseworker responds by giving attention to the reality situation. If the reality factors that have already affected the client have been favorable, the worker takes advantage of the initial rapport thus created to get on with the case. If he encounters antagonism, he will look first at the factual nature of the client's immediately preceding experiences. In such cases he will seek in himself and in the agency environment the objective situations, delays, misunderstandings, and so on, occasioning this negative reaction, and will seek to remove them and replace them with stimuli conducive to satisfaction, liking, and trust.

In relatively normal people, reality factors, that is, the real situation and the real attitude of the worker, are the determining ones in establishing the quality of the early client-worker relation. The client's feelings toward the worker are fairly directly caused, are conscious, and are subject to relatively easy control. Genuine transference feelings, on the other hand, although they may be currently stimulated, are remotely caused, are largely unconscious, and require considerable skill for their control.[1]

Transference

When a client's problem is in part a personality one or requires considerable time for its solution, the influences that bring about

[1] Thomas French gives a succinct statement of the nature of the transference relationship. "By 'transference' Freud meant reactions to the analyst as though he were not himself but some person in the patient's past. According to this definition a patient's transference to the analyst is only that part of the patient's reaction to the analyst which repeats the patient's reactions to a person who has, at some previous time, played an important role in the patient's life. . . . It is important to distinguish between such transference reactions and reactions that are adequate to the present real situation. A patient does not react to the therapist only as though the therapist were somebody else, only as though he were some important figure in the patient's past. Sometimes he reacts quite naturally to what the therapist actually does or says, to the therapist's actual personality characteristics and behavior." (Franz Alexander, M.D., and Thomas French, M.D., *Psychoanalytic Therapy*, Ronald Press, New York, 1946, p. 71.)

transference are increased, and transference occurs to a correspondingly greater degree.

The need to ask for help recreates to some extent in anyone a dependency situation analogous to one's infancy and thus tends to reactivate the characteristic way of handling problems which was developed at that time. As a child seeks help from his parents, as a patient seeks the aid of his analyst, a social work client asks for assistance from the caseworker. Even a simple request for financial assistance places one in the position of seeking a favorable response from a person in power. When the help requested is more extensive than this, the feeling of dependency is proportionately greater. It is impossible for a person to place himself for long in such a dependency situation without a transference to this new situation of his infantile attitudes. Part of this transference will be positive, corresponding to the love felt for the parental figure; part of it will be negative, corresponding to the fear of anyone's possessing such power over one's own destinies.

Often transference feelings are not direct projections of a parent or other childhood figure onto the worker. In the course of the client's life he may have projected this momentous early figure onto a number of other people—teachers, acquaintances, employers, and so on. The projection onto the caseworker may then be from one of these later persons, or derivatives, as they are called. In the successive transfers that have occurred, the original figure may have become modified or even quite distorted.

Thus the caseworker may be the recipient of the feelings the client has currently toward an aunt, an employer, or a child, as well as, or instead of, those he had in childhood toward a parent. Hence, often a caseworker must ask, "With whom is my client identifying me?" Actually, to an alert caseworker, clients are very generous with their clues. "My mother never understood me, but I could always confide in my aunt." "My neighbor is always snooping into other people's affairs." In the first instance it behooves the worker to make special efforts to avoid misunderstanding what the client is trying to say and thus to avoid identification with this trait of the mother. In the other instance he will do well to watch his tempo in seeking to elicit information.

When, as is so often the case, a client's problem is to a considerable degree an emotional problem requiring for its solution some modification of his own attitudes, transference tends to develop more rapidly or even to occur to a marked degree in the initial interview. Such clients are less able to respond to the reality factors of their situation, including the actual attitude of the worker. They tend rather to live in a world shaped by their past. Anyone on whom they are dependent is readily endowed by them with the attitudes they once attributed to a mother or a father and is reacted to as they earlier reacted to that parent.

Transference development proceeds with characteristic differences in relatively normal clients, in neurotics, in psychopathic personalities, and in psychotics. Within each of these main types there are further differences of detail which are informative to the trained observer. Children, again, have their own characteristic ways of developing transference, ways that serve as clues to their underlying personality problems. Because of the special technical complexities of transference in children, in psychotics, and in psychopathic personalities, this discussion will be concerned primarily with transference as it occurs in normal or neurotic adults.

Client-worker transference in the sense described approaches in nature the analytic transference so characteristic of the early stages of psychoanalysis. It is, of course, a complicated phenomenon, involving dynamic unconscious forces which operate through such mechanisms as projection and identification. In casework such transference, in so far as it is positive, has among others the obvious advantage of attaching the client to the worker with sufficient strength to keep him from terminating treatment prematurely.

Transference Neurosis

A principal danger, on the other hand, in the development of transference is that the client will get such satisfaction from assuming the infantile role that the transference will grow into the stage of development which normally occurs next in analysis, the stage known as transference neurosis. In this stage the analytic patient comes to value the transference emotions and the satisfactions resulting from indulgence of them as more important than permanent health, the search for which led him into analysis. As Ives Hendrick puts it,

This is the point where the . . . unresolved, unconscious problems of childhood begin to dominate. They are now reproduced in the transference with

56

all their pent-up emotion. The patient is unconsciously striving for what he failed . . . to gain or to do without in actual childhood. . . . The three outstanding characteristics of the instinctual life of childhood, the Pleasure Principle, Ambivalence, and the Repetition Compulsion, govern the situation. . . . It was the full recognition of the significance of this period by Freud, as a result of failure with a case he analyzed in 1899 and reported in 1904, that marks the beginning of modern psychoanalytic technique. And it is its full comprehension and management that sharply differentiates the adequately trained from the untrained analyst, and tests the skill of the best.[2]

The development of transference neurosis, which plays such an important role in analysis and whose resolution requires such trained analytic skill, must be guarded against by the caseworker. His competence and skills fit him for a needed and valuable treatment of a different range of human problems. The vast majority of clients who come to a social agency for help are not seeking the comprehensive personality exploration and therapy that only a trained analyst or psychiatrist can give. They want realistic help with relatively limited problems. In order to be able to cope with their difficulties, they need the kind of discharge of emotional tension which they can gain from development of a limited transference, but they are not prepared to accept, nor the worker to give, the more complete personality reorganization of analysis.

A caseworker needs to know about transference neurosis so that he can prevent it, when possible, by not allowing the transference to develop to this stage. And he needs to be able to recognize incipient signs of it should it occur despite his efforts, as might easily be the case with a highly neurotic client. For its occurrence, in spite of precautions to the contrary, constitutes a good sign that the client is not suitable for casework treatment.

One of the dangers of drifting into a transference neurosis is the great amount of hostility that is released by the reversion to childhood attitudes. The relatively uninhibited force of childish aggression, combined with the power and skill of an adult, makes possible such violent antisocial or suicidal action that it is imperative that the caseworker learn how to control the intensity of the transference and avoid the transference neurosis.

This warning seems particularly necessary at this time, for clients coming to social agencies since the war seem to display more deeply

[2] Ives Hendrick, *Facts and Theories of Psychoanalysis*, Alfred A. Knopf, New York, 1934, pp. 208–209.

neurotic symptoms than prewar clients. Particularly in such agencies as the Red Cross and the mental hygiene clinics of veterans' hospitals, caseworkers must work with very sick people and often, because of the shortage of psychiatrists, without sufficient psychiatric consultation. When strong unconscious forces are operating without the worker's awareness, the situation may easily get out of hand. The use, for example, of a permissive, unguided interview technique may, with a neurotic or psychotic client, bring so much unconscious material to the surface that only a skilled psychiatrist can effect a re-establishment of necessary defenses. A caseworker must know enough to avoid such developments. Should they occur despite his efforts, a psychiatrist should take responsibility.

Countertransference

Since any relationship between two persons is a two-way one, there is also an unconscious tendency on the part of a psychotherapist to transfer onto the patient feelings growing out of earlier experiences. This psychoanalytically discovered phenomenon, countertransference, also operates between a caseworker and his client. As in the case of transference, these countertransference feelings, both positive and negative, are unconscious and hence are not easily recognized or controlled. Similarly again, there is a distinction between the conscious reality-determined feelings of the therapist or caseworker toward the patient or client and true unconscious countertransference. Mere liking or disliking, irritation or sympathy, distrust or confidence do not necessarily involve countertransference. They are often simple, conscious responses and in so far as they do not have their sources in irrational projections and identifications, they are relatively easy to control. A caseworker quite readily learns that he has a professional responsibility not to react to, or let his behavior be guided by, such personal feelings toward a client as whether he would like him for a personal friend or not. More challenging and difficult to the worker is the responsibility gradually to gain control over his unconscious feelings. Analysts protect themselves from letting their own unconscious feelings interfere with the patient's progress, by being analyzed themselves and by an extended period of supervision and rigid discipline. In 1910, Freud gave this as a reason why all

58

analysts should themselves be analyzed. For most caseworkers supervision is the only safeguard available. Through an objective discussion of his cases with a skilled supervisor, a worker gradually becomes aware of his own blind spots and achieves a modicum of recognition and control of countertransference.

Casework experience is replete with examples of countertransference. Thus a woman working with a mother may easily overidentify with the client's child. Then the mother becomes the recipient of the worker's negative countertransference feelings— feelings that originated in her attitude toward her own mother. Again, there is a natural tendency for a caseworker, whether a man or a woman, to overidentify with one spouse or another in marital problems. In such cases, the countertransference, although often positive, will falsify the worker's picture of the situation. In other instances, unconscious positive countertransference may complicate the worker's successful termination of treatment. In countertransference a worker may identify the client with some person in his past or may identify directly with the client. But since regressive feelings always occur in transference and countertransference, it tends to be the child in the adult client with whom the worker identifies. He tends to react to the child in the client as a child himself. In such cases unconscious regressive childish attitudes dominate both client and worker.

With the aid of the various distinctions we have been making, we can now turn to the primary question that arises for the caseworker out of the various relationships between the client and himself. How can they be handled most effectively to further his efforts to help the client to solve his problems? The reality relationship, transference, and countertransference all occur. How can they best be used? A transference neurosis may occur. How can it be avoided?

Reality Relationship

Establishment of a positive reality relationship between the client and himself is one of the caseworker's first concerns. This done, the worker may find his client getting enough support from conscious confidence and security so that the case progresses satisfactorily. If so, he tries to keep the interpersonal relationship at that level, minimizing transference tendencies as far as possible. Even when transference must be allowed to develop, a positive reality relationship will help to make that early transference positive.

The chief pitfalls at this early stage of client-worker relationship are two. The worker may mistake a reality-induced negative attitude on the part of the client for negative transference and thus neglect to remove its objective sources. Late or early arrival of a client for an appointment may be objectively rather than emotionally determined. Negative attitudes may be due not to transference but to a mistake on the part of the worker. Or, secondly, a worker may unnecessarily proceed beyond the reality relationship and promote a deeper transference when it is not needed.

Transference is not an end in itself as is, say, the reinforcing of ego strengths, but a means and often a necessary means to successful diagnosis and treatment. For example, its operation, whether consciously controlled by the caseworker or not, accounts for success in those cases where the client's adjustment is blocked not alone by reality but at least in part by emotional difficulties. Its operation also accounts for many casework failures, as in those instances where the worker, unaware of its presence, either unwittingly fosters too much transference too rapidly, or fails to develop enough to hold the client through rough going.

In view of the basic importance of transference and its practical ubiquity in any complex casework situation, it becomes desirable for caseworkers to acquire greater knowledge of its nature and operation, greater ability to recognize and understand its manifestations and to increase or dilute it as the situation requires, greater understanding of its function in diagnosis and treatment, and greater skill in avoiding the pitfalls inherent in it.

Recognition of Transference

A caseworker may be overly transference-conscious and may, like the thief who sees a policeman in every doorway, find "clues" to transference in every favorable or unfavorable word or action of the client. Most early and obvious reactions are much more likely to be reality-induced and should be so understood and taken care of. Indications of transference, especially at first, are apt to be quite subtle. It is difficult even to notice them at this stage, and their understanding must be deferred until later. Clues to transference require for their adequate comprehension a good deal of knowledge about the client, often including knowledge that can be attained only after quite a bit of transference has already occurred. For example, in a child-placing agency a woman, who in her first interview discussed her problem in an apparently objective and adequate manner, failed to return. Active follow-up by the worker recovered the case, but it was not until much later that he realized that the client had identified him with her own father who had always required too much of her and hence could not be counted upon for satisfactory help.

Although understanding of transference often requires slowly acquired knowledge of the client, and always requires subtlety and skill if misinterpretation is to be avoided, a well-trained worker alert for clues may notice signs of transference fairly early. Thus a worker three minutes late at his first call at the home of a woman whose husband has recently deserted, properly notes for checking the woman's reproachful greeting, "Oh, I thought you had forgotten me."

Few general guides can be given for the discovery of transference. Perhaps the best is: Be alert for manifestations of transference, but distrust them. Check them against the reality situation, against all known information about the client, and especially against other apparent manifestations to see whether these "clues" nullify each other, or on the contrary coincide in their signification.

Regulation of Transference

The regulation of transference presents another difficult problem. Although some factors inherent in the casework situation tend inevitably to promote transference, others normally tend to dilute it. The initial reality dependence of the client seeking agency help leads easily to the transference of many of the unconscious feelings of childhood. The permissive, nonjudging attitude of the caseworker tends to facilitate transference because it leaves free play for the fantasy of the client. Because the caseworker does not immediately react with condemnation or advice, the client has little objective data on which to judge his attitude. The client's imagination then tends to endow the worker with feelings originat-

61

ing in his own unconscious. In general, the less activity the worker undertakes, the freer is the field for fantasy and the more readily transference occurs.

In so far as the worker focuses attention on the reality core of the client's problem, interest is diverted from the emotional area, discussion of which tends to promote transference. When it is specifically desirable to increase the intensity of transference, the worker can often do so by turning the interview from factual material to a discussion of feelings. This again dissipates the reality aspects of the situation and lets the atmosphere become hospitable to the development of feeling and emotion. The fact that expression of feelings is not rebuffed or condemned by the worker then tends to promote further expression and development. Often a client remarks, "I never could talk to anyone this way before."

In psychoanalytic therapy, where free association and dreams are used, a maximum of opportunity is provided for unconscious expression, and the intensity of transference increases apace. The caseworker, on the other hand, although he notes such occasional free association as occurs inadvertently, does not encourage it as a systematic procedure. The degree of transference promoted by the interview situation is thus very much less than that stimulated by the free association method of analysis.

Again, the fact that a patient on an analytic couch is not talking face to face with the analyst tends to minimize the reality factors of the analyst's appearance, his age, sex, and general personality. The patient is left relatively free to fantasy as he wills. In the face-to-face situation of the casework interview, it is less easy for the client to ignore such obvious features as the worker's age or sex. These are reality factors that tend to influence whatever transference takes place.

In general, a greater frequency of interviews steps up transference. In the usual procedure, when a worker sees a client not more than once a week, the intensity of transference is decreased by the intervening activities and other relationships of the client. When greater transference is required, it may often be induced by a period of more frequent contacts. On the other hand, an increase of the frequency of interviews may serve the opposite purpose. If a client has developed too intense a transference, absence from the worker

62

may pile up his feelings dangerously, and it may be necessary to give him more opportunities to drain these off and thus diminish the intensity of his transference.

Again, in the area of transference, personalization serves as a stimulus for further transference, and generalization tends to dissipate it. Thus, "Often people feel dependent" serves to dissipate transference, whereas "You feel dependent on me" centers attention on transference feelings and tends to increase them.

For effective control of transference, a worker must be aware also of his own countertransference and in reasonable control of it; for uncontrolled countertransference stirs up an emotional reaction in the client resulting in the accumulation of further positive or negative transference feelings.

Transference and Interpretation

Closely interwoven with transference and its regulation is the basic casework method of interpretation. Interpretation cannot be therapeutically successful unless it rests on the solid foundation of an established transference relationship. At the same time interpretation serves as an effective means of regulating the intensity of transference. Further, the object of interpretation may be either the transference feelings themselves or other dynamic factors in the client's personality.

Interpretation consists primarily of the discernment of hidden relationships among the various aspects of a client's personality which his behavior and conversation have revealed. It consists in putting two and two together, in taking account of the various clues the client has given and recognizing that they are all expressive of an underlying pattern of feeling or attitude of which the client has not before been fully conscious. It involves translating the client's manifest behavior patterns into their dynamic significance.

This is interpretation in the sense of recognizing and understanding relationships that have not been clear before; it is *interpretation by the worker to himself.* In another sense, and this is of more importance in reference to transference, interpretation occurs on those occasions when the caseworker, with appropriate safeguards, *interprets to the client.* Such interpretation must be less intellectual so that the client will be able to feel its appropriateness and accept it emotionally. A correct interpretation made in the right way at the right time enables the client to recognize the actuality of the underlying relationship to which the worker is calling attention. It makes it possible for him to give up his resistance to accepting a possibly unpleasant fact about himself and to reorient his current attitudes and behavior in the light of this new emotional self-knowledge.

Proper interpretation of a client's emotions and attitudes as they underlie his problem serves the important therapeutic effect of enabling him to recognize that his current behavior is appropriate only to some other situation perhaps long past, and thus to modify it to meet more satisfactorily the present reality situation. Interpretation as used in casework usually has this reality reference; it is designed to help a client understand his behavior in reference to his reality problem and hence to modify it appropriately. For example, a client who has revealed a lot of hatred toward a cigar-smoking father and who then says of his boss with whom he is having trouble, "He's always smoking one of those big foul cigars," may be helped if the worker remarks, "Just like your father?"—helped to recognize that he has been projecting his dislike of his father onto the boss for no better reason than this similarity of habit.

The chief dangers in the therapeutic use of interpretation to the client are that the worker may interpret too soon, too deeply, or too much, or that he may interpret inaccurately, or may use the interpretation as an attack.

Since interpretation reveals to the client facts about himself which he had previously resisted, it should not be undertaken until he has gained confidence enough in the worker not to fear that this revelation of the unpleasant will turn the worker away from him. In the absence of such confidence, interpretation may easily feel to a client like an attack. The previous establishment of positive transference will avert this danger. An added responsibility falls on the worker to ensure that his own countertransference feelings are not accusatory, that he is not really gleeful over his "discovery" and is not inadvertently using detective methods to "prove" his point or convince his unready client. Interpretation is helpful only if it is felt as a sympathetic and understanding aid to self-discovery. It succeeds best if the client can be helped to make it himself, to see for himself the relationship hitherto unnoticed by him, or is able to do so with a suggestion, "Do you see any relationship between such and such?"

It seems obvious that interpretation should begin at the top conscious layers of the personality. No one can see or accept a relation between elements of which he is still unconscious. Interpretation is easiest when it calls attention to a previously unnoticed relationship among factors of which, separately, one is clearly aware. It functions well when one or more of these factors is in the preconscious stage and needs only a slight additional stimulus to bring it to the full light of day. One sign that attempted interpretation is too deep is increased resistance. A client's resistance varies directly with the strength of his unconscious conflict. An increased resistance may be a sign that the caseworker is threatening to uncover such basic unconscious material that he had better retreat, either leaving that aspect of his client's problem unsolved, or delaying and approaching it by more gradual stages.

Again, interpretation cannot be too comprehensive. The client does well to discern one previously concealed connecting link at a time and only becomes confused if a worker attempts to direct his attention to a number of them at once. To overinterpret is an easy mistake. A young worker, thrilled by his own new knowledge, may be inclined to try to pass on all he knows about his client to him. Clearly this is both unnecessary and undesirable. A worker must interpret to himself. But he need not and usually should not seek to communicate his interpretation to his client. It may be helpful for the worker to know that a woman is a rejecting mother, but ordinarily it will be of no help to try to convince the woman of this. Two good questions to ask before interpreting to a client are, "Will this new insight, if it occurs, help him?" "Is he ready to accept it, or will he feel it as criticism?" Only when the answer to both is favorable should interpretation be undertaken. Thus, for example, it might be helpful for the rejecting mother to realize that she is thinking of her son too much in the image of her ne'er-do-well brother, for this may enable her to realize that she is projecting onto a boy feelings of aversion that were appropriate only

65

to his uncle. But if she regards such an interpretation as a criticism, she might well respond not with appropriately modified behavior, but with increased negative transference to the worker.

Interpretation should not be confused with explanation. In its therapeutic sense, interpretation refers to the entire process of the worker's activity that is followed by spontaneous insight by the client. The worker's activity to produce this may be only a nod, the repetition of what the client has just said, a brief question, or a comment. An explanation is seldom an interpretation as it elicits an intellectual rather than an emotional response. The place for explanation in casework is in reference to the objective reality factors of the client's problem. Only here is it likely to be helpful.

It is sometimes forgotten that a caseworker does not and cannot give insight to his client. In interpreting to himself, he gains insight into the underlying dynamic significance of the client's behavior. But he cannot pass this on directly to the client. He can offer him an interpretation, and if the client is ready for it and is not too resistive, he may then gain a corresponding insight.

To put it positively, a caseworker may interpret helpfully to a client under the following conditions: He must be sure that positive transference feelings have developed sufficiently to support the client in his new self-knowledge. The worker must know diagnostically that the client's ego strengths are great enough to enable him to forestall too great an eruption of feeling and to handle satisfactorily such excess of feeling as does accrue. The worker must interpret only conscious or preconscious factors, relating only things the client has recently been talking about. His interpretation must be tentative enough to give both himself and the client a chance to check its validity and to drop it if it proves incorrect. He must allow enough time between interpretations to permit the client to integrate his new understanding and to modify his behavior in the light of it.

An analyst, through his greater knowledge of the patient's unconscious, due in part to his use of dreams, has more material on the basis of which to forecast the accuracy of the interpretation and the patient's ability to accept and use it. The caseworker, limited for the most part to outward manifestations, must proceed more

66

slowly, checking carefully at each step along the way the clues he is thus offered.

As important in its effects on transference as the method of interpretation is the sort of material interpreted. Ordinarily interpretation will be of emotional relationships underlying the client's reality problem. Interpretation of this sort is of most direct help and normally increases the degree of transference. But there may also be interpretation of the transference feelings of the client toward the worker. Ordinarily these are not interpreted. But if the client is blocked or is in danger of breaking off treatment because he cannot tolerate the intensity of his transference feelings, either positive or negative, or if he begins "acting out" these feelings beyond the treatment situation, or if psychosomatic symptoms develop, discussion and interpretation of the transference feelings themselves may be necessary.

In summary, interpretation requires transference if it is to be acceptable and therapeutically efficacious; and interpretation in turn tends either to increase or dilute transference, depending on how it is used and on what subject matter. Interpretation that seems critical to the client will ordinarily diminish positive and increase negative transference, whereas a sympathetic helping of the client to self-knowledge will promote identification with a benevolent parental figure. Interpretation of the transference feelings themselves can help in reducing transference but should ordinarily be avoided by not allowing transference to develop to such an extent.

Use of Transference in Diagnosis

When a client's problem is due primarily to external factors, he is likely to be conscious of them and to have little resistance to discussing them with a receptive listener. In such cases a positive reality relationship suffices for diagnosis. When, however, emotional factors complicate his problems, transference becomes necessary. He is less fully aware, or perhaps quite unconscious, of the existence or nature of his personality difficulties and of their relation to his reality problem. He cannot talk about them directly because he is to such a considerable degree unaware of them himself. And even in so far as he is dimly conscious of them, the same

67

resistances that operate to keep him from becoming more fully and clearly aware of them serve to inhibit his talking about them. Transference diminishes these resistances to some extent and thus helps him to talk more freely than he otherwise could. But even more important, transference gives the worker clues by which he can infer the nature of the underlying difficulties.

Transference, in giving the worker increased insight into the client's personality, helps not only in identifying his weaknesses, those aspects of his nature which are the sources of his difficulties, but also, and perhaps more important, his strengths, those features of his ego which can form a sound basis for further growth. It is on the basis of these ego strengths that the worker will have to help him to build. Only as these are freed and allowed to assert themselves can the client modify his attitudes.

When diagnosis is unclear, there is sometimes a tendency to stimulate more intense transference than the worker realizes. If too much transference is developed too rapidly, the client may be plunged into deep despondency or into irrational hostility even before the worker is aware of what is happening. Should the client be a homosexual or a psychotic, such a stimulation to transference may release far more feeling than the worker can control. In such cases reinforcement of the defenses is indicated rather than diminution of them through transference. Even in less severe neuroses, care must be taken to avoid so much revelation of feeling that the client becomes frightened, perhaps filled with guilt or shame, and either runs away or becomes overdependent in a way that approaches the transference neurosis.

Use of Transference in Treatment

The caseworker's use of transference in treatment differs markedly from that of the analyst. The latter encourages it to the full, including the intense manifestations of the transference neurosis. He wants the patient to live through these intense feelings, and he helps him to become conscious of them. An important part of the analytic process is the analysis of these transference feelings themselves. The caseworker, on the other hand, seeks to keep transference at the minimum necessary for his purpose. He rarely offers even interpretation, let alone analysis of transference feelings.

He operates at the conscious, or, at most, the preconscious level, not trying to unearth and bring to the light of consciousness the deeply unconscious transference or other emotions of the client. Since only a person who uses the method of psychoanalysis can acquire a full knowledge of the unconscious, the caseworker's understanding of the unconscious, in general, is less rich than that of the analyst. Further, he lacks the detailed knowledge the latter acquires of the unconscious of the person under treatment. Again, since the caseworker's attention is focused on the client's reality problem, he does not seek to bring about the fundamental personality adjustment that is part of the aim of the analyst.

Although different in these respects, transference functions in casework, as it does in analysis, not as an isolated process but in manifold interrelation with other treatment procedures. Only the necessities of discussion and elucidation justify its artificial abstraction.

Much of the effective power of transference results from the parental role with which the client's emotions often endow the caseworker. The worker in his role of parent surrogate is able to give needed additional courage and strength to his client. A child, confident of his parents' love, will face difficult problems and new experiences unflinchingly, whereas one dominated by anxiety will cower away from the new and seek security in the old. Similarly, a client supported by his confidence in the strengths of the caseworker is willing to give up his old and worn patterns of behavior which have proved futile for the solution of his problem and dares to attack it by new and more hopeful methods.

Again, just as a child's affection for his parents makes him willing to try their suggestions, so his attachment to the caseworker renders a client amenable to suggestions from him. So effective indeed is this force that the caseworker must exercise caution if he is to avoid exploiting it by overguiding his client. But often a client is at the end of his resources with regard to his problem, and a worker can provide necessary aid by calling attention to a number of courses of possible action among which the client can then choose. Suggestion in this sense, far from controlling a client, instead enlarges the breadth of his choice and consequently his freedom of choice.

Transference promotes a feeling on the part of the client that his problem is being shared, that someone who is genuinely interested in his welfare is helping him to work to a satisfactory solution of it. This feeling is symbolized by the worker's frequent use of "we" in discussing the situation with him. This feeling of sharing itself mitigates the burden and eases the tasks that must be undertaken in working toward a solution.

This feeling of sharing is but one aspect of the identification of client with worker which transference develops. This identification functions importantly in treatment in a number of ways. The mature ego strengths of the worker serve to reinforce the weak ego strengths of the client. With their support he is better able to bear frustration for the sake of future benefit. He becomes more willing to abandon his resistances to facing the emotional disturbances of his personality which are contributing to his problem. He becomes better able to recognize and then modify the contributions his own personality has been making to his reality difficulties. Further, the worker who serves as a parental surrogate may differ from the original parental figure by not responding neurotically to the client's neurotic behavior. He thus breaks the vicious circle and enables the client to give up his own neurotic response to others, such as his employers, who also have the parental role projected upon them. Further, the worker, through being tolerant, becomes an idealized parent, identification with whom then becomes an increasing source of strength.

Identification with the worker helps the client not only in making use of the greater ego strengths of the worker, but also in modifying his own overly severe superego to match the more tolerant and accepting superego of the worker. Thus a superego that has been surcharging him with guilt and driving him to neurotic self-punishment may, through such identification with the less exacting superego of the worker, be able to relax and allow him to pursue a course of action which is more satisfactorily oriented to the reality situation.

For example—and this is typical of situations that occur in a child guidance clinic—a mother may complain with undue vehemence about her child's "intolerable" behavior, and later inadvertently reveal that her own mother was very severe with her, demanding rigid adherence to a strict code. Through sharing in the feelings of the idealized mother that the woman caseworker through transference has become for her, her own superego gradually relaxes, and she finds, often to her surprise, that she is less worried and anxious about her child's behavior and is much more tolerant and permissive of childish infractions.

Again, the very fact of the worker's being not only a parental surrogate and thus a creature of fancy, but also a real person helping in the solution of reality problems, helps the client to focus his attention on these, to use his increased knowledge of himself in their solution rather than as an excuse for further introversion and escape from the reality situation.

These various effects of transference in treatment never occur in isolation, but rather in close interrelation with each other and with the other aspects of treatment. The effect of any one by itself may be small, but it is not unusual for the whole process to integrate in such a way as to set off something resembling a chain reaction. The client, through increased confidence, freed ego strength, relaxed superego, or abandoned neurotic displacement, may come to behave somewhat more rationally toward some of the figures involved in his reality problem. This more rational behavior on his part meets with a better response, which gives him further confidence and security, makes possible less neurotic counter-response, and thus further increases his ability to deal with the reality rather than the delusive aspects of his problem. Increased success in reacting to the worker because of transference to him and his own reasonable behavior in the face of it, presents the client with a new and more satisfying experience which then serves as a model for improved behavior toward the persons connected with his problem. Any success then achieved with one of these increases the likelihood of success with others, and so on.

The effects of transference, although considerable and often far-reaching, should not of course be overemphasized. It is but one aspect of treatment procedure. It is but the leaven of treatment, not treatment itself. Yet only through the development of a casework method designed to utilize this universally present phenomenon will its dynamic force be directed to the realization of treatment goals. As remarked earlier, although the use of trans-

71

ference in casework often produces more satisfactory behavior, it does not result in the sort of fundamental personality readjustment that follows successful analysis. The caseworker, with the aid of transference, helps his client to make the best use of the ego strengths he has.

The worker does not necessarily make the client such a new man that he will solve any other problem that may later confront him. But the worker does stimulate the capacities for growth which seem to be present, if only latently, in everyone. By helping him to reach for himself a satisfactory solution of his current problem, the caseworker helps him also to make some progress toward a maturity with which to face and conquer later problems. In this casework process, knowledge of worker-client relationships, and especially of transference, is of inestimable benefit.

4. The Impact of the Client's Unconscious on the Caseworker's Reactions*

Ner Littner, M.D.

THERE IS NO QUESTION but that a shock effect may occur when one is first exposed to unconscious material. Nevertheless, I feel that the future of casework is inextricably tied with the further understanding by each caseworker of the unconscious feelings of his clients. It really is insufficient for the caseworker to have memorized stereotypes about personality functioning. If he is to do full justice to his desire to help troubled people, he must be prepared, when he is with the client, to understand what is bothering him at that very moment. In view of the fact that the main feelings that disturb the client are unknown to him because they are unconscious, it becomes the caseworker's responsibility to understand what lies behind the client's verbal and non-verbal communication so that the worker will know what is bothering the client, even though he himself may not. It is only begging the question to suggest, as some do, that the unconscious is the private domain of the psychiatrist and that no poaching by social workers is allowed. The fact of being a caseworker rather than a psychiatrist need not set any limits on how much of the client's total feeling he is entitled to understand. Regardless of what the worker does with this under-

* Presented at a meeting sponsored by the Chicago Chapter of the Smith College School for Social Work Alumnae Association, Chicago, May 6, 1957, as a discussion of Miss Hamilton's paper (Chapter 1).

standing, or the kind of therapy he uses—whatever its semantic definition—the therapy then will logically develop from the worker's appreciation of what is really occurring between him and the client.

The Unconscious Request

My discussion pertains to the use of Freudian theory in recognizing how a client's unconscious feelings may manifest themselves in his relationship with the caseworker. Specifically, I wish to comment on how some clients unconsciously seek to provoke certain feelings and behavior in the caseworker, and to describe how, when the client is successful in this provocation, he is able to conceal from himself either the presence or the true nature of some of his own feelings.

A basic contribution of Sigmund Freud and those who have followed in his footsteps has been increased knowledge of the many feelings one person may experience toward another, of the origins of these feelings, and of the methods by which one handles the feelings that are too painful to tolerate in consciousness. In the field of social work, the application of this knowledge has vividly illuminated many of the subtle interactions between the client and the caseworker. It has always been recognized that a client's request for help and the caseworker's provision of specific services do not occur in an emotional vacuum. Yet only today are we beginning to appreciate some of the complex meanings of the two-way emotional interchange between client and worker.

A client who asks for a specific service consciously may think that this is all he wants. However, if there are sufficient contacts with the caseworker and an emotional relationship begins to develop—or sometimes even in the first interview—the client unconsciously may wish for far more from the caseworker. This unconscious request usually is not verbalized and both the client and the worker may be completely unaware of its existence.

Some of the client's feelings and anticipations about the caseworker are realistic reactions to the worker as he really is. Many others, however, are not realistic but are a result of the fact that the relationship with the caseworker and the behavior of the caseworker tend to stir up in the client unresolved conflicts from his childhood. These reactivated desires, concerns, and anticipa-

74

tions are now unconsciously experienced toward the caseworker. The client is then placed in a dilemma since, in order to satisfy these unconscious wishes adequately, he must somehow become aware of them. This he is unable to do, for at least two reasons. First, the impulses and worries currently being aroused once were realistic reactions to painful experiences in childhood, but are now, in the relationship with the caseworker, completely irrational and unrealistic. Second, if the client should consciously experience these feelings as his own he would be threatened with some of the pain and fright which in childhood had caused him to repress them.

The client, therefore, as part of his developing relationship with the caseworker, not only consciously asks for a specific service but unconsciously seeks gratification for the wishes and reassurance for the concerns that are parts of the unresolved conflicts now stirred up within him. He may attempt to relieve this inner tension in many ways. For example, he may use the proffered services of the caseworker as a smoke screen to hide the fact that he is unconsciously playing out with the worker a reassuring version of an emotional scene from his childhood. If a client is able to use the casework relationship in this manner, he may be able to avoid facing the fact that he is currently experiencing with the caseworker feelings and concerns that really belong to painful childhood experiences.

Unconscious Provocation

Generally speaking, there are at least three ways in which a client may make unconscious use of the feelings and behavior of the caseworker in order to help himself control the anxious and unacceptable feelings aroused within him by the relationship. These three methods are: (1) discharging his unconscious feelings directly, but only after setting up a situation with the caseworker in which his feelings appear justified; (2) discharging his unconscious feelings indirectly, by causing the caseworker to experience them instead; (3) provoking behavior from the caseworker which reassures an unconscious concern within himself.

Discharging unconscious feelings directly by provoking a justifying situation: In order to discharge his unconscious feelings directly, the client attempts unconsciously to create a situation in which his currently illogical and unrealistic feelings can be made to appear

75

realistic. By inducing the caseworker to exhibit behavior to which his own unconscious feelings would seem a natural response, he can allow his unacceptable feelings to become conscious since, as an apparent reaction to the caseworker's behavior, they now appear completely justified.

Mrs. A had never made peace with her upset feelings about her mother whom she had experienced as being distant, angry, and rejecting. When her son was treated by a child guidance clinic for his own problems, Mrs. A was also seen in collaborative therapy. In time, the caseworker came to dread the interviews because she was constantly being angered and frustrated by Mrs. A's unreasonable demands and provocative attacks, and by her repeated accusations that the caseworker, rather than helping her, was actually depriving her of vital information about her son's progress.

Mrs. A was thus successful in pushing the caseworker into an unrealistic corner so that the worker really did feel angry and rejecting, and really did believe that she was depriving the client. By unconsciously forcing the caseworker into a mold that actually fitted her experiences with her own mother, Mrs. A felt justified in experiencing and expressing angry feelings that currently seemed logical to her but that actually belonged to her unresolved childhood conflicts about her mother.

In another paper [1] I have discussed various examples, from the child welfare field, of the placed child's similar attempts to control painful feelings by unconsciously manipulating his caseworker's feelings to evoke a desired response. Let me give one of them here.

Jimmy was so provocative one day in his therapy session that he made his caseworker obviously angry and restrictive. He then accused her of being very mean and proceeded to stalk out of the room, loudly proclaiming that he would never come back. And he didn't, for a long three months. The caseworker, who was completely taken aback by how angry she had felt and acted, secretly agreed with Jimmy's evaluation of her meanness. What was thus completely missed was the recognition that Jimmy, as his method of handling his unacceptable feelings about the caseworker's approaching vacation, had rejected her before she could reject him. Because of his inability to tolerate consciously

[1] Ner Littner, M.D., *The Strains and Stresses on the Child Welfare Worker*, Child Welfare League of America, New York, 1957.

76

how he really felt about her leaving him, he provoked a situation that appeared to justify his angry feelings about a mean person, and only then could he experience and express them. He was, of course, completely unaware of this mechanism.

I have given two examples of one way in which a client may attempt direct discharge of conflictory feelings that are stirred up by his relationship with the caseworker. By unconscious manipulation of the worker's emotions, the client tries to evoke from him behavior that will allow him to cover with the cloak of current reality unpleasant feelings derived from his past.

Discharging unconscious feelings indirectly by causing the caseworker to experience them instead: A client may also try to conceal his conflicting feelings from himself by unconsciously manipulating the caseworker's emotions so as to displace onto the worker feelings and concerns that really belong to himself. He tries to avoid experiencing a consciously unacceptable emotion by causing the caseworker to experience it instead. He can thus indirectly discharge his pent-up feelings by satisfying them vicariously through the caseworker.

For example, the client who cannot accept his own curiosity about the caseworker may try to make the worker curious about *him*. Or the anger that a caseworker feels toward a client's husband may serve to discharge indirectly, and so to conceal, the client's own anger toward the husband. A client may be able to avoid facing concern about himself and his own feelings if he can get the caseworker to become concerned instead.

Natalie, an inhibited 15 year-old adolescent, had many anxieties about her sexual feelings. She told her caseworker such hair-raising stories about planned sexual escapades that the caseworker, alarmed lest Natalie start acting out sexually, repeatedly and unnecessarily warned Natalie about the dangers of sexual promiscuity. As long as Natalie could evoke such concern in the caseworker about her sexual feelings, she could avoid consciously facing the fact that basically the anxiety was her own and not the caseworker's.

I have been considering, thus far, how a client unwittingly may attempt to set up a casework relationship that will enable him to drain off, either directly or indirectly, some of his consciously unacceptable feelings, while simultaneously avoiding recognition

77

of their true nature. Frequently, however, he tries to provoke behavior from the caseworker not only for the purpose of justifying or indirectly discharging his currently unrealistic feelings, but also to reassure himself about the inner concerns being stirred up.

Unconscious provoking of behavior to reassure concerns: The provoking of *anger* in the caseworker and the worker's resulting behavior may have many reassuring meanings for the client.

Mr. B had been raised by a mother who had put a great deal of pressure on him to learn quickly. When he could not live up to her unreasonable expectations, she went through a cycle of getting angry at his stupidity, then punishing him, and finally forgiving him. When, as an adult, Mr. B unconsciously experienced feelings toward the caseworker that he felt were unacceptable to her, he would suddenly seem quite stupid and completely unable to understand what she was attempting to explain to him. It bothered the caseworker that at such times she became quite provoked with him. However, her obviously angry reaction to his apparent obtuseness actually served a very reassuring function to him, because of his unconscious expectation that her anger would be followed by forgiveness of his external misdeed. Thus temporarily he could ease his deeper guilt over his internal feelings of badness. As long as he could find inward reassurance by evoking this angry response from the caseworker, Mr. B could avoid completely any conscious knowledge of the conflict raging within him.

Mr. C, on the other hand, had been brought up by a depressed mother who seemed interested in him only when she was angry at something he had done. Emotional contact between them seemed to exist only when she was enraged. As an adult, when he experienced unconsciously a feeling that he felt would cause his caseworker to lose interest in him, he would provoke her to anger in order to gain the kind of emotional contact that for him was reassuring. But of course his success in producing an angry caseworker meant that consciously he also remained unaware of his inner conflict.

Mr. D also used anger as a reassuring device. One of his major emotional problems was fear of his wish for closeness. As he became more involved in a relationship with the caseworker, his wish to be cared for by her became stronger and therefore more threatening to him. At such times, he would unconsciously provoke her to anger, causing her to draw away and reject him, thus producing for him a safe emotional distance.

Other Responses

There are many other kinds of behavior which clients unconsciously may attempt to evoke in their caseworkers for inner self-reassurance. I have stressed angry behavior because it usually is considered socially unacceptable for a caseworker to feel the emotion of anger toward a client, and he may therefore be ashamed to mention it. There are, however, other responses which seem quite acceptable for a caseworker to make but which also may be unconsciously sought out and used by the client for his own emotional self-protection.

Mr. E had been *overprotected* by a mother who had dressed and bathed him far beyond the necessary time. In contacts with his caseworker, whenever an unacceptable impulse unconsciously caused him to become inwardly concerned about her reaction to him, he would become the caricature of a co-operative client. He would ask for and use specific advice and help; he would subtly push the caseworker into taking authoritative stands, and almost induce her to assume the direction of his life.

Mr. F had been raised by a mother who was extremely interested in his bowel movements and who was highly pleased whenever he did a good job of producing for her stools of the right size, amount, color, and consistency. Similarly, in his relationship with his caseworker, whenever he unconsciously expected disapproval, he would "produce" for her in order to reassure himself by getting her *pleased reaction*. His fecal productions, of course, were dressed up in suitable adult guise. He would produce therapeutic results, specially adapted for casework consumption. He offered copious insights into his problems and colorful stories of his progress on his job and in his marriage.

Mr. G, as a child, quickly discovered that his mother secretly enjoyed his stealing escapades but would severely reprimand him for them. As an adult, when he was inwardly troubled about an unacceptable feeling toward his caseworker, he would boast about his delinquent dealings, which would provoke her to lecture him about his misconduct. However, she could not help inwardly being quite intrigued by his manipulations.

Mrs. H, as a child, had a mother who unconsciously enjoyed her daughter's sexual acting-out. To her caseworker Mrs. H told such intriguing stories of her life as a prostitute that the caseworker always looked forward eagerly to the interviews with her.

79

Such *angry, overprotective,* or *pleased* reactions from the caseworker are not the only emotional responses which clients seek to evoke as a subtle method of quieting inner turmoil.

Mr. J had learned unconsciously how to evoke *boredom* as a self-protective device. Whenever he was inwardly troubled his voice became monotonous and his conversation uninteresting. His caseworker, despite her best intentions, found herself almost falling asleep.

Mr. K had been brought up by a mother who was so preoccupied with herself that he felt she had little thought for him. Whenever he unconsciously anticipated a similar uninterested reaction from his caseworker, he became so upset and so demanding that his caseworker spent a great deal of time between their interviews thinking and *worrying* about him. In this way, Mr. K unconsciously reassured himself that his anticipated concern about the caseworker was not true. The present reality that he had provoked with the caseworker unconsciously reassured him about his inner, unrealistic, childhood-derived fears.

Mrs. L had been raised by parents who constantly *quarreled.* As an adult, she had learned unconsciously how to get two people quarreling by the discreet selection of what she told each about the other. Whenever she was troubled by the tension of an inner conflict, she would paint for her caseworker a most unsympathetic picture of her husband, would indirectly blame him for all her troubles, and casually mention his angry disagreements with the caseworker's suggestions. The caseworker's anger at the interfering husband was matched only by his anger at her, since his wife, of course, was unconsciously provoking him in the same way.

John was a child who was being treated in group therapy by a male worker and in individual therapy by a woman caseworker. Although John was very fond of both, he rarely mentioned one to the other. Suddenly one day he told his woman therapist that since he liked both of them so much, he would like to be seen by both workers in his individual therapy sessions.

This request stirred up the woman therapist considerably, but she rationalized to herself that perhaps it would be a corrective emotional experience for John to see that a mother and a father figure could get along well together. Therefore, she complied with John's wish and persuaded the group worker to join her in John's treatment interviews. What this very skilled caseworker was blind to, because her own problems were being stirred up, was that for some time she had been thinking of leaving the agency, that she had finally made up her mind to do so, and that John had sensed it because of her unconscious withdrawal from him, although she had not yet told him. To John, separation from a loved woman had a very early unconscious meaning. When he was 17 months old, his father—whom he had never seen—returned home from overseas and displaced John in his mother's affections. Therefore, for John, separation from his caseworker unconsciously implied that a father figure was about to enter his and her life. John attempted to master his concern about this unconsciously anticipated event by taking the bull by the horns and being the one responsible for the event.

Caseworker's Use of His Own Feelings

I have discussed the importance of understanding some of the subtle interactions in the client-worker relationship, from the client's point of view. Such understanding is a result of the illumination first provided by Sigmund Freud and later maintained and strengthened by his followers. Certain casework practices— giving advice, being directive, being pleased by the client's accomplishments, or showing concern about the client—may be subtly provoked responses used by the client to protect himself from consciously experiencing some of his own painful feelings.

The caseworker must fully appreciate *all* of the meaning of his behavior toward the client, if he is to gain a better understanding of what *really* is transpiring between them. He will appreciate that the client actually is asking for service on two levels. Consciously, he is trying to persuade the worker to meet his needs as he is aware of them. Unconsciously, he is trying to persuade the worker to meet needs of which he is totally unaware. The latter include: (1) satisfying his unconscious desires, (2) reassuring his unconscious concerns, and, simultaneously, (3) helping him keep from conscious awareness the presence or true nature of these desires or concerns.

The caseworker who is able to use his own feelings to help him understand what the client really is trying to say, may find his thinking going through six steps:

(1) A critical self-awareness of what he is feeling, thinking, and doing when he is with the client, while still retaining spontaneity; (2) a recognition and conscious sorting-out of the feelings that he experienced prior to seeing the client and which, therefore, may not be related to the client; (3) an increasing awareness that some

of his feelings are present only when he is with this particular client; (4) an understanding of what the client is saying and doing to evoke these feelings; (5) an attempt to understand the feelings that are probably present in the client to cause him to need such a feeling and behavior response from the worker; and, finally, (6) a consideration of the origins in the client's past life experiences of this particular emotional interchange.

I have said nothing about the fact that some caseworkers are more vulnerable than others to having their feelings and behavior manipulated in such a way. This vulnerability is due partially to current stresses in the caseworker's life but basically to the sensitivities originating in unresolved conflicts derived from his own childhood experiences.

Ideally, the caseworker should be sufficiently at peace with his own feelings to recognize that some of them, when he is with his client, belong in effect to the client. He will then be able to derive from his own self-awareness invaluable diagnostic clues that will help him reach an understanding of what is troubling the client and how to help him with it. The more vulnerable the caseworker is to the client's self-protective manipulations, the longer will the client be able to avoid the ultimate goal of facing up to and conquering his own emotional problems.

In this connection, I think it is vitally important for us to consider Miss Hamilton's comments on supervision.[2] I fully agree that the supervisor plays an important role in providing the caseworker with the emotional support, encouragement, and information that will enable him to gain increasing tolerance of the emotional demands made upon him by his clients. It is important that the supervisor help the caseworker identify the nature of the client's unconscious manipulations, and recognize the fact that he may be vulnerable to these manipulations in certain areas. But I definitely do not believe that it is within the function of the supervisor or the agency to deal directly with the caseworker's childhood-derived personal difficulties. Obtaining direct help with his own internalized emotional problems is, I think, the sole responsibility of the caseworker; it is his prerogative to know as much or as little about himself as he wishes.

2 See Chapter 1 of this volume.

5. Personality Diagnosis in Casework *

Florence Hollis

THE ONLY SENSIBLE APPROACH to questions of personality diagnosis in casework, it seems to me, is through asking ourselves: "What do we need to know in order to do the kind of job that casework considers itself responsible for doing?" Diagnosis and treatment have an extremely close relationship—in fact, they are different facets of the same problem. The treatment of any problem is inevitably determined in large part by one's understanding of its nature, and that, essentially, is what diagnosis is. In casework, diagnosis is the attempt to define as accurately and fully as is necessary for casework treatment the nature of the problem, its causative factors, and the person's attitude toward the problem. From this formulation we design our treatment plan—our picture of the way in which we shall proceed in offering help to the client.

Obviously, the only purpose of diagnosis is treatment. Therefore, the nature of casework diagnosis can be discussed only in the light of the nature of casework treatment. There seems to be considerable agreement about the nature and scope of casework treatment as a whole. The different subdivisions or sub-types of treatment, however, are defined and understood in several different ways and designated by a variety of terms. In the hope of clarifying these

* Presented at a meeting sponsored by the New England Chapter of the Smith College School for Social Work Alumnae Association, Boston, January 14, 1955.

83

matters somewhat further, I should like to propose a slightly different classification from those used heretofore.

The Two Forms of Casework Treatment

I am inclined to think that there are really only two major forms of casework treatment which, for lack of better terms, I should like to call "supportive treatment" and "development of self-awareness." My definition of the former is "treatment that aims to improve general functioning of the person without substantial increase in the ego's understanding of previously hidden aspects of the self." My definition of the latter is "treatment that holds as a major aim the improvement of the individual's functioning by seeking to better the ego's direction of behavior through enabling the ego to gain more accurate and more complete understanding of previously hidden aspects of the individual's own feelings and behavior."

Both these forms of treatment have the aim of improving the *individual's functioning.* I think we have confused ourselves quite unnecessarily in the past by pretending that supportive treatment did not have the aim of improving adaptive patterns, but rather was concerned only with maintaining current adaptive patterns. I am convinced that considerable improvement in adaptive patterns occurs as the result of using purely supportive measures. Likewise, we confuse ourselves by trying to define certain types of casework, particularly "insight development," as those that bring about so-called "basic changes" in the personality. In the first place, we have not defined what we mean by "basic change." If we mean the kind of change that occurs when previously unconscious, infantile, psychosexual phenomena are relived in the treatment context, obviously nothing short of psychoanalysis or intensive analytic psychotherapy can bring this about—and this is not casework. If this is not what we mean by basic change, then it will have to be defined in a way that tells us how basic a change has to be to be awarded that title. It is more fruitful to describe the *nature* of the change we are seeking and the means by which we seek to obtain it.

In supportive treatment the change we are seeking is one that may occur either without the client's awareness of change in functioning, as such, or with his better evaluation of the reality situation but without substantial increase in his knowledge of *himself*. The improved functioning is brought about by environmental changes, by the effects of catharsis, by the influence of an encouraging, anxiety-relieving relationship with a caseworker, and by better perception of external reality. Supportive treatment does not involve, by intent, any uncovering of hidden material.

In development of self-awareness, on the contrary, the personality changes do involve greater self-understanding and require that the client examine previously hidden aspects of his own thoughts, feelings, and behavior. I am increasingly inclined to think that in casework we are principally uncovering suppressed, preconscious material rather than unconscious material, though I would not rule out some small use of the "near-conscious unconscious" material. Here I would follow very closely the lines laid down by Dr. Greta Bibring and Dr. Edward Bibring in the Symposium on Psychotherapy and Casework [1] in which they participated in Boston in 1949. Many of us in the past have not been altogether clear about the distinction between preconscious and unconscious material and we have tended to regard as "unconscious" some material that actually belonged among the more remote preconscious thoughts, feelings, and memories.

The Use of Unconscious and Preconscious Material

The term "unconscious" refers to memories, thoughts, and fantasies which, upon entering consciousness, were so anxiety creating that they were automatically repressed, and material of a similar or even greater anxiety-producing potential which was never even allowed to reach consciousness. These consist of memories, thoughts, and fantasies representing infantile destructive and sexual impulses and wishes, material concerning matters strongly prohibited or invoking punishment by parents especially in pre-school years, later traumatic events, and derivatives so closely related to these matters that to recall them would involve danger of a break-through of the associated material. If casework deals with unconscious material at all, it is only in a minor way with these derivatives.

The term "preconscious" covers a wide range of memories, thoughts, and fantasies. It includes, first, material that differs in no

[1] *Journal of Social Casework*, Vol. XXX, No. 6 (1949).

way from conscious material except that it is not at the moment the the subject of attention. Second, it applies to material that has relatively little cathexis, either because it originated very long ago or was not very important to the person. Third, it refers to suppressed material—that is, ideas that were so anxiety arousing that by more or less conscious choice or effort they were pushed out of consciousness. Fourth, it refers to material that has never been fully conscious but would arouse anxiety comparable to that of suppressed ideas if it entered consciousness. There is a vast amount of content in these last two types of preconscious material and it is primarily this content, I believe, that casework deals with in the second method of treatment—that is, in developing self-awareness.

The most important distinction between the two forms of treatment outlined lies in whether or not an attempt is made to bring suppressed material into consciousness; for as soon as we move in the direction of uncovering hidden material we move in the direction of arousing anxiety. In order to reach this material we need, at points in treatment, to permit the continuance of some degree of tension within the client, otherwise there is no seeking for the answers that lie hidden below readily accessible material. In supportive treatment, on the contrary, we are primarily reassuring and attempt to lessen the client's anxiety as promptly as possible rather than to delay this for therapeutic reasons.

Development of self-awareness comprises a wide range of efforts—from the unveiling of current feelings of which the person is unaware (for example, the anger of a mother toward a child when that anger is inhibited and suppressed because of the mother's ideal of herself as always sweet and loving) to the bringing to light of suppressed memories about childhood attitudes and experiences which have lain dormant for many years. Such efforts may constitute quantitatively a small part of treatment with only one small facet of the person's life examined, or they may be extensive both in the range of life experiences examined and in the thoroughness with which they are gone into. The more extensive such examination is, the more anxiety will be involved for the client.

Thus, in deciding upon what treatment to offer a client, as part of the process of studying his situation, personality, and needs, we must estimate carefully his general capacity for bearing anxiety and his ways of dealing with it, the degree of anxiety likely to be aroused by exploration of certain areas, and the areas in which such uncovering can profitably be undertaken.

I do not need to stress the fact that we do not *impose* treatment on a client. We offer it and he either makes use of our efforts or rejects them. It is part of our job to foresee what he is likely to accept and to modify our offerings accordingly. If we misjudge his desire for help after we have done what we can do to help him work through his fear of accepting help, we must try to find a new basis that will be more acceptable to him. In the end, an implicit or explicit decision to engage in treatment must be arrived at mutually; no other course is either desirable or possible.

The Nature of the Information Needed

A limitation of this paper must be made clear at this point. I am concentrating upon the effort to delineate the client's personality for the purpose of selecting the general form of treatment which is to be offered him. Stress is therefore being placed upon the nature of the information needed in making such a delineation. There is another important area of diagnosis with which this paper does not deal directly—that of describing with equal care the nature of the *situation* of which the client is a part. A thorough understanding of the situation is necessary, in part to determine whether changes can be brought about in the situation itself and, in part, to analyze specifically what changes the client himself needs to make in order to relate himself more constructively to his total life situation. Whether such adjustments as the client himself can make are to be achieved through supportive methods or through development of self-awareness, however, depends upon the worker's estimate of the nature of the client's personality. It is on this latter concern that the present paper seeks to shed light.

What do we need to know in order to guide ourselves in offering casework help? Obviously, we need first to know what he sees as his problem, what he has tried to do about it, what he wants to do about it, and what he hopes we can do about it. We must, therefore, secure a sufficiently rounded and detailed account of his problem as he sees it from which to draw some conclusions about the reasonableness of his appraisal of his own situation. Within limits set by the function of our agency, we then broaden our inquiry beyond the presenting problem to include matters which he reveals to be additional problems or which our observation of him or our general knowledge of similar situations leads us to believe might be problem areas for him. If his need seems to be one that cannot be met by concrete services or by supportive services of rather brief duration, we must explore the nature of his personality and his adjustment with great care.

Although such an exploration requires a number of free-flowing interviews which follow, in large part, the client's own lines of thought, the process is by no means an unstructured one. In fact, one of the greatest weaknesses of casework as it is practiced today lies in our failure to pursue lines of inquiry that give us the answers to certain basic questions about the personality of our clients.

There are three main areas from which information can be drawn: (1) the actual life situation, that is, the external reality life factors to which the client is reacting; (2) the client's physical condition; (3) the way in which, as a personality, the client is reacting to his life situation. We must look at these three aspects of the client's life as they reveal themselves in his current life, in his past life, and in the treatment relationship.

We often fail to get an accurate picture of the first two of these areas, and it is impossible to evaluate the third except in relation to the first two. We rely too much on the client's spontaneous productions and we are satisfied with generalizations instead of inquiring about the specifics on which the generalizations are based. I cannot overemphasize the importance of getting from the client the concrete details of the daily and past events of his life—of his actual functioning. We must not let him generalize; we must ask for specific narrative detail. It is the "I said, he said, she said" of life that we need in order to do our own evaluating of what occurred. We cannot rely solely on the client's subjective reaction. It is only in this way that we can check for the internal consistency of his story, and estimate the adequacy of his reactions to life's events and his interpretations of them. Furthermore, when it comes to treatment itself, only specific material can be used in helping the client. Generalized observations lead only to intellectualization or confusion.

88

The method by which caseworkers secure the information they need for casework diagnosis often needs to be understood. Just as our treatment is almost entirely concerned with conscious and preconscious material, so the data on which our diagnosis rests are also conscious or preconscious. We definitely do not have access to deeply unconscious material and therefore cannot use it in diagnosis, although we do use our general knowledge of the unconscious as a frame of reference for understanding the individual and we can draw inferences about his unconscious mental processes from conscious and preconscious data.

We do not use true free association in casework interviewing. Rather we rely on the voluntary production of material in a permissive atmosphere which often overcomes suppression but by no means carries the power of free association for bringing repressed unconscious material to light.

The Social Study and Diagnosis

Returning now to the *content* of our social study, from the three areas of information—life situation, physical condition, and psychological reactions of the client to his situation—what are we seeking to know? What sort of diagnosis are we trying to make? We seek: (1) to answer certain questions about the nature of the client's personality and the dynamics of his functioning; (2) to understand something of the etiology of the client's behavior; (3) to answer certain questions about the significance of the problem for the client; and (4) to classify his adjustment. I should like to consider each of these four subjects.

1. Concerning *the nature of the client's personality and the dynamics of his functioning,* we secure information on the following points:

    a. What is the quality of his libidinal relationships? To what extent is he capable of warm object relationships? To what extent is he dependent, and to what extent is he narcissistic?

    b. What is the nature of his sexual identifications? His attitude toward his own and the opposite sex? His specific sexual adjustment?

    c. What is the quality of his aggressiveness? How extensive

89

and how primitive are his hostilities? What direction do they take? How much of his aggression is channelized into problem-solving?

d. What is the nature of his superego? To what extent is it overly severe or overly lax? How consistent is it?

e. How well does his ego function in the following respects: How accurate are his reality perceptions? How accurate is his image of himself? What capacity does he show for self-criticism? How good is his judgment? How efficient and effective are his controls of his own behavior? What is his ability to secure reality gratifications? How intelligent is he? How great is his anxiety, and how does he handle it?

f. On what defenses does he characteristically rely?

g. What symptoms has he needed to develop?

h. What are his principal character traits?

Systematic exploration of the possible symptom picture especially tends to be overlooked by many caseworkers. The picture of defenses also is frequently not carefully delineated. Knowledge of the major defenses upon which an individual relies and of his character traits gives an essential key both to the nature of his difficulty and to the choice of treatment method, area, and depth.

All these questions can be answered only as we appraise the inter-action between a person's external reality, his physical condition, and his personality. This appraisal is based on knowledge of his functioning in his current life, observations of his responses in the treatment situation, and knowledge of his past functioning. All three sources of information are of great importance.

2. The social study also must help us to understand *the etiology of the client's difficulty.* The chronology of changes in the client's behavior and their relationship to life events are our major concern as we seek to establish cause and effect in the development of his personality. We look also for the characteristics of periods of better functioning and for the precipitating factor in the present acute phase of difficulty. Symptoms, defenses, and character traits also provide etiological clues.

3. Concerning *the significance of the problem for the client,* we wish to know the degree of discomfort the problem causes him,

the nature of his desire to change it, and the effect that change may have upon other members of his family and on his ability to satisfy his needs in the world of reality. Here again we must think very specifically and concretely about the interrelationship between the individual's personality characteristics and their effect on his actual life. There are situations in which an overly severe superego is not a great handicap. Certain defenses work havoc for a person under some circumstances and do little damage in others. Inhibition, for instance, is a much greater handicap in some marriages than in others, and the same holds true for intellectualization, for turning against the self, and so on. It is not enough to say a person acts in such and such a way. We must also determine whether or not his acting in such a way causes actual suffering for him or for others in his life.

We must look with particular care at the interactions within the individual's immediate family. Social workers carry responsibility for the well-being not only of the client who originally applied for help but also for other members of the family even though *direct* treatment responsibility may be taken for only the original applicant. To fulfil this obligation we must, in effect, include an appraisal of the family interaction—family diagnosis it is sometimes called—in arriving at a total understanding of the problem. Family diagnosis has particular importance in our estimate of the significance of the problem for the client and the values that a change in his adjustment may have for him as a member of a family.

4. We seek also *to classify the client's adjustment.* It is in this area that we run into a good deal of controversy on two scores: first, on the grounds of the danger of categorizing, and, second, on the question of appropriate terminology. "Categorizing" can be used in a derogatory sense to descibe the *mis*use of classification. Certainly we all want to guard against such misuse; for example, distorting a situation to make it fit into a classification to which it does not belong, failing to take into account newly emerging information which calls for a change of classification, failing to recognize mixed classification, or using classifications to destroy the individuality of a person. But these abuses are not necessary; they can be guarded against. When properly used, classification

91

simply brings to bear on the understanding of one individual what has been learned from the experience of other individuals who have had similar life experiences or who tend to react in similar ways. We human beings have much in common in our maladjustments, and we might as well put this commonness to good use. Certainly classification should not be allowed to destroy the individuality of the client. In truth, each person is unique. The suffering of no two people is ever exactly alike, nor is their treatment ever identical. The nuances of treatment are highly individual and the art of treatment lies in our adapting it to the subtle, unique differences that defy classification; but the science of treatment rests upon our bringing to the help of one person what has been learned from the suffering of another.

As to the second area of controversy about classification—terminology—perhaps it is the phrase "clinical diagnosis" that has so confused us on this issue because of its medical implications. Some people claim that when a caseworker states that, in his opinion, a client has a compulsion neurosis, he is making a medical diagnosis. Actually, all he is doing is using the same term that a doctor would use to express the same ideas. It is impossible for a social worker to make a medical diagnosis; a medical diagnosis is made by a physician for the purpose of medical treatment. We are not doctors and we do not express our opinion for the purpose of medical treatment. The real question is whether the use of the same terminology as that used by physicians will facilitate or hamper our ability to help our client. Granted that doctors themselves are still formulating their terminology, it is true, nevertheless, that they have reached at least a measure of common understanding about the words they use for classification. Since we collaborate extensively with psychiatrists, I see no particular advantage in our developing a different terminology to add to everyone's confusion.

The more we use a common language, the greater will be the possibilities of fruitful and accurate interchange of thought between the two professions. In many instances collaboration is necessary before we can arrive at a reasonably satisfactory diagnosis. Since the social worker is untrained in understanding physical phenomena, this part of the diagnosis must be contributed entirely by the doctor. The doctor usually has greater training and experience in detecting and identifying the psychoses and in evaluating intrapsychic phenomena. The social worker usually has greater training and experience in evaluating phenomena of social behavior. The analytically trained psychiatrist obviously has deeper understanding of unconscious phenomena than either the social worker or the psychiatrist of ordinary training. Whatever insight each has, let him contribute fully to the final opinion; but surely common language will help rather than hinder the process. In the communication of diagnostic opinions to other agencies, care must be taken not only to use language appropriate to the use of the inquirer (with due regard for confidentiality), but also to make clear whether the opinion is a physician's opinion, an analyst's opinion, a social worker's opinion, a psychologist's opinion, or one arrived at in consultation by all or several of these practitioners. It would certainly be inexcusable for a casework diagnosis to be transmitted with the implication that it is a medical opinion.

One important point about the social worker's use of terminology is that it is essential for him to understand the whole conception behind any term he uses. He should know its significance in terms of what kinds of feeling the client has; how he is likely to react; why he feels and acts as he does; how he can best be helped. Knowledge of classification helps the worker in knowing what to look for in order to understand another person with accuracy, and tremendously sharpens his understanding of personality.

Collaboration between casework and psychiatry is highly important whenever the development of self-awareness is contemplated, and certainly in any situation in which organic involvement or psychosis is suspected. It is also frequently of great value in supportive treatment.

Selecting the Treatment Method

I should like to turn now to the question of the significance of this type of diagnosis for casework treatment. An early decision must be made as to whether to rely primarily on supportive work or on developing self-awareness.

Frequently the client's ability to handle his problems does not appear to be adversely affected by hidden feelings, drives, or reactions. In such instances supportive treatment is wholly adequate. In other situations, even though hidden factors do exist, the client shows no interest in examining these but may be willing to use supportive help. This should by all means be given even though the worker may be disappointed in the client's lack of motivation for understanding. A third type of client for whom supportive help is most suitable is the very seriously disturbed person. Certainly if psychosis is either present or suspected, the worker does not want to promote the uncovering of hidden material. Rather, his aim becomes one of helping the person to keep disturbing material suppressed and of emphasizing reality relationships and problem-solving in the context of reassuring rather than anxiety-creating relationships. Certain seriously disturbed neurotic clients would also fall in this group, as would also the oral type of character disorder.

It is persons with the less severe neuroses and the neurotic characters of various sorts who can make most use of the development of self-awareness. The extent to which awareness of hidden material is promoted again depends upon the worker's diagnostic understanding of the client's ego strength, including his capacity to bear anxiety, and of the accessibility for casework treatment of the hidden material, better understanding of which may alleviate his suffering. Obviously, the caseworker must maintain a continuous diagnostic process as he observes the client's response to treatment. Sometimes the worker moves into uncovering treatment and, finding the process unrewarding for the client or unbearable to him, returns to a supportive approach.

Thus far we have been considering the use of diagnosis mainly in relation to its bearing on the over-all treatment method. The details of treatment, either supportive or by development of self-awareness, rest just as directly on our diagnostic understanding. Does this client need help in strengthening or lesssening the force of his conscience? He can be influenced either by the direct effects of the client-worker relationship in supportive work, or by the development of self-understanding as uncovering methods are used; but in either case the diagnosis must tell us whether his conscience constitutes an area of maladjustment which creates trouble for the individual, and something of the factors that have contributed to the development of his problem.

Often one or more of the defenses is creating special trouble for the individual—turning against the self, or intellectualization, or projection, or displacement. Again, these can be modified to a degree by either supportive or uncovering methods. Work often centers largely around a particular set of relationships. A woman's hostile feelings about her mother may need to be explored thoroughly to illuminate the displacement of these feelings on either child or husband. Or, in supportive treatment, the direct experience with the worker may help to counteract the effect of a destructive mother-daughter relationship.

In the person suffering from a character disorder the worker may need to promote guilt feelings, while in the compulsive neurotic every care may need to be taken to avoid the increase of guilt, especially in the early stages of treatment. One person may need help in seeing the consequences of acting out, while another is helped to acquire greater spontaneity.

In every instance the worker must understand the major outlines of the client's characteristics; estimate what aspects of his characteristics are causing discomfort or maladjustment in his actual life situation; and to a certain extent foresee what areas of current and past life experiences must be explored in order to give the client some relief and enable him to function more effectively.

We have a major responsibility to understand the dynamics of the client's adjustment in order to avoid explorations and comments that will have a harmful effect on the client's functioning. The client must not be subjected to more anxiety than he can tolerate constructively. Above all, defenses must not be modified except as either his actual need for them is reduced or their role in his emotional economy can be taken over by other less harmful defenses. Otherwise he will become more disturbed and regress to an even less adequate adjustment, unless he succeeds in withdrawing from treatment—as he often does—without being much affected by our efforts.

We cannot escape responsibility for contributing in a major way to the direction treatment takes. Interviews do not flow on

95

without guidance. The worker's direct or indirect expresssion of interest or disinterest can definitely affect the course of the client's associations and in casework should definitely do so. Both the fundamental nature of our treatment and the area of adjustment in which we work rest directly upon our diagnostic understanding and, in my opinion, that diagnostic understanding must be thorough. It must be broadly based on social, physical, and psychological data; it must lead to a personality delineation including an attempt at formal classification; it must throw light on etiology; and it must culminate in a tentatively held and broad—but nonetheless definite—conception of the help to be offered to the person who is seeking aid in improving his social adjustment.

Part II

Selected Applications
In Casework Practice

6. Therapeutic Considerations of the Borderline Personality Structure*

Irving Kaufman, M.D.

THE NUMBER OF REFERRALS to casework agencies of clients with severe ego disturbances has been steadily increasing. Many of these clients fall in the diagnostic category of "borderline" cases. The major focus of this paper will be a consideration of their personality structure and its relation to the psychodynamics of the therapeutic process.

These clients manifest their difficulties primarily in their inability to handle the realities of living; they have emotional difficulty in handling a job, a marriage, a relationship to a child. They may apply to the family agency because the husband has lost his job, or the wife has lost her pocketbook with the rent money, or the child has run away. A considerable part of their lives is made up of recurring crises.

The borderline group of clients are those who demonstrate: (1) overt depressions; (2) an inability to handle the realities of living; (3) the acting-out behavior of the delinquent, the alcoholic, and the drug addict; (4) psychosomatic reactions, such as ulcerative colitis; (5) borderline, but not committable, psychotic reactions of the schizoid, paranoid, and hypomanic types.

*Reprinted from *Smith College Studies in Social Work*, Vol. XXVI, No. 3 (1956). This paper and the three following ones by Dr. Weinberger, Miss Nicholls, and Mrs. Barry, were published in the same issue as companion articles.

These people who characteristically express their problems in environmental and behavioral patterns are in contrast to the less disturbed clients who express their difficulties in symbolic symptom formation. Persons in the latter group, who are suffering from the neuroses, are functioning at a more organized level of ego development and require the more familiar techniques used in the treatment of hysterical, obsessive, and phobic reactions.[1]

Within the neurotic group, however, there may be some clients who show some of the elements of the disturbed patterns of the borderline group, but to a much less degree. The diagnostic evaluation of the individual client will then be based on an appraisal of the organization of the ego structure, of the mechanisms of defense, and of the presence of pathologic nuclei within the personality. Consideration of the personality structure of these clients with severe ego disturbances includes the concept that all areas of function, in the course of normal development, come under the service of the ego. This control includes dealing with perceptions of reality and developing effective means of discharging tension. The ego also normally controls and directs the tension-discharging routes—the affects, motor activity, the visceral discharge mechanisms, and the intellectual processes. Looking for evidence of disturbances in any or all of these areas represents the major method of detecting pathology in ego development.

Use of this method introduces consideration of the criteria for assessing ego strengths and weaknesses. Not only must one note evidences of disturbance in reality testing and in the functioning of the discharge mechanisms, but one must consider how much of the total personality is involved in the pathology. The evaluation is not difficult in the case of a severe schizophrenic who curls up in a corner, but may be so when the client has a job, a wife, children, and a social life. One of the bases used in evaluating ego strengths, however, is related to the concept of what various activities or relationships mean to the individual. For example, a job may not represent ego strength if it is used for acting-out, as may be true in the case of a truck driver who needs to be away from his family. There is considerable range in the degree to which

---

[1] See Chapter 10 of the present volume.

all these aspects of living represent a repetition compulsion needed to handle some core anxiety.

The following case illustrates behavior based on the repetition compulsion: A woman who, as a child, had been deserted by her parents, married a truck driver who was away for days at a time and was drunk the few days he was home. She herself deserted her children by alcoholism, promiscuity, and frequent literal abandonments. She had been unable to hold a job, always getting into an argument with her boss because he was too demanding, and then quitting. She was thus handling her anxiety over desertion by taking both roles, being deserted by her husband and deserting her children. Her compulsive need to cope with this anxiety influenced all the major areas of her life.

From another point of view, however, it is necessary to realize that many of these clients demonstrate different levels of ego organization at different times and places, ranging from severely disturbed to quite well organized, depending upon the specific area of function. For example, one woman would go into a depression when she came home from work. She was not able to decide whether to have broccoli or carrots for supper and remained helpless until her husband made the choice for her, yet she was able to hold a job and function relatively well in that situation. This latter factor has considerable bearing on therapy because the areas of more adequate ego functioning can be utilized as a basis of strength and relatedness to reality while the therapist attempts to treat the other more disturbed portions of the personality.

Persons in the borderline group have certain common characteristics in ego organization:

1. They reveal severe disturbances in reality testing, which are manifested in several ways. These include the anticipation that certain acts will magically solve their problems. For example, many clients in the acting-out group really believe that if they get into difficulty a parent figure will come to save and take care of them. One patient in analysis repeatedly created such a crisis. He would get himself apprehended by the police for speeding, or he would start an argument with his boss. Always, to his amazement, the police or the boss, instead of considering him "charming" or "cute," as his parents had, would get really angry.

101

An important technique in working with this man consisted of predicting when he was about to act out in this way and understanding the meaning of the action as an attempt to re-establish the infantile parent-child relationship. Ultimately one might hope to help with the disturbance in reality-testing by establishing with the patient the meaning of the fantasy behind the behavior as well as by defining the reactions of persons in his environment to this type of acting-out.

2. Disturbances in reference to omnipotence represent an especially important aspect of pathology in this group of clients. This fact has considerable bearing on treatment technique. The normal stages of development of the infant involve a first stage where he feels that he is omnipotent; he controls the world and obtains his own narcissistic supplies. With further ego development and the separation of self from non-self, the omnipotence is invested in the parents; they have the power to control, to give and withhold what is necessary. Many of these borderline persons are struggling with the problem of giving up their fantasied omnipotence or investing it in a parent figure. This fact accounts for the paradoxical features of the object relationships these people form. On the one hand they berate the therapist for not solving all the problems immediately and, on the other hand, are certain that no one can give them anything. This situation is related to the whole question of whether they feel they can find their gratification in any reality experience.

Although the normal individual certainly obtains direct gratifications from his reality experience, he is governed by an ego organization in which the basic sense of well-being comes from his ability to fulfil his own standards; he is then functioning in an ego-syntonic way. In these more disturbed borderline people this sense of well-being is related to an earlier stage of development in which the world is pictured as peopled with babies and giants. Although the giants take care of the babies they have enormous, frightening power of life and death over them.

These clients simultaneously wish for both roles, baby and giant. One patient stated that he had fantasies of someone big and strong enough to take care of and control him; he was fearful, however, lest such a person would also be so powerful that he would destroy him. This patient's pathologic solution to his dilemma was to establish a minimal relationship with any individual and, by a series of devices, to test the strength of the other person in a brief foraging operation, at the same time allowing himself safe avenues of escape.

The therapeutic task in resolving such infantile omnipotence is a complicated one, involving problems in establishing a therapeutic relationship without, at the same time, being drawn into the dangerous fantasies of the client regarding omnipotence.

One cannot in reality take over the management of the client's life. However, by understanding the needs of the client and working out the patterns of behavior, one can help remove his feelings of fear and awe about the internal and external forces acting on him. Such feelings include his attitude toward his own emotions and instinctual drives, as well as his feelings toward such external phenomena as schedules, and authority figures such as police and bosses. Of utmost importance in helping such a client handle his fears about omnipotence is the organization of events into a sequential cause-and-relationship pattern. For example, one patient, following any successful venture, showed a need to get himself into trouble. After this pattern was elaborated, it was possible to point out that when something had gone well he had the tendency to cause trouble for himself. He replied with a sheepish grin that he now understood why he was not going to prepare the assignment for his next class even though it was his turn to be asked to discuss the material. Bridging the gap between the unconscious force that caused the trouble and the fact that he was about to produce it again made it possible over a period of time to help this patient see that not only was there no all-powerful force trying to cause difficulty for him, but that this type of acting-out was based on his unconscious wish for such a force—which is equated with the omnipotent parent—while he became a helpless baby.

The working through of the problems of omnipotence includes dealing with the fact that the client invests this omnipotence in the therapist. The therapist attempts to handle this through the techniques of prediction by relating these concepts to the patterns of life experience of the client, but he needs to be able to tolerate

103

the mass of explosive feelings associated with this concept. Aichhorn,[2] in his work with delinquents, willingly accepted this position and, in fact, conveyed the idea that he was potentially a more clever and powerful thief than the delinquent. This was a method of offering a superego figure for identification which could cope with the pathologic forces within the delinquent. The implication involved in this process is related to the fact that the therapy that helps the patient remove some of the omnipotence from the environmental phenomena also leaves him afraid. The support of the therapist helps to sustain him through this phase.

The wish for an omnipotent parent takes many forms. One of the most typical is illustrated by the client who said he had headaches and shortly afterward revealed that his father died of a cerebral hemorrhage and that he felt guilty for having been such a bad son. One may be inclined to give such a client reassurance that he was not a bad son and did not cause his father's stroke. During the course of therapy, however, it was possible to elaborate the concept that he had the need to feel that he could cause people to have a cerebral hemorrhage. If reassurance were given, it would not only rob the patient of a defense but would interfere with his opportunity to work through his feelings about this type of problem.

Special Problems in Relation to Depressions

Clients in this group are fixated at a level of infantile relationship to their parents. An awareness of the reality aspects of the pathologic features in their relationship to their parents would probably precipitate a severe depression. Much of their behavior, such as job choice, marital relationship, and specific pathology such as acting-out, delinquency, or alcoholism, is related to their need to ward off depression. One can anticipate that, during the course of treatment, these clients will demonstrate both the wish for the infantile relationship to their parents and the fear that the giving up of this relationship will lead to a depression. In order to deal with these fears and grow up, these clients require the support of a caseworker to help them cope with the overwhelming anxiety. The worker's technique of relating to these clients and helping

[2] August Aichhorn, *Wayward Youth*, Viking Press, New York, 1935.

104

them work out their fears is based on the techniques of dealing with any depression. These include building up a relationship that involves placing the therapist in the role of the substitute parent. Once this has been accomplished, the client then has the courage and support to face the frightening loss of the infantile fantasy relationship to his parent, and work through the depression associated with this loss. An amazing tenacity is manifested in the client's wish to retain this fantasy relationship, and one should not be discouraged if it takes considerable time to resolve even a portion of this pathology.

One patient in analysis quite clearly understood this struggle within herself in which she felt her mother was a powerful force described by her as a dinosaur or prehistoric monster that was controlling her and making her act like a baby. The patient felt that unless she continued this pattern she would lose everything in spite of the fact that as a drooling, incontinent baby she had a minimum of what was available to her in reality. A considerable portion of the therapy was devoted to her need to test repeatedly whether this baby behavior, which she felt was what her mother wished, would really provide her with loving parents. One of the characteristics of this patient and of many of the others of this group is the strength of the drive to test out this fantasy. In terms of the therapy, one tries, by such methods as predicting and suggesting, to prevent the patient from creating so many reality troubles for himself. One of the pitfalls of treatment can occur if the therapist gets overanxious about the acting-out. The therapist's anxiety repeats the pathologic aspect of the patient's relationship to his parent, and may precipitate further acting-out rather than prevent it.

One should realize that it is not always possible immediately to prevent acting-out. For example, the therapist of an adolescent girl in treatment saw, after the second interview, that she might have the need to become pregnant out of wedlock in order to handle her wish to stay close to her mother. Because the relationship had not advanced to the point where this girl had begun to incorporate the superego values of the therapist, it was not possible to prevent the pregnancy from occurring. It was necessary to give all possible support to this girl during her pregnancy and

105

utilize the experience as an opportunity to help her to see what it meant, especially in terms of her ambivalent fantasy wish to be close to her mother in the mother-baby-daughter relationship, and to separate from the mother by giving her the new baby in place of herself.

Sometimes the therapy can prevent the pathologic process, such as acting-out, from occurring and sometimes it cannot. One of the important procedures is to draw the pathologic behavior into the total picture so that the ego can gain control and the individual is not repeatedly swept away by the fantasy that his disturbed behavior will really give him the parent-child relationship he is seeking.

Special Features Related to the Aggressive Instincts

In general, there has been more careful elaboration of the libidinal forces than there has been of the aggressive ones. There are, however, some characteristic features associated with the development of the aggressive instincts which have special bearing on the treatment of these clients. A brief review of some of the phases of the development of the aggressive instincts may help to clarify these concepts.

In the early phases of the child's development, aggression, like libido, is bound up in the undifferentiated ego. Gradually, with the differentiation of the self from the non-self the aggressive strivings become organized under the service of the ego into purposeful, goal-oriented activities. The differentiation of object aggression from auto-aggression is a complicated process involving the development of ego capacity to differentiate one form of instinctual tension from another and to allow finely differentiated activities to occur. These concepts can be understood by observing the child whose initial response to frustration is a massive one with crying, thrashing of arms and legs, and so on. The later manifestation of this gross reaction is demonstrated in the temper tantrum. Interference with the development of the ego in relation to the aggressive impulses not only reduces the energy available for constructive activity, but this aggressive energy gets tied into pathologic processes and is repressed as a force which maintains the pathology and gives the disturbed features their viability.

106

Persons in the borderline group show two opposite ways of handling their aggressive energy, and these often occur within the same client. There may be a fear of releasing too much aggression or there may be an absence of well-defined methods of organizing and controlling the aggression. These clients demonstrate this pathology either by an inhibition of action or by outbursts of intense hostile behavior such as destroying property, beating a child, or self-destructive activity such as getting one's self fired. These clients' disturbances in the area of the aggressive instincts can be described in terms of a failure to develop effective ego mechanisms wherein the aggressive drives are used in goal-directed, purposeful, and meaningful activities.

The following are examples of a few of the more frequent clinical features found in this group of clients as they demonstrate ego pathology in relation to aggression, and of the dynamic implications these features have for treatment.

1. *Aggression as a role concept:* To some clients hostile activity and overtly aggressive behavior represent a role such as the masculine role. An illustration of this concept was given by a client who thought of men as angry and shouting, and women as weak and soft-spoken. Once when he had raised his voice and was shouting, I asked him if he were angry with me. He looked puzzled and said, "Of course not." But this, he explained, was the way he remembered his father. In fact, his memory of his father's shouting and forceful behavior was expressed with considerable fondness and admiration. It was possible, during the course of treatment, to convey the idea that to people like myself who had not met his father, the angry shouting would not necessarily convey such a fond image but might be interpreted by them as anger. For such a patient, as with all patients, the important technique was not the process of bringing out his anger but helping him to understand what purpose it served in his psychic economy.

To some clients the angry hostile role represents a strong parent who will desert or hurt the weak child. Many of these clients act out both the parent and the child role. They may beat or desert their child, or precipitate a desertion or abandonment within their marriage, or attempt to provoke the therapist into anger. Again, the treatment technique is based on the relationship of the

107

client's anger—whether it is directed outward or provoked against himself—to the unconscious need to resolve the anxiety he feels at being in a weak and helpless position.

2. *Aggression as a defense against overwhelming anxiety:* There are many examples of this type of reaction. One of the commonest is seen in an instance in which a client comes to an agency and describes in great detail his need for a job, money, food, a bed, and so on. The caseworker tries to relate this need to various conflicts and at the same time may help with some of the reality needs, perhaps by getting clothes for an ill-clad child. The client then responds with an outburst of hostility. One of the reasons for this paradoxical reaction is based on the client's sudden awareness of all his unmet needs, which has been stimulated by his receiving something. The hostility in this instance serves as a defense against the underlying depression. In treatment, it is most important that the therapist not respond with counter-hostility or to try to bring out further aggression; he must realize that the aggression is a defense mechanism designed to keep the ego intact.

3. *Aggression as a means of maintaining ego boundaries:* This concept has several components. Two examples will serve as illustrations. One patient said he continually got into fights with people because only then did he feel alive. He described such action as analogous to pinching himself to see if he were awake. Another manifestation of this disturbance is exemplified by the patient who projected his impulses onto the environment and had an aggressive interaction with these projected impulses.

This type of reaction is most manifest in paranoid clients who are either fighting for or against a cause, a concept, or a person, and whose struggle is clearly a projection of their own conflicts. This defense mechanism often includes the infantile technique of giving impulses human form, placing them outside oneself and then struggling with them. This was illustrated by a child who was seen in therapy. This child asked the therapist if he would like to join his secret club. It was suggested that before joining an organization, one should understand what it was all about. It turned out that this club membership did not represent people to the child but the hostile destructive forces which he had projected onto the club. The child, in reality, was asking about his relationship to these

108

instinctual forces. Was the therapy going to help him deal more effectively with them or was the therapy going to give greater strength to these aggressive forces?

Dynamically, the manifestations of the aggressive impulses expressed by clients with ego disturbances cannot be handled directly but only through the process of helping them work out more effective object relationships. In general, then, this entire group of clients have not evolved a successful method of utilizing their aggressive energies in solving their life needs. The normal use of aggression is related to the process of mastering and altering one's environment. The process of learning and achieving includes the aggressive drive. Most of these clients dissipate their aggressive energies in the service of more infantile fixations and hence are unable to release this bound aggression for more effective functioning. The dynamic process of therapy in relation to the aggressive drives includes the therapist's understanding what the aggression means to the client, how it is utilized in his life, and then, once this diagnostic aspect is elaborated, helping him in the ways that seem indicated to utilize the aggressive drives more effectively in ego-syntonic, goal-oriented activities through the process of establishing a new ego-ideal and providing a different model of functioning.

Disturbances in Libidinal Development

The clients in this group show many disturbances in libidinal development. The major disturbances are based on their pregenital infantile fixations. The unconscious wish to retain the parent-child relationship has already been mentioned. The present discussion will be limited to a consideration of the relation of these libidinal disturbances to the dynamics of the treatment process.

The way these clients attempt to relate to the therapist is based on their previous pathologic experience. For the therapist to sit back and wait until the client becomes aware of his unconscious need for, and resentment of, his parents is not enough. Many of these clients are either too fearful or are too certain of a repetition of their previous life's disappointments to allow any relationship to develop. Others cling to the therapist in a hostile, dependent way which interferes with the attempts to help them.

The psychodynamics of a relationship, therefore, must be considered. In a general sense, a relationship is based on a series of shared affective experiences. This particular one includes an awareness, by the therapist, of the content of the client's life as well as the emotions associated with the content. Many of these clients, after presenting themselves and their current crisis, will attempt to draw the therapist into doing something for them immediately. Sometimes he finds it necessary to do something in the reality sphere to convey his sincerity and willingness to give support. However, it is eventually essential to get to know as much of the details of the client's daily life as possible—the day-by-day activities, the people he sees and how he feels about them. This type of reality material is of the utmost importance to the therapist in the process of working out a relationship. It gives a reality basis from which one can work and in an active way establishes the therapist as a meaningful figure. To a very large extent the libidinal distortions of such a client will be resolved by the therapist's relating to these reality events with expression of the affect that is associated with them.

It is through this process of developing the relationship that the problems of omnipotence, aggression, and depression will be resolved. A considerable part of the basic treatment will be accomplished by such non-verbal measures as making one's self available when the client is upset, and by not reacting in a hostile or punitive way to the client's provocative behavior. Many of these clients are struggling desperately with their need to develop or identify with ego strengths that will help them channelize their instinctual forces and relieve them from the pressures and anxieties that dominate their lives. Ultimately this will be accomplished through the relationship, based on the techniques suggested above for building up an affective interaction with the reality aspects of the client's life.

7. Basic Concepts in Diagnosis and Treatment of Borderline States*

Jerome L. Weinberger, M.D.

I SHOULD LIKE TO CONSIDER some of the conflicting views in relation to the term "borderline states" and the basic concepts in the diagnosis and treatment of borderline cases.

The increase in the number of persons with severe ego disturbances is not confined to clients referred to casework agencies, but has also been noted in the treatment of patients in psychiatric clinics as well as in private practice. Some feel that this diagnostic group is increasing. On the other hand, we do not see as many cases of hysteria as in the earlier days of psychoanalysis. Cultural changes such as the relaxation of strict morality of the Victorian age, the loosening of family ties, the greater mobility of people, the stress of living in our modern civilization, and especially the urbanization of the population have been held responsible for this change. I believe that our greater diagnostic acuity and the larger number of people coming for help may be additional factors. With our more comprehensive knowledge of ego psychology and the mechanisms of defense, we are able to assess more accurately fragments of primitive thinking and acting. From this point of view it is interesting to note that some of Freud's early cases would be termed "borderline" today.

Although we understand and can delineate psychosis and neurosis

* Reprinted from *Smith College Studies in Social Work*, Vol. XXVI, No. 3 (1956).

111

more specifically, the term "borderline state" is not to be found in any psychiatric nomenclature. As a diagnostic term it does not convey a precise understanding of the state, course, treatment, or prognosis of the illness.[1] The diagnosis, when used, indicates that it is difficult to determine whether a client is neurotic or psychotic or whether features of both are present. In our general categories of normal, neurotic, and psychotic, the borderline group would then represent an area between neuroses and psychoses.

Because of the difficulties in the use of the diagnostic term "borderline state," Dr. Kaufman and most other writers on this subject deal with it clinically. They show the various aspects of the primary process present in clients together with the secondary process which includes the various deficiencies of the ego function in reality perception, in social adaptation, and in the integrative processes, as they present themselves in clients. However, there are two points of view concerning borderline states. One is that there is no such state but rather a continuum based dynamically on the psychoanalytical principles concerning the stages of development and the concepts of ego psychology. Inherent in this concept of a dynamic spectrum is the view that, given certain conditions of stress, individuals may move from normal to borderline state or to psychosis. For example, during World War II soldiers who were psychiatric casualties overseas were returned to this country by plane or boat. Those who arrived by plane still showed severe psychotic states, while those who had presented the same picture earlier, but who returned by boat, often had recovered during the long voyage. The situation can be compared to one in which a weight on a cork pushes the cork under water but when the weight is released the cork is allowed to come to the surface again.

The second view stresses the quantitative differences between the various categories of neurosis, borderline state, and psychosis; there is movement in the borderline group but it is limited—some patients staying borderline and some fluctuating between this area and the others. Those who hold this view believe that psychoanalytic psychology has enlarged the descriptive diagnostic categories, but has not done away with them.

[1] R. P. Knight, M.D., "Borderline States," *Bulletin of the Menninger Clinic,* Vol. XVII, No. 1 (1953), pp. 1–12.

The two points of view indicate differences in prognosis and treatment. Those who hold the former would necessarily maintain that with treatment the process is reversible and that treatment can gradually approach more classical psychoanalytic methods. The latter viewpoint is less optimistic and its proponents would probably urge in some cases a more supportive type of therapy which would not gradually approach more classical methods.[2]

The assessment of the strengths and weaknesses of clients may furnish us with an estimate of the degree and type of ego disturbances in the total functioning of an individual. Disturbances in reality perception may extend from hallucinations and delusions to subtle manifestations in the client-caseworker relationship.

For example, a 27-year-old male patient flunked out of college. He had excellent intellectual equipment but did not attend classes. In therapy he stated that if he did not go to class, the professor would not see that he was absent. If he was present, the instructor would then know that he was not there previously. This corresponds to the primitive, concrete thinking of the early years of life. It is the basis of magic—if you think something, it will come true. It is best illustrated by the child's game of peek-a-boo. "If I don't see you, you can't see me." This patient would not open his mail for such long periods of time that his mother would become alarmed and would send him telegrams. In this role he was the small boy who, by the denial of the existence of letters, classes, responsibility for his clothes or for his body hygiene, became in fantasy the "infant king." He regressed to the early years of his life when he, an only child, was cared for by a doting mother and a devoted nursemaid. These periods of regression were initiated by any success which brought him into competition with his father, who was famous in his field. It is interesting to note that he cut classes immediately after he received 100 per cent on an examination. At times he would become efficient in his work and competent in the handling of his affairs. He would speak with authority and impress his colleagues. During those periods he would occasionally limp. His father limped, and it was in the role of his father that he became the successful individual. His

[2] Scientific Proceedings, Panel Reports, "The Borderline Case." *Journal of the American Psychoanalytic Association*, Vol. III, No. 2 (1955), pp. 285–298.

fantasies, which referred to his displacing his father, dealt with becoming the great man. His successive loss of positions resulted from his provoking his superiors by acting the role of the "infant king," messing, coming late to work, and in general being inefficient.

An appraisal of his total functioning would reveal his defective reality adaptation, socially, intellectually, and emotionally. However, the central feature of what may be termed his borderline reality adjustment was the brittleness of his ego defenses and his regression to early modes of behavior under everyday stress.

The various aspects of primitive processes, such as magical thinking, feelings of omnipotence, and impulsivity are present in all of us. It is the amount and the degree with which they contaminate normal ego functions of secondary process thinking, realistic planning, and maintenance of object relationship which is significant. For example, a patient who was late for her first appointment berated the therapist, saying "You made me late. Why don't you have a parking lot?" Another patient would say that the therapist was angry when she herself was angry. The first patient identified with and "became" her very strict mother to avoid the anxiety for being late, scolding the therapist as a projection of herself. The second patient projected her feelings on the therapist and acted as though they came from him—the scolding father—and she during the interview became the bad girl.

These two fragments represent features of primitive thinking and acting. The first patient became identified with the powerful mother to protect herself from overwhelming anxiety in relation to her mother. The second patient shows beginning paranoid features and more severe stricture of reality perception.

During an initial interview the neurotic defenses and the intact adaptive ego functions may enable the "borderline" client to present a relatively conventional neurotic maladjustment. It is after repeated interviews that the other features of the personality may intrude themselves, however subtly. In an interview these elusive features may make the caseworker feel that he is out of tune with the client. What occurs is essentially a subclinical break in the relationship, which may happen from time to time, caused by the intrusion of the primitive elements of the personality of the client.

Treatment of this broad group of patients must of necessity be related to the individual. For example, one individual, because of overgratification in his early development, may not have developed the ego functions of control over his instinctual wishes. He may present feelings of omnipotence, gigantic fears and anger, and feelings of marked deprivation.[3] A similar picture may appear when a client has not had the gratifications and identifications necessary for him to form models. In either case, however, primitive aspects of functioning are present. Although they may appear similar in symptoms, one individual needs to develop ego control through the acceptance of frustration while the other needs consistent gratification to develop ego strength.

Our mode of casework treatment would therefore depend upon the extent and degree to which the client is impaired in his adaptation to reality, his ability to deal with people, arrange his affairs, and take consistent responsible action.

The more infantile the client, the more the worker must serve as the bridge to reality. The aim of the worker is to help the client develop by dealing with the everyday realities, by being the steady available support in cases of stress. Insight, whether correct or not, is of little value. It serves mainly as a means of emotional contact. It should be added that insight, by removing some areas of resistance, can aid in the forward movement of the client, but in general it serves mainly as a means of relationship rather than a tool of understanding for the client. In some cases insight can have an adverse effect on a borderline patient by undermining some of the defensive aspects of his symptoms. Because of their immaturity and narcissism, these persons are reluctant to accept responsibility for their acts. They are poorly motivated in their wish to change. Acting on the pleasure principle and employing concepts of omnipotence and denial, they are not pushed to adapt to reality. For a great number of these patients, initially, insight therapy would be a weak means to effect change.

In working with the borderline group, the relationship between the worker and the client is the main method of developing and

[3] Helene Deutsch, M.D., "The Impostor: Contribution to Ego Psychology of a Type of Psychopath," *Psychoanalytic Quarterly*, Vol. XXIV, No. 4 (1955), pp. 483–505.

strengthening the impaired capacity for feelings for others.[4] Through identification with the worker, dealing with the "bread and butter" of everyday living, the client can develop new identifications. He will gradually accept controls and attitudes more appropriate to reality. The client's aptitudes and potentialities should be carefully assessed so that realistic goals may be reached. A major requirement of these clients is their need for a steady, constant relationship over a long period of time. Ego growth and integration requires time, as it does in normal development.

One of my patients, after three years of analysis, said during a stormy period in which she was quite angry at me, "You have not made me understand anything new, but you are always here and you don't change." She was referring to her parents who vacillated in their attitude to her, so that she never knew how they would react.

Many of these patients because of their difficulty in forming relationships are not ideally suited for insight therapy. We might phrase it that they require "developmental therapy"—a therapy of relationship. It is in this area, where the need is great and other resources for help are meager, that the caseworker with a psychoanalytic orientation has a great deal to contribute in a decisive fashion. But in the end the therapist's best tool for successful treatment of the borderline group is persistence.

4 M. Schmideberg, "Principles of Directive Analytic Therapy for Borderline Patients," Scientific Proceedings, Panel Report, presented at the Annual Mid-Winter Meeting, American Psychoanalytic Association, New York, December, 1955.

8. Treatment of a Disturbed Mother-Child Relationship: A Case Presentation*

Grace Nicholls

THE PAPER PRESENTED by Dr. Kaufman reveals the essential similarity of personality structure among clients who exhibit on the surface such striking differences of behavior. It is revealing to see the common ego problems expressed by people who present symptomatology as varied as that of the alcoholic, the person with psychosomatic symptoms, and the typical neglectful parent who is known to the protective agency. Although there is such a core of similarity, these clients may express their difficulties in diametrically opposite ways.

I should like to present casework with the mother of a child who had psychosomatic illness. She was one of those deprived, infantile mothers who, like the patients themselves, tend to resort to subterranean ways of handling their intense, primitive feelings. If one is to help them one must respect their much needed self-protection.

Mrs. M was referred to the hospital social service department a week after her 14-year-old son, Willy, was admitted to the Pediatric Ward with a diagnosis of ulcerative colitis. His symptoms, in a mild form, predated his admission by eight months. There appeared to be no precipitating events coincident with the onset of his illness. Because of the psychosomatic implications of this disease, a child psychiatrist was asked to see Willy. His mother was reputed to have gone all to pieces when she learned his diagnosis.

* Reprinted from *Smith College Studies in Social Work*, Vol. XXVI, No. 3 (1956).

117

Mrs. M seemed eager to come and talk to me about her son. She was a short, dark, middle-aged woman, plainly dressed in black, wearing a kerchief over her head. I was immediately impressed with her quality of deep sadness, her lined face, and her look of having worked hard and suffered a lot. The pediatrician's comment that she reminded him of someone out of Dostoevski seemed very apt. Although her voice was quiet, she spoke in a feverish way, almost gasping for breath. She said that she was glad Willy was seeing a psychiatrist if the doctors thought it might help him. She knew that he kept things to himself too much, because he did not want to worry her, and it might be good for him to get his worries off his chest. She could not see what he had to worry about, however.

In tears, Mrs. M described Willy as a good, quiet, agreeable boy, clever at school and happy just staying around the house, making things or working on his stamp collection. She gave a detailed account of his symptoms and previous medical care, reproaching herself bitterly for not having brought him to the hospital sooner. When she learned that he had ulcerative colitis, she felt as if his whole life was ruined. She and her husband had never had anything but trouble, but she wanted everything for her children. There was one younger child, who was spoiled and saucy, but apparently a fairly normal, active 6-year-old boy. To my questions about Willy's early years, Mrs. M responded with the story of her husband's hospitalization for tuberculosis when Willy was two or three. She and the child had to take a furnished room and live on relief. They were forced to move from house to house by landladies who did not like children. Even after her husband returned from the sanatorium they always had a struggle to get along, but she lived for the children. They were her whole life. She never told Willy about his father's illness, but he managed to find out. She answered specific questions about his early development readily, but in a surprised, absent-minded way, as if I were breaking into her real preoccupations, so I did not press her.

In the first interview she alluded briefly to her own unhappy life, particularly the death of her mother when she was quite young, and her mean stepmother, with whom she and her sister lived for a short time, adding "If we had stayed with her we would have been sick." Her husband's early life had been similar to her own,

118

and each of them had married to find a home. Her only close relative was her younger sister, who had so many troubles of her own that Mrs. M could not bother her with hers.

For the first four months that I knew her, Mrs. M came in two or three times a week, and we had frequent telephone calls between visits. She could see no point to regular appointments, preferring to come to my office whenever she felt like it. Because I felt that she was acutely depressed and needed constant support, I would manage somehow to see her whenever she appeared. Willy's medical course was very uneven and whenever there was a minute change for the worse she called me in a panic. I tried to tell her that the doctors expected ups and downs, but she could not be reassured unless I went down to the ward to see him with my own eyes, and reported to her at once that he was all right. She seemed to need literal proof that he was still alive and that her unconscious wish to kill him was not fulfilled.

Throughout this period she checked up on the doctors constantly, irritating them with her unsolicited advice, her inability to accept their explanations, and her need to go from one to the other to collect conflicting opinions. I encouraged her to call me so that I could get information from them for her, in the hope that it would spare her further rebuffs. She told me that she realized she alienated people by her constant complaining, and knew she annoyed the pediatricians as she did her own relatives. "No one wants a person around who complains all the time."

Willy's condition was concerning the medical doctors gravely. They debated the question of surgery, deciding finally to postpone it for the time being. Although no one told Mrs. M that surgery was a possibility, she knew that it was in the wind, and became more terrified. There were conferences of the various medical personnel almost every other day which were attended by Willy's psychiatrist and myself. The medical doctors blamed Mrs. M for impeding her son's recovery and were determined to cut down the frequency of her visits and place him away from home on his discharge. We spent much time interpreting the fact that both Willy and his mother needed a sustained relationship with one person whom they could trust, and who gradually could help them to express negative feelings so that these could be handled without recourse to physical symptoms on his part, and to depression and clinging, hostile demands on hers. I also stressed the fact that although her life had been hard, she had always managed to function reasonably well before this illness, which seemed to mean the end of all her hopes.

There was no recent history of contacts with clinics and social agencies. Mrs. M cared for her home and family and, although her marriage was not gratifying, she was apparently able to compensate through her relationship to the children. I felt that she would not always be so depressed, and that, although she upset Willy with her tears, the bond between them was a strong, close, mutual one, so that to separate them might well be still more disastrous. In time the pediatricians blamed her less, and began to talk with her willingly, rather than try to avoid her. The doctor in charge of Willy's case assured her that Willy looked forward to her visits, which helped him. She was greatly relieved by this and, characteristically, attributed the change in his attitude to my having talked with him. It was very important for her feeling of safety that not only the child psychiatrist, but also I, should attend medical conferences.

During this period there were many magical elements in her relationship with me. On one occasion when I had to be away from the hospital for a few days, she carried my name, address, and telephone number with her, so that if she should collapse on the street, people would know where to bring her.

Throughout this turbulent period of about three months she was unable to talk about anything but her fears for Willy, how awful she felt herself, and how she was responsible for his getting sick. Realistic reassurance or questions of what she could have done differently were brushed aside, and I felt that my contribution was to accept her, to be available constantly, and to help temper the hospital environment so that other personnel would not retaliate against her. This attitude seemed to convey to her that we did not share her opinion of herself as a bad person who had made her son critically ill.

Willy began to show some medical improvement at about this time, and she became calmer. For the first time she was able to discuss her relationship to him, and to indicate a little of her concern about it. She talked with genuine pride of his accomplishments and gentleness. He was just the kind of son she always wanted. In response to my interest in where he got his many talents, she replied that he was good with his hands just as she was. He helped her around the house "just like a girl," and she was "more like a sister to him than a mother." Her husband complained of this and felt left out. She went on to talk again of how she was always fearful and overprotective of Willy, keeping him close to her and away from rough companions or the dangers of the street. She thought that mothers who were not so anxious had better luck with their children. She had never had a mother herself, and felt she had missed a great deal. She tried to give her children what she had never had. I told her that I thought it made it harder for her to deal with her children because she had had no help from her own mother in growing up and she had had to learn a lot by trial and error. I felt that she began to see me as a protective mother figure and that this had much meaning to her owing to the loss of her own mother early in her life.

Following a few weeks of relative calm, Willy had an increase of symptoms, coinciding with a change of pediatrician and psychiatrist, and once more surgery was considered. Mrs. M immediately became deeply depressed and terrified. She begged me in a desperate way to take her to the head doctor, so that she could save Willy. I arranged an appointment and accompanied her to the office of the director of the children's service, an older man with an imposing manner. She clung, weeping, to his lapels, begging him not to let them operate. He was kindly and understanding with her and, although she obviously did not follow any of his explanations, she was comforted by his warmth and patience, and told him he was like a father to her. Her feeling of omnipotence was again reflected when she told me later that she had saved her sister from a brain operation several years ago in the same way, and that she knew when surgery was not necessary even though she was not a doctor.

When the medical situation was quiescent again, and Mrs. M continued to reproach herself in a guilty, frightened way, I insisted that she was harder on herself than she needed to be, and wondered why. For the first time she was able to talk about her deprived childhood in detail. I thought it was because she now felt safe in the hospital and our relationship was sufficiently strong for her to tolerate the unhappy memories. She told me that her mother had died through lack of medical care in a small town in Russia where she grew up in extreme poverty. She could not remember how old she was when her mother died, but she thought about 6 or 8 years. Her father had come to this country to earn a better living, and in his absence some of her cousins died of starvation. Finally he sent for the family. They had their passports and were about to leave when her mother took sick. She was so determined to get to America that she refused to go to a hospital, insisting that she was all right. When she died, Mrs. M and her younger sister stayed on in the town for a few years, with no one to care for them. Then they got as far as Moscow where a woman took them in. Later they moved on to England where strangers looked after them. Finally they reached America and found their way to their father who had remarried. She thought she had reached early adolescence at this time. Their stepmother did not welcome them and they were sent to various foster homes, but apparently she made no meaningful relationships in any of them. She married young to get a home, and then her husband took sick. She had often dreaded getting sick like her mother, but had never dreamed her son would be the one, rather than herself.

In succeeding interviews Mrs. M spoke of her husband, whose life was like her own. He had always been critical of her and ungiving, resentful of her close attachment to the children. She still thought of him as a sick man and sterilized all his dishes, although his tuberculosis had been in remission for many years. Several times she wanted to leave him, but stayed with him for the sake of the children. Now that Willy was ill she felt her sacrifice had been in vain. She had kept the knowledge of the poor marital relationship from Willy, but wondered if he sensed it. From time to time I tried to suggest gently that he might very well do so, and that it might relieve both of them if they could talk more frankly. She concluded this account of her past by telling me that if one's life has been full of unhappiness, each new misfortune just brings back all the other bad things that have happened. There was then no further reference to her background through all the rest of our contact.

The account of her gross poverty, her losses, and homelessness was confirmation of my earlier impression of a person with a life-long lack of nourishing relationships, without the inner resources to bear exploration of her past or interpretation of her disproportionate feelings of guilt and depression.

There were other examples of her need to ward off feelings. When a doctor attempted to discuss with her the fact that Willy thought the atmosphere in the home was gloomy, she agreed that the kitchen had no window and decided to buy a brighter light-bulb. On another occasion, the possibility of my interviewing her husband to get a more rounded picture of the family situation was suggested tentatively. She made no direct reply but went on to consider a divorce. Needless to say, the subject was dropped.

For the next four months both Willy and Mrs. M showed progress. She occasionally skipped seeing Willy on a visiting day, and began to see me once a week on a definite schedule. She seemed less depressed, and gradually her behavior on the ward changed. Instead of making hostile, clinging demands she became more openly critical about Willy's care; she disliked a nurse who was hard on him, felt that some parents were allowed to visit longer than she, and so on. I encouraged her to express her irritation to me as fully as possible, since this seemed to be a safe place for her to drain off some hostility. It encouraged her to learn that another boy who was admitted to the ward with ulcerative colitis was in very bad shape physically. His mother was a nurse, and Mrs. M decided that she should not blame herself so much, since she was a simple, uneducated person and even a nurse had let a serious condition develop without consulting a specialist. At no time was she able to express any negative feeling toward me, except through her excessive demands, nor did I attempt to provoke any. I thought her hostility was so great and so buried that to bring it into the open would be overwhelming. She became acquainted with other mothers who had children on the ward, and they shared their worries, competed for privileges, and vied with each other about the extent of their misfortunes. From time to time she brought me gifts, which I accepted without question. As far as I could tell, they had no specific connection with anything that was going on in our relationship at the moment. The gifts became less frequent, and their character changed from glittering jewelry and high-heeled purple shoes to doilies made by the mother of another patient and homemade apple strudel.

Eight months after his admission, the doctors began to think of discharging Willy. Mrs. M professed to be delighted, but gave many evidences of her extreme fear of having the responsibility of his care. She thought he should remain in the hospital until the weather got warmer. She brought up many physical symptoms of her own, which she had mentioned often, but now she wanted to go to the medical clinic herself to be sure the doctors considered her strong enough to care for him. It was possible to arrange for a long preparation, consisting of visits at home before his permanent discharge. This gave them a chance to readjust to each other, and showed her that nothing catastrophic happened when he was with her again. Just prior to his return home I had to leave the hospital for the summer, and she was seen by another caseworker during my absence. She was able to make the transfer successfully, but spent much of the time going from clinic to clinic. Prior to my return she spoke of her longing to see me again, but decided to see both of us, as if she needed to keep anyone who had any meaning to her, as a safeguard against loss.

The second year of treatment was a marked contrast to the first. Willy remained well, returned to school, quickly made the honor roll, picked up with his friends again, and began to talk to his psychiatrist about his future choice of a career. Mrs. M looked like a new person, ten years younger, and for the first time I saw that she had a really attractive smile. She seemed to have no pressing concerns, and decided to see me only when she felt the need, or was in the hospital for some other reason. I went along with this decision, because I felt that she needed to protect herself against the danger of getting into any exploration of the source of her concerns, now that she no longer needed me to help with the acute crisis. She began to go to family gatherings, resumed her bridge club, and took in a small child to board. She felt that it was evidence of her strength to be able to care for another child. I also thought that, in turning her energies to this baby, she was able to free Willy and let him grow up. Now, when some of her own infantile needs had been met, she startled me by asking what most mothers ask in the first month of casework, "Why is Willy seeing a psychiatrist? Does it mean that there is anything wrong with his head?" She accepted realistic reassurance about this.

In conclusion, one might say that there was no basic change in the personality structure of Mrs. M, but rather that she had a corrective experience which diminished her expectation of loss and her distrust of her relationship to those close to her. Should she experience a further serious threat to her defensive system, one would anticipate that she would need more help, and feel confident that she would seek it. Had the caseworker attempted more inquiry and interpretation with a view toward effecting greater change, this attempt might well have precipitated more disorganization, severe depression, and a frantic search for safe parental figures in clinic after clinic. The choice of treatment that provided emotional support in line with Mrs. M's life experiences was aimed toward strengthening her necessary defenses and filling some of her basic needs, so that her fears of her omnipotent power and annihilating hostility were diluted, and she could allow Willy to grow toward greater health and independence.

9. Some Problems in Protective Casework Technique: A Case Presentation*

Elizabeth Barry

In CONSIDERING THE PROBLEM of neglect in disintegrated, acting-out, family groups, the protective agency discovers repeated evidences of ego pathology in the parent, pathologic interaction between parents and children, and the ever-recurrent pattern of repetition of the same disturbed behavior from one generation to the next. These pathologic symptoms appear not only in parents' relationships with the children, but in their reactions to their own impulses as well. The deprivations that these parents themselves have experienced cause them to seek infantile gratifications which are in competition with the children's needs. Even the basic elements of the child's physical care are overlooked since the parents' own impaired sense of reality pervades the whole family functioning.

In view of such imperfectly perceived reality, the protective agency must become the figure of what is real, and the worker becomes the funnel through which the real world outside the home can be channeled into the disturbed family situation. The following case illustrates these problems and related casework considerations.

The protective agency received a complaint from a person who lived in a multiple dwelling, and who for weeks had been concerned about the neglect of a 2½-year-old child in the same building who was routinely tied to a rope in the barren, graveled

* Reprinted from *Smith College Studies in Social Work*, Vol. XXVI, No. 3 (1956).

backyard where he ate dirt and removed his clothing. The complainant described the family set-up as including a young mother who worked and a grandmother who was supposed to watch the children—a baby in addition to the 2½-year-old Sam, who was the complainant's main concern. She believed the family was constantly in desperate financial straits, because Sam was always hungry and poorly dressed. Once he had dangled by the rope around the waist over the railing of the third-story porch, until another tenant had rescued him. The grandmother did nothing but smoke and read. The neighbor said that she often slapped and screamed at Sam. There seemed to be no husband, but men came at late hours, and frequently knocked on the wrong doors. The mother and the grandmother fought, and the language was very bad. Sam's daily exposure to the dangers of the backyard for long hours when he was unattended had all the tenants of the house nervous and upset.

Because of the particular responsibility of the protective agency to both family and community, the worker checked both names with the social service index and found that the grandmother was Mrs. B, whose former married name had been N, which accounted for the young mother's name, given as Louise N. The children were identified by the use of the social service index as Sam and Joseph, both illegitimate, the latter three months old. The public welfare agency had helped two months ago, and the family service agency was registered five months ago. Neither agency was now active. Public assistance had been granted briefly but the family had legal settlement in another state and had been told to return there. The request to the family agency had been by the grandmother, for employment as a housekeeper. It was a short contact, because there was no job available, and no other area of family need had been mentioned. In both agency records Louise's age was given as 17.

The first visit of our worker was unannounced, because the public welfare agency had mentioned that the family had moved frequently, presumably to avoid "investigation." That agency also told us there had been a threat of arrest and institutionalization in the other state when Louise's last pregnancy was discovered, and we feared that our usual approach by letter would cause them to flee again.

On the home visit we found the grandmother alone, smoking and reading; her stack of about twenty light novels was the only orderly item in the house. The apartment was crowded, cluttered, dirty, with beds unmade, dresser drawers open with contents spilling out, foodstuff piled on tables and chairs, dishes unwashed, cigarette butts and ashes everywhere. The grandmother's clothing was soiled, her bare feet were dirty, and all exposed portions of her body grimy. The infant lay face down, asleep, on a soiled couch near her; Sam was found at the end of a rope, one end of which was tied to the grandmother's chair, from which it extended through the apartment, across a porch, and down three flights of winding stairs to the hot, garbage-filled, gravel-surfaced backyard. The baby was fairly clean, but Sam's body and clothing were extremely dirty. He did not look undernourished, but was chewing on his sock which he had removed. When he was brought upstairs he was fretful and whining, pulling at his grandmother until she roared at him, slapped him away from her, and fetched an uncooked frankfurter for him to munch on. The baby had a scarred area just under the right eye. Mrs. B explained that it was a burn from her cigarette which she had accidentally laid against his face while feeding him. The baby's head had to be supported because it was large and heavy. The doctor had told them an operation might be necessary.

Beyond some slight weariness in her manner, the grandmother did not obviously resist the worker's arrival or the explanation of why she had come. The worker put emphasis on the fact that she had come to the family (a proof of giving), and would continue to come until things were better. (We know that neglectful parents are extremely deprived people who must be given to before they can give.) The grandmother immediately projected the responsibility of their trouble onto "people who couldn't mind their own business." This included the caseworker, no doubt. They had had trouble with the neighbors, who picked on them and who complained that Sam hit the other children. The grandmother said she could not run up and down stairs all day, so the rope had seemed to be the solution.

The young mother was working. She had two jobs, one at a hospital from 7 A.M. to 3 P.M., and the other at a roadside stand from 5 P.M. to 1 A.M. The grandmother hoped nobody would interfere with this arrangement, because for the first time there was money enough to pay their bills. When the worker inquired about the girl's age, the grandmother hesitated briefly, and then said she might as well tell the truth; it would be found out anyway. The girl had had her sixteenth birthday a week ago.

In the course of the next half hour the following story was elicited. Mrs. B's response to the worker was chatty and superficial, strikingly like a child. She said that she had been raised in a strict religious home from which she had run away and been married at 16. She was now 56. She had had three marriages in all, and left her last husband, a 75-year-old man, when he had threatened to leave her because of Louise's second illegitimate pregnancy. She and Louise had come to this community to escape authorities in another city, where they threatened to take Sam and put his mother "away." Louise was the youngest of nine children born to Mrs. B in her first two marriages, and she was the only one of the children who had "stuck by her." Some of her children, including Louise and her older half-sister Edith, had been in a foster home until, with the help of a lawyer, Mrs. B had been able to get them back. It was for that reason only that she had married her third husband, who had a house. She now expressed contempt for him, but he occasionally visited and paid her for going to bed with him. "After all he is my husband, and we need the money." He was believed to be responsible for the current illegitimate pregnancy of Edith, another daughter who had left her husband and two children and was now living with Mr. B in another state. Mrs. B's attitude about this was simply annoyance that he would spend money on that girl instead of giving it to her.

The 16-year-old mother, Louise, had to work because there was no other income. The father of her first child was in jail, and the second man, married and supporting his family, had agreed to pay hospital costs if the girl did not take legal action about paternity. He still called on them occasionally and brought money when he could. The grandmother's remarks about him were tolerant, with emphasis on his agreement to pay. "Everybody was quick to find fault, but nobody was willing to do anything to help"; yet later the grandmother showed the worker a fur coat and several

129

dresses contributed by neighbors who had also supplied food. Her emotional affect throughout this was bland, except as she referred to incidents of hostility directed against her and her family.

The reality hardships in the situation were recognized and discussed with Mrs. B. Suggestions for an immediate adjustment in the care of the children were made, the worker assuming responsibility for some areas (such as a day-care plan for Sam), and the family's job was also outlined. Their part included keeping a clinic appointment later the same day for the baby, and the young mother's being available to meet the worker after that. The grandmother was helped to face the validity of the complaint which had brought the agency in, and the function of the protective society was gone over simply but completely. The grandmother's response to this was to smoke in silence for a moment, and then say, "Well, now maybe somebody will do something for us."

On the return visit later in the day, the worker saw the young mother, who looked older than 16, but was too slender in build and had great circles of fatigue under her eyes. She was hostile to the worker and profanely denunciatory in her comments about the community. Following the clinic visit the baby had had to stay in the hospital and might have to be transferred to a children's hospital one hundred miles away. The diagnosis had been mentioned as "water on the brain," which might kill him. His mother said it was the fault of the community, which would not give relief when she was pregnant, and she had almost died of starvation. (This was true.) "The kids would get better care if there was a decent place to live" (they were being evicted), "but nobody would help with that."

The worker sympathized with the family's concern about the baby, realizing that the mother's reference to the baby included her feelings about herself. The caseworker verbalized that the agency's arrival now must now seem like another problem on top of so many others; she then suggested that this time, when the baby was out of the home, was a good time to look for new quarters, with which the worker would help. Sam could go into the day-care center tomorrow without cost, and the grandmother could look for the job that she was sure she could get. The family then asked if the worker could find the minister who had visited the

130

hospital during the girl's confinement. They wanted him to baptize both children. Plans were worked out for the family to list potential vacant apartments, which the worker would take them to see on Louise's day off the following week. The importance of taking Sam to the day-care center the next day was stressed, and specific directions for doing this were gone over. The family followed through on the plan, and twice phoned our agency in the next week to talk about the baby's progress in the hospital. In the next few weeks the minister was located; he baptized the children and stayed in touch. An apartment was found; the family service agency agreed to pay the moving costs, also to meet material needs as they arose in connection with moving.

The baby underwent brain surgery, and returned two months later in obviously better physical condition, able to lift his head and give other signs of normal development. Louise got a better paying job which made a second job unnecessary; Sam continued in the day-care center where, after a difficult beginning, he ceased to bite and hit the other children, and adjusted fairly well. In the interviews the family revealed certain facts about their previous experiences with welfare authorities in another state; contradictions appeared but these seemed due to faulty perception on their part rather than to a deliberate attempt to confuse. The worker discussed with them the need to know exactly what had happened, so that she could be most truly helpful, and permission was secured to write to other agencies. The casework objective at this point seemed to be to keep the family in one place long enough to allow for some exploration of dynamics, which might indicate how and to what extent the disorganization could be corrected. To this end, frequent contact was made with them, obviously focused on the environmental changes, while behavior, attitudes, and conversation were carefully noted.

The reports from out-of-state described a long pattern of impulsive, self-gratifying, acting-out behavior, on the part of Mrs. B and her three husbands. The first two marriages had been replete with physical abuse, non-support, drunkenness, and promiscuity. Her first husband, by whom five children were born, deserted after much strife, and was later presumed dead. During her second marriage, of questionable legality, four more children were born.

131

This man, Mr. N, the father of Louise, had molested his stepdaughters, one of whom, Edith, mentioned earlier, had been sent to a school for the feebleminded, when prolonged sexual activity with her stepfather was discovered. He finally deserted, and the grandmother had then secured an Enoch Arden divorce in order to marry Mr. B. In the interim, legal action to remove the minor children from the home during the second marriage had resulted in their placement. The grandmother had made repeated efforts to get them back, but her behavior was known to be morally questionable. She therefore married Mr. B, with whom she had been living, in order to get her daughters back.

Louise had done fairly well in a four-year placement. Her I.Q. was measured at 117; school work was satisfactory; social contacts were comfortable, but a tie to her own mother remained strong. When she was 11, the court had returned her to Mrs. B, and within a few months the social agency observed a developing sullenness in the girl, a fall-off in school attendance and performance, and marked "deterioration in personality." At 12 years and 9 months she was pregnant. Another attempt to remove her by court action was foiled when Mrs. B got a lawyer to fight the case. The baby was born, and a second attempt to bring Louise before the court as delinquent was defeated. This was due to her mother's need to perpetuate the acting-out behavior. Louise almost married at 13, with her mother trying to manipulate it, but so many boys had been involved that no one boy could be held, and finally a married man with a court record was arrested and served a sentence for the offense.

The family then moved to another city, where the grandmother cared for the baby, while Louise, 14½, had come to this city alone to work. At 15 she was pregnant again. This time another married man agreed to pay the hospital bill. When the agency in the other city tried to bring action to remove the first child from the family and plan for the second, the grandmother came here too. This was the setting in which we found them five months later.

The recorded facts, plus our own observations, pointed up the pathology that was mentioned earlier. These people could not learn by experience, nor could they make adequate plans for themselves or the children. Their behavior remained disorderly, disorganized, dependent, hostile, and demanding. Object relationships occurred on a hostile plane, the motivation being "What can I get?" Functioning remained on a level of marked infantile fixation, with impulses having to be gratified immediately. We also observed interaction between Mrs. B and Louise (and later between Mrs. B and Edith when she moved in), which suggested that these girls had some special pathologic meaning for their mother, and were being used to act out her own conflicts. Mrs. B displayed a leeching dependence on Louise, who had to work to support her, the children, and finally illegitimately pregnant Edith, who had moved in after being ejected from another state where she was believed to have been prostituting. Louise had to do all the planning, all the housework, and was eventually pushed by her mother into a marriage with a 40-year-old punishing man who could help support them. He then became the focus of all the aggression of the three women. Even after Louise's marriage Mrs. B would say to the girl, "Go out and find somebody to take us for a ride."

The castrating impulses which had characterized all Mrs. B's relationships to men were being repeated in the behavior of both her daughters. This hostility to men had even extended to the now 3-year-old Sam who was physically abused on one occasion by his Aunt Edith, and who was routinely screamed at, cuffed, and ignored by his grandmother. The young mother seemed to be functioning like Trilby, with no ego strength of her own, jumping as her mother pulled the strings, and displaying signs of increasing depression. The pressures on her mounted, and the future of the two children—unfortunately males—in this setting was a foregone tragedy.

The agency then faced its responsibility to bring an end to the chain-like reaction in the group by removing the children and separating Louise from the grandmother, if possible. Because legal evidence of the children's neglect was too thin to stand up in court, the young mother was worked with directly. We pointed out the unreality of her trying to give the children acceptable care while she remained buried under her mother's and sister's needs. We indicated our interest in her own future, as well as in better plans for the children, and said, in effect, that we could not let her go on like this because her action was self-destructive, and we cared what happened to her. Voluntary placement of the children was suggested, so that she could be relieved of the responsibility for them, while we helped her work out what she want to do about her marriage and a living plan. We emphasized her right to be protected as well as the children, and we tried to help her minimize the guilt she felt over any attempt to break away from her mother. She responded briefly, but could not sustain the effort, and displayed a helplessness to act at all. She became more depressed and preoccupied in expressing hostility against the new husband for his sexual demands. We knew that she was frequenting drinking places with other men and getting drunk. Attempts were made to help her control the acting-out, but we did tell her that the agency, as a responsible part of the community, would have to report the situation to the police if she continued to act in this way. In telling her this, we emphasized the social protections that were available to her if she could use them. On the other hand, she knew that if she was arrested the children could be taken, and she seemed to need to precipitate this.

Within forty-eight hours after this discussion with her, Louise got herself arrested for adultery; the evidence was not directly secured by the police, but on her own statement made to them. She took the stand in court and described the activity in detail, while the man in the case denied that it had ever happened. At the hearing she lashed out at those who "talk about helping but when you make a mistake go against you," but at the same time she signed a placement order for the children to cover the period between hearings. The legal routine here required an interval of two weeks between her trial for adultery and a subsequent hearing of the children's neglect, based on her being found guilty of the adultery.

Although the agency had not actually initiated the first court action, it was clearly identified with the court procedure. The caseworker talked with Louise and her lawyer together and separately before the hearing, informing both about information we had submitted to the judge. The worker was also present throughout the hearing. The minister, too, was present, and reinforced with Louise what we had been saying to her. At the neglect hearing, instituted by the agency, the children were committed to the

134

Department of Child Welfare, and Louise was committed to the State Youth Division.

At this point, the protective agency had carried out its responsibility in several areas. It had accepted the community's assignment to act in an unacceptable situation involving children. It had determined that the children were now neglected and would be worse off later in this set-up. It had looked for causes, diagnosed what was happening at present, and tested the potentials for change. If Louise could be helped at all, help could be given only in a controlled environment, free from the influence of her mother. Louise herself picked up this idea and actually precipitated a situation requiring casework intervention.

Meanwhile, with placement, it seemed possible that the children's developing awareness of themselves as individuals in a social group could proceed under circumstances which did not distort reality and in which they might learn to control their instinctual drives and develop personality structure with ego and superego strengths. Although Louise might love her children, she could not be a good model for identification. The same distorted concepts of which she was a victim would be passed on to them. In their home environment they would never know how parents should function, and therefore could not be good parents themselves. They would, by reason of their sex, have been destroyed in the family pathology of hostility to men. Their removal, however, was motivated and carried out, not as a punishment to their mother for bad behavior, but because of agency recognition that some parents are too sick to be able to give their children the love, care, and protection that are a child's right. When this situation exists, society must relieve the person of parental responsibility, help him to get well if possible, and, meanwhile, meet the children's needs.

The protective intervention is a first step. In this instance the mother and children are now in different places, in situations where long-range therapeutic measures may now begin to operate. What we have been able to do is to set the stage for a task to be carried out by other agencies. The eventual outcome will depend upon the potentials of Louise and the children as these can be developed through the skills of workers who have further responsibility for them.

In other situations, when the family is not broken up and the agency can continue in the role of the parent substitute, we may feel somewhat surer that the type of behavior that leads to neglect can at least be modified. An example is an aggressive, potentially abusive father of two adolescent boys who had tremendous guilt about his wife's death. He identified one of the children with her and the other with himself, and he regarded the latter child as a potential delinquent. In the father's periodic outbursts of near violence, to which he was pushed when threatened by something in the environment, the special meaning that this child had for him and his own need to punish and get rid of the delinquent part of himself became evident. The role of the protective caseworker here involved some of the techniques Dr. Kaufman mentioned.[1] This man expressed the ambivalence of wanting someone to take care of and control him, yet fearing that such a person would be powerful enough to destroy him. The caseworker had to convey the feeling that she would not let the man injure himself or his son, and would help him reduce the omnipotent forces of his environment without leaving him defenseless. In such a case the role of active, supportive treatment may have to be sustained for a long time. The goal is not an attempt to bring about a radical personality change, but to help the client sustain a capacity to deal with reality problems with greater efficiency, so that the situation involving himself and his children may be improved.

The development of protective techniques is based on the need to help this generation of parents, and is directed toward salvaging the children who will be parents in the next generation. Protective casework can, then, be conceived as within the matrix of generic casework responsibility; it is geared to helping the borderline, acting-out client acquire greater ego strength which will allow him to handle the reality pressures of his life with greater effectiveness. Understanding is the basis on which all progress must be founded, and we are beginning to understand neglect.

[1] See Chapter 6, p. 99 of this volume.

10. Dynamics and Treatment of the Client with Anxiety Hysteria*

Lucille N. Austin

THE FIRST ATTEMPTS TO UTILIZE psychoanalytic psychology in case-work were associated with the neurotic client and his punishing superego. Guilt-relieving techniques, together with permissive and nonjudgmental attitudes on the part of the caseworker, came to be accepted casework procedures. Over the years, there has been a tendency to use these procedures in an all-inclusive way, rather than selectively. It is now clear that treatment techniques must be based on a clear understanding of the relationships between the various parts of the personality structure and of the underlying unconscious conflict, and that these dynamics differ in different clinical entities. In the various neuroses, as well as in psychoses and the character disorders, there are wide variations in ego strength, the severity of the superego, defenses, symptoms, and characteristic modes of behavior.

A re-examination at this time of treatment formulations about casework with the neurotic client, and particularly those with anxiety hysteria, may be useful. Although there are indications that the caseloads of social agencies and clinics are made up increasingly of clients with character disorders and "borderline" problems, it seems likely that a large number of clients are still in the neurotic category. In many instances, these cases are incorrectly diagnosed as character disorders. I believe, too, that anxiety

* Reprinted from *Smith College Studies in Social Work*, Vol. XXVII, No. 3 (1957). This paper and the three following ones, by Dr. Gardner, Miss Perry, and Miss Hunt, appeared in the same issue as companion articles.

hysteria is sometimes confused with compulsive neurosis, to the disadvantage of persons in the former category.

In this paper, I shall highlight the clinical features of anxiety hysteria and then discuss (1) the nature of the problems that clients in this category present in initial contacts; (2) the typical features of the life history as a diagnostic aid; and (3) some treatment considerations.

The Clinical Picture and Dynamics of Anxiety Hysteria

In Freudian terms, the central conflict of all the neuroses is the oedipal conflict.[1] Capacity to love is established but remains partial under the influence of the oedipal ties to the parents and the incomplete resolution of the problem of bisexual identification; the neurotic does not accept masculinity or femininity. His ego is relatively well organized and developed, but it is weakened by the conflict between the demands of the id and the prohibitions of the superego.

Whereas the compulsive neurotic reacts to the oedipal disappointment by regression to the anal level of operation and manifests problems of anger, the anxiety hysteric reacts by regression to the phallic period, that is, the conflict remains focused in the psychosexual sphere. In the phallic stage of development, heterosexual desires are strong but they are blocked by castration anxiety, fear of punishment, and oedipal guilt. Furthermore, the genital organ of the heterosexual love object is refused full recognition, as if recognition of the difference would be an admission of inferiority. The hysteric handles these conflicts by maintaining bisexual identifications, repression of sexual strivings, and the development of symptoms that are, in themselves, abnormal sexual expressions. Sexual feelings are also displaced on nonsexual relationships and situations, so that a kind of pseudo-sexuality pervades all activities and contacts.

The problems of aggression in the hysteric are predominantly those of erotic aggression, rather than the hostile aggression of

[1] Otto Fenichel, M.D., *The Psychoanalytic Theory of the Neuroses,* W. W. Norton & Co., New York, 1945, Ch. XI; Helene Deutsch, M.D., *Psychoanalysis of the Neuroses,* Hogarth Press, London, 1932, Parts I and II; Sigmund Freud, *Collected Papers,* Vols. I and II, Anglobooks, New York, 1952, *The Problem of Anxiety,* W. W. Norton & Co., New York, 1936.

the pre-oedipal stage. In the child the aggressive and sexual feelings are intertwined when he perceives his parents as a couple; his resulting anger is in response to the oedipal situation and not to frustration because of unmet dependency needs. Some of the aggressive feelings are conscious or preconscious but they may be somatized or turned against the self.

The characteristic defenses in anxiety hysteria are repression, displacement, and projection. The characteristic symptoms are pervasive anxiety; anxiety as a neurotic symptom attached to a special situation that represents the neurotic conflict; conversion symptoms; fears of abandonment, death, and mutilation; phobias; and sexual inhibitions ranging from shyness with the opposite sex to impotence and frigidity.

Hysterical "acting out" is a marked feature. It is a turning from reality to fantasy and is an attempt to induce others to indulge in daydreaming in order to obtain some relief from anxiety and guilt or to evoke punishment. It is sometimes confused with the "acting out" of the character disorders; in anxiety hysterics, the behavior is neurotically determined by the oedipal wishes.

In character structure the anxiety hysterics are in many respects most nearly "normal." They show vivid dramatic qualities associated with the excitement and exhibitionistic features of the neurosis. They have lovable qualities, based partly on their fear of losing love which makes them eager to please others. They are more capable of love than the ambivalent compulsive, who provokes rejection as a justification for his own hatreds. Hysterics have considerable charm, imagination, feeling, and sensitivity. They may indulge in chaotic behavior but it has a romantic and colorful flavor. The extensive fantasy life, which they develop as a refuge and as a substitute for unpleasant reality, gives color to their conversations and actions. Their child-like qualities, such as seeking protection, are often acceptable and appealing, particularly in women. Their many real strengths and abilities, combined with a defensive capacity to simulate more adequacy than they feel, enables them, more often than not, to conceal their illness.[2]

The degree of character disturbance ranges from the relatively outgoing person to seriously repressed, restricted, disorganized, help-

[2] Karl Abraham, *Selected Papers on Psychoanalysis*, Hogarth Press, London, 1949, Ch. XXV.

139

less, and anxiety-ridden individuals whose neurosis is not held in bounds. In some cases, pregenital factors are in the foreground; in others, compulsive features are mixed with hysterical features, making for a more complicated illness and character structure.

Etiologically, anxiety hysteria may be based in part on a constitutional predisposition but is chiefly rooted in sexually stimulating events—in infancy and in the period between three and seven years —which make for sexual precociousness. Childhood sexual seductions, which are reported in the life history as conditioning factors, are kept secret by the hysterical child because of guilt about his complicity and his wish for sexual excitement and pleasure.[3] His attitude is different from that of other children who speak more freely of sexual matters because they were not responsive to seduction. Karl Abraham says, "The tendency to experience sexual traumas repeatedly is a peculiarity which we can often observe in adult hysterics. . . . Hysterics are those interesting people to whom something is always happening. Female hysterics in particular are constantly meeting with adventures. They are molested in the public street, outrageous sexual assaults are made on them, and so forth. It is part of their nature that they must expose themselves to external traumatic influences. . . . People of this kind have a similar tendency in childhood."[4]

In all neurosis there is suffering; the suffering, combined with the transference capacity of the hysteric, provides the leverage for both casework and analytic treatment. It is possible to work with the ego if the ego feels pain and the person senses the irrationality of his feelings, symptoms, and behavior.

The case records of these clients show certain clinical features and the influence of the neurosis on their social functioning. I shall now present some material on the nature of the expressed problem and conflict in the initial contact, and the typical features of the life history.

[3] Freud's original formulation concerning sexual trauma and childhood sexual seduction (Collected Papers, "The Etiology of Hysteria," Vol. I, p. 183) was later altered (Collected Papers, "Sexuality in the Neuroses," Vol. I, pp. 276–277) to take cognizance of "the deceptive memories of hysterics concerning their childhood" and the fact that often a fantasy of seduction was a defense against the memory of sexual activities practiced by the child himself, for example, masturbation.

[4] Op. cit., p. 57.

The Nature of the Expressed Problem and Conflict

In the initial contact, these clients show marked anxiety, ranging from an acute anxiety state to diffuse and pervasive anxiety feelings. The anxiety is accompanied by feelings of inadequacy and inferiority, of not being loved and appreciated. In general, the anxiety hysteric, at the point of the intake interview, gives an appearance of being sicker than he is, while the intact paranoid schizophrenic or the person with a character disorder may appear healthier than he is.

The presenting problems may take the form of difficulties in family relationships, in the job situation, or in personal adjustments. They have a special meaning, however, for the anxiety hysteric. The external event which touches off the anxiety can be seen to be overdetermined by the neurosis. To the anxiety hysteric, certain problems with a child, a marital partner, an employer, or the circumstances of a physical illness, loss of work, and so on, signify a psychosexual danger. He anticipates the loss of love and the verification of his unfitness and inadequacy as a whole man or woman, as well as punishment for trying to exercise sexual rights and privileges. The compulsive neurotic, in contrast, tends to interpret similar events as attacks or as attempts to weaken his controls and to expose his anger and retaliative wishes. Because the hysteric has not regressed to the same level, his psychosexual conflicts are partially conscious or, when repressed, are thinly disguised. In the treatment of these cases, the caseworker must endeavor to bring the conscious sexual conflicts into focus, since the client will continue to suppress, project, and displace them until he is given permission to talk openly about them.

The hysteric frequently presents his marital problem in terms of differences and incompatibilities in all areas other than the sexual. He usually states that the other partner is the one at fault.

In a typical case, a wife reported that she had decided to separate from her husband because they could not agree on ways of raising their children and quarreled over money. She said she had lost interest in sex because her husband had hit her several years before. Only later could she talk about her sexual problem and the fact that she had grown up without a father in the home. She had heard only negative talk about men from

141

her mother and she did not know how to relate to them. She said she had not learned to give herself in the sexual relationship and achieved an orgasm only occasionally.

Many times these clients will make a beginning contact and then become frightened. They minimize the problem they came with or make a "flight into health" as a resistance to going on with treatment.

In one case, after a few interviews the woman said that "it is best to forget it all" and that she was doing all right and did not want to continue. With encouragement from the caseworker, she was able to tell about an early sex experience in which "a man took advantage of her when she was intoxicated." Then she was able to tell that she was the aggressor in current sexual relationships with her husband, and that he was often impotent, which was disturbing to both of them. Later she arranged for him to come to the clinic for help.

Sometimes the conflict is expressed in terms of not being able to choose between a home and a career.

One woman at the beginning of contact was in an acute anxiety state. She said she had a wonderful home, husband, and baby but that she "felt cooped up and as though there were no escape." She had become pregnant immediately after marriage and had had to give up an art career. In later interviews, she described her childhood and told about her father's violent temper. Her mother had been an unhappy woman who felt tainted by sex and she had conveyed these ideas to her daughter who had always been afraid and inhibited sexually. Going to work, obviously, was safer than being a wife.

Some women express their problems initially in terms of feeling pulled between husband and children or between the husband and mother; others have conflict about managing money and difficulties in homemaking.

A man's problem may be expressed in the work situation. The conflict is often centered on employers who, he thinks, belittle him; or he may have anxiety about not doing his job well or feelings of dissatisfaction because he has not found himself vocationally. This group of cases, because of the clear displacement of the oedipal rivalry with the father onto the employer and the sexualization of the work situation, might well be classified as "work difficulty—oedipal type."

142

In child guidance cases, where the mother's predominant concern is about the child's sexual interests—whether he is four years old or adolescent—the problem is unmistakably a displacement. If the child is young, the mother is fearful of injury to him and is over-anxious about his illness. If he is an adolescent, she fears he will get into sexual difficulties and therefore frowns on heterosexual friendships. These mothers often take pride in being frank about giving sexual information to their children but reveal that they are either inhibited in answering questions or seductive in their over-emphasis on sex and in their discussion of inappropriate sexual material. The compulsive mother, on the other hand, usually focuses the problem on her fear of losing control over the child and her fear of his aggression and destructiveness.

In the medical social work setting, hysterical clients tend to be difficult and fractious. They shop from clinic to clinic when the doctors find nothing wrong organically, or when they cannot accept a diagnosis and relax under competent medical care. Illness produces undue anxiety because it is associated with castration fears. Sexual fantasies are clearly evident in their exaggerated fears of body injury. Illness is also viewed as punishment for sexual pleasure.

In the initial interviews, the client is not likely to mention symptoms other than his anxiety. He does not think of phobias, conversions, or obsessive thoughts as symptoms but as idiosyncracies. He may not mention situations he completely avoids, but in talking about less dangerous situations he may reveal the presence of organized symptoms. Phobias particularly are obscured by the avoidance measures which he uses to keep them quiescent. Incidentally, I think the caseworker's failure to recognize symptoms and to inquire about their presence frequently results in inadequate data for use in psychiatric consultations. The absence of data may be a contributing factor to the idea that symptom neuroses are not frequently found in agency caseloads.

The client in early contacts often succeeds in leading the caseworker away from the path of building a sound treatment relationship into a morass of transference gratifications. His neurotic need for love and his phobic need for protection form the basis for an initial positive transference. The hysteric often shows marked improvement even after the first interview. His appearance improves and he is vocal in his gratitude for the help he has received. He does this to create a bond between himself and the caseworker as well as to ward off further work on his problem. He usually has extensive fantasy about the worker. Through permissible flattery and conventional interest, he tries to satisfy his curiosity about the worker as a person. As he weaves his fantasies, he is able to blot out any facts that he wishes to ignore. A transference goal—to be loved for himself—supersedes the goal of securing help with his family relationships and other problems of adult adjustment.

The narcissism and the defense of wish-fulfilling daydreams lead the hysteric to an avoidance of hearing anything he might construe as negative criticism; the compulsive, in contrast, provokes criticism and rejection. The hysteric has a tendency to volunteer only a few factual details and has difficulty in giving a consistent, coherent account of what is actually going on at home or at work. He skips from topic to topic. He talks in such a vivid, interesting way that the caseworker may fail to note that he is giving an exaggerated dramatic version of what happened. He demonstrates that he is a talented person, worthy of love and recognition. He produces feelings, not facts. This way of communicating differs from that of the compulsive neurotic. The latter chooses words carefully. He underplays rather than overstates, and gives detailed facts without apparent feeling because the feeling has been isolated.

In many respects, at the points of early contact as well as later, the hysteric seems to be repeating much of his early behavior with his parents. In childhood he had to pretend innocence in order to keep the parent from knowing how much he knew about sexual matters and how intense was his sexual life. An element of scorn for adult stupidity is also reflected as a transference response, especially when he senses naivete and repression in the caseworker.

The client tends to hide his negative transference reactions because he cannot take the chance of losing a source of gratification and protection. When he does venture a negative response, it is often in the form of a childish attempt to let the caseworker know he is displeased. These responses take the form of play in order to disguise the extent and reality of the negative feelings.

As a last comment about problems in the initial contact, I should like to note that it is not always easy to recognize panic anxiety or acute anxiety states. Certain common errors are made in diagnosis. The caseworker may think the client who cries and expresses despair is deeply depressed. The degree of depressed affect, however, cannot be measured by the amount of anxiety expressed. The hysteric's tendency to exaggerate—to believe that all is lost and the worst has happened—must be taken into account; often self-pity, rather than depression, may be the prevailing affect. The phobic client who is seeking protection may give the impression of being a deeply dependent person. Immobilized by his anxiety, he seems uncertain, childlike, and helpless, and, at first, gives no evidence of his real ego strength. In some instances, the caseworker may suspect that the hysteric is psychotic; he may talk wildly and excitedly, show signs of disorganization, and express fears of insanity. A premature referral of such cases to psychiatrists will only add to their fears.

In the early interviews with hysterics, the caseworker should remain calm and supportive, in order to test out the client's ability to regain his ego strengths and to get treatment started with a correct diagnostic appraisal.

The Typical Features of the Life History

The life history is an invaluable tool in the formulation of both the clinical and the psychosocial diagnosis of persons suffering with anxiety hysteria. I therefore will present some typical features of their histories.

Childhood

The life history of these clients usually reveals the presence of the neurosis in childhood. They were fearful, anxious children. They were afraid to go to school, afraid to be away from mother, afraid of the dark, and afraid of new experiences. The women frequently speak of themselves as "good little girls, too afraid to be anything else." They were frequently depressed and moody and took things hard. Toys and pets were overinvested with libidinal significance. The men were often enuretic into latency. They were onlookers rather than participants in sports and frail in

145

physical build, at least in their own comparison to their fathers. They were mothers' boys, not just in the passive, effeminate sense, but "mother's little man" with good manners and consideration for the mother's friends.

Most of these clients remember some of their sexual curiosity, fear, and preoccupation. They express anger because their parents did not give them sexual information. Most of them remember being discovered masturbating and being caught in sexual experimentations with siblings or playmates. These memories are still sources of guilt in adult life because of the parents' excitement, threats of punishment, and predictions of dire consequences. They were sometimes taken to a doctor for examination and were often the object of family concern. The client's memory of such events sometimes goes back only as far as his adolescence, but it seems likely this is a screen memory covering earlier sexual traumas and experiences. These memories, because they are fraught with guilt, are usually brought up only when treatment has advanced and the relationship to the worker is well established.

One man, who later became mentally ill, had an overdeveloped sense of responsibility for his young sister; he was obsessed with a feeling of responsibility for not having told his family about a man who molested his sister when she was 11 and he an adolescent. He had come downstairs at dusk and saw a man attempting to rape his sister. The man ran and he chased him. He knew him but he did not report the episode to his parents or to the police. Sex was a tabooed subject in his family.

The women often report being molested by men in the neighborhood or by relatives.

A woman client reported that she remembered being taken to a doctor at the age of 6 or 7. The doctor gave her an internal examination and she felt a sharp pain in the genital region; she had always believed that he pierced her hymen. He had become hostile because her neck was dirty. Her mother had come in at this point and, instead of siding with her, had sided with the doctor. She had always wanted to express her anger at her mother for not protecting her. She thought her husband had always suspected that she had had sex experience previous to marriage. She was not able to tell her mother that she was pregnant with her first child until after three months. She showed shame and anguish in telling these incidents.

Adolescence

The life histories of both men and women in this group show a difficult adolescence. Menstruation for women and pubescence for men were fearful experiences.

One woman, who began menstruation at 14, had no difficulty at first; she said it proved her womanhood and she used it to get out of housework. Then she began to have little fainting spells, but was not clear about the details. In adulthood she still felt depressed and irritable during menstruation.

One man reported that he was completely unprepared for changes that took place in his body when he approached puberty. He said that he had grown up in complete ignorance about sex. When nocturnal emission occurred for the first time, he did not know what it was. He had earlier been enuretic and thought the emission was a form of the same thing. As it continued he became worried about his health and at last mentioned it to his father who merely shrugged and said, "Well, now you're a man." A kindly family doctor later explained the matter to him.

In adolescence both sexes were shy, had marked feelings of inferiority, and had problems in dating. The girls had crushes on teachers and older women which were more intense than is usual for girls of their age. They had more girl friends than boy friends, and in several cases the girl dated only the man whom she subsequently married; frequently he was an older man. The husbands are described as gentle and understanding, "not sexual like a lot of men." The woman usually seemed grateful to the man for marrying her, feeling that it was unlikely that anyone could have loved her.

The men also had been slow in dating and showed a tendency to separate sexual and tender feelings in their discussions of premarital sexual relationships. They often married women who were sexually inhibited. Neither the men nor the women were promiscuous before marriage and generally did not have extramarital relationships. Rather they would form strong nonsexual attachments which aroused guilt because of their oedipal nature.

These clients have many fears about the effects of adolescent and childhood masturbation, including the fear of insanity which often continues into adult life. The women clients usually do not talk easily about masturbation, but they give evidence of their guilt.

147

One woman, early in contact, mentioned her fear of becoming psychotic. She had marked feelings of inadequacy and had always felt second to her brother, who had graduated from college. When she finished high school, she felt unable to decide anything for herself and had been unable to make her wishes about employment or possible further education known to her parents; she felt hurt because of their lack of interest. Through an aunt she obtained a job as an attendant in a state mental hospital, remaining there for a year and a half. She frequently felt panicky and spent many sleepless nights wondering whether she would become psychotic. She pictured herself as socially awkward and dumb.

Relationship to Family Members in Childhood

From early childhood the relationship of the hysteric to the parent of the same sex is characterized by hostile competition, with an accompanying overdevotion to the parent of the opposite sex. Both sets of feelings are guarded through defenses of rationalization and projection. The woman frequently says, "No one liked my mother," and "Everyone loved my father." Overdevotion to the parent of the same sex is a defense against the underlying hostility. The oedipal feelings toward both parents are usually so apparent that caseworkers have difficulty in believing that the clients themselves are not conscious of them.

It is not uncommon for a woman to recall incidents of being embarrassed in adolescence because her father was mistaken for a boy friend. In some women, the negative feeling toward the father may be high, particularly if he had deserted the mother and the daughter; if he remarried, the daughter feels it as a double insult. In one case, the woman said that her father had beaten her with a strap and connected her fear of being a woman with her father's treatment of her. Yet she vaguely sensed that she loved him.

In general, the complaints of the hysteric against his parents are in terms of their unwillingness for him to get ahead, rather than in terms of neglect, which is the chief complaint of borderline and psychotic clients. The hysterics believe that the parents stood in their way. The women feel that their mothers did not train them in housework, did not prepare them for marriage, and did not give sex information. Basically they feel that the mothers did not want them to marry or to have babies.

In many cases, these clients are still in touch with their parents; after marriage many live near them and often live with them for a period. They usually are psychologically overinvolved with them; they are concerned about the affairs of family members and dependent on them for advice in making decisions. The women clients often resent the closeness to their mothers and what seems like their interference, but are unable to tell them so. They sometimes neglect their own families to help their parents.

Sibling relationships are also marked by extreme rivalry, since a particular brother or sister often plays a role in the oedipal conflict. The hostility toward the sibling may carry over to their relationships with their own children, particularly if one child becomes identified with the hated sibling. In the case of women, we find the birth of a brother often had increased penis envy and made feminine adjustment more difficult. Both men and women show strong reactions to having had a crippled or retarded sibling, since the actual presence of handicap heightened their castration fears.

Health Histories

In all age periods of the hysteric, health problems are prevalent. These clients have a tendency toward illness and they overemphasize ordinary illnesses when they occur; after illness, they usually require a long convalescence. Childbirth is fraught with changes for the women and surgery is frightening for both men and women. They have fear of cancer, tuberculosis, and various infections. They worry about nourishment and their weight; obesity is a frequent problem. Some are afraid to go to doctors and others go at the first sign of any sickness.

School Histories

Learning difficulties are frequent in latency and adolescence as a result of sibling rivalry and of preoccupation with daydreams. Also, learning itself is sexualized since it is connected with childhood sexual curiosity.

Work Histories

The choice of a career is complicated by rivalries with parents and fear of competition. Work that involves exhibitionistic qualities, or that calls attention to the person, is often given up in favor of a more anonymous role; if it is not given up, it is carried

149

with anxiety. Work activities are sexualized for both men and women, with resulting anxiety. When the person does succeed in school or work, he feels that something is wrong. He believes that he does not merit the success, or that he got it by cheating, or that his superiors did not evaluate him correctly. The women are torn between homemaking and having a career, often alternating between them and unable to combine them comfortably.

In the women, the motivation to work is in part a masculine identification, but in part a defense against the fear of the feminine role. Their frequent use of their mothers to care for their children while they work is again related to the oedipal conflict; they feel they must turn the children over to their mothers. At work the women are competitive with men but not in as revengeful a way as the compulsive women.

Friendships

The woman hysteric often maintains a friendship with an older woman, or with a series of them in turn. Such friendship is motivated by an overcompensated hostility to the mother. Others find women friends dull and prefer the company of men; with them they may be provocative and flirtatious or they may establish platonic friendships. The men maintain relationships with other men through clubs or informal groups which have in them a strong, unconscious sexual element. The marital partner in both instances senses a threat to the marriage and is likely to quarrel about the other's friends.

In summary, the life histories of persons with anxiety hysteria have similarities to histories of persons with other disturbances. On the whole, however, persons in this group have a stronger tendency to grow and develop than many other clients. They make achievements in spite of problems, largely because there is less ego impairment. Oedipal problems, rather than pre-oedipal problems, are predominant in childhood, in adolescence, and in adult life. Fear of sex and preoccupation with sexual matters and the separation of sexual and tender feelings are their chief problems.

Treatment Considerations and Techniques

The treatment of this group of clients, in general, should be designed to help them to develop some self-awareness as a means of strengthening the ego. Not all, of course, have the ego strength, the motivation, or the supporting favorable conditions to make such treatment possible; these persons, however, can benefit markedly from supportive treatment because of their transference capacity. The choice of treatment should be determined by the evolution of the content and the extent of the neurotic conflict and of the transference and countertransference factors.

I should like to discuss first the countertransference problems that enter into the treatment of these clients.

Caseworkers often have difficulty in engaging clients in a discussion of sexual problems. In a way, caseworkers have acted as if all of sex is unconscious. Since caseworkers do not work with the unconscious, they have tended to rule out sexual matters. Hostility seems to be an easier topic for them to discuss, perhaps because the values of helping clients express anger have been more adequately formulated. The caseworker is able to elicit anger with a feeling of safety and with assurance about the correctness of his technique. Also, the extensive experience in working with the compulsive neurotic has added to the sense of safety; the compulsive's many defenses against complying with the caseworker's suggestion that he vent his anger serve as a protection. The caseworker in these cases may "chip away" at the hostility, but it comes forward so slowly that nothing very frightening happens.

In any event, the hysterical client, with his emotionality and sexuality, appears to frighten the caseworker. The current generation of caseworkers, as well as clients, have been brought up by parents who retained the repressed attitudes of the puritanical previous generation, even though many give lip service to new sexual freedoms. Thus client and worker alike are likely to be wary of talking about sex. In working with the hysteric, whose central neurotic concern is sexuality, the worker should focus on sexual matters relatively early in treatment. If this is not done, the client is likely to terminate contact, using whatever help has been given to relieve his guilt and raise his morale. Such help may be useful but it does not have the value of sustained treatment of the core problem.

When we read case records, we see that the hysteric is seldom able to take the initiative in talking about sex. He hints at it or reveals it through projection or displacement. For example, a

151

client talking about his work frustrations may also be expressing feelings about his sexual inadequacy. The caseworker, therefore, must feel free to ask about possible sexual problems, thereby giving the client permission to talk about them. In order to do this, the caseworker must overcome any feeling he may have that sex is a fearsome topic or that talking about sex is a form of seduction. If the caseworker fails to give the client an opportunity to explore his disturbing sexual problems, he will represent the disapproving or repressive parent who made the child feel guilty, or sent him elsewhere for help, or forced him to hide his sexual concerns.

Handling the anger of the oedipal conflict is doubtless more frightening to the caseworker than handling the hostile aggression related to the pre-oedipal period. Since there is considerable justification for the anger of the client who was deprived in his earliest years, the caseworker can agree with his feelings and offer sympathy. The "unjustified" anger of the neurotic presents more complex problems, for both client and caseworker. The caseworker's own anger, fear, and guilt associated with the oedipal situation may block his ability to help clients with their feelings. He must be able to tolerate his own anxiety and guilt if he is to help them reduce the power of their punishing superego.

In the treatment of the hysteric, the transference relationship is of particular significance. Freud identified the hysterical neuroses as transference neuroses and therefore amenable to standard psychoanalytic procedures. In casework treatment, the positive transference response of the hysteric places the caseworker in a position of primary influence. Certain standard casework techniques, therefore, may have a deeper influence with this group of clients than with others. I shall discuss briefly four techniques: (1) manipulation, (2) emotional release, (3) clarification, and (4) selected interpretations.

1. Manipulation

By manipulation, I refer to the technique delineated by Dr. Grete Bibring.[5] The main elements are the construction of a corrective relationship and intervention in the client's environment.

[5] Grete L. Bibring, M.D., "Psychiatric Principles in Casework," *Journal of Social Casework*, Vol. XXX, No. 6 (1949), pp. 230–235.

The anxious or phobic client needs a calm and consistent relationship because his own anxiety and his tendency to misconstrue or distort relationships keep him stirred up. He needs to be sure he is appreciated and respected, since he feels inferior and unworthy of love. He wants love so badly that frequently in his life he has paid too high a price for it; he often sacrifices his own individuality and his reality wishes. He will tend to repeat this pattern in his relationship with the caseworker. He needs a relationship in which sacrifice is not demanded of him; instead, he needs attention and an opportunity to voice his hopes and aspirations as well as his despairs. The caseworker should construct a relationship that will contain the elements both of a corrective parent and of a kindly person who operates on an objective reality level. A link with the ego, with the person's strivings to improve his functioning, should be established early. The client's problems in functioning must be defined and the goal of working on them must be established and kept in the foreground in order to give a boundary to the treatment and to help in controlling the transference.

The sex of the worker may be an important consideration in casework with these clients, but this question needs further study. In some cases, there has seemed to be a readier response when the female client has been assigned to a male worker.

In one case, after an initial embarrassed beginning, a woman client clearly responded positively to a nonseductive man worker, who showed respect for her as a wife and mother and who encouraged her to improve her relationships with her husband and son. She believed that her father had belittled her and as a result she had felt unattractive and unable to compete as a woman.

In another case, it is probable that improvement was accelerated when a man client was assigned a fatherly caseworker.

The client's current work difficulty was tied up with his rivalry with his father. He had repressed his negative feelings about his mother, who died when he was 17, and spoke of her in idealized terms. The worker played the role of an encouraging father who wanted the client to succeed; he made active job suggestions that were in line with the client's capacities. Later he also had contact with the wife so that she could continue to give her husband the support she had given him during the courtship and early days of the marriage. A woman worker might have reactivated a complicated attachment to the mother.

If a woman worker works with the woman client, careful steps must be taken to prevent the client from regressing into an over-dependent attachment. Such an attachment can best be avoided by dealing with her as a grown-up woman and a mother. She should be supported in her maternal role and be helped to work out conflicts that interfere with her assumption of it. Problems of child rearing can be profitably discussed with the expressed aim of helping her be a better mother. If the problem is a marital one, the caseworker should make it clear that the aim is to help her get more out of her marriage. If both partners are involved in a treatment relationship, separate workers may be desirable to avoid recreating the oedipal triangle.

The caseworker's intervention in the management of family life can serve a useful function in both marital and child guidance cases.

> In one case where the mother was reacting to her son's growing independence and attempts to free himself from her seductive love, the worker encouraged the father to become more active in doing things with the boy. The father's participation in the boy's life not only supported his attempts to develop normally, but it also brought relief to the mother by reducing the temptation to cling to her son.

Giving advice about such matters as moving away from irritating parents, changing jobs, and the use of social resources can be psychologically helpful. Changes in their reality situation can give clients protection from phobic stimuli and can reduce the opportunity for neurotic gratifications. When this kind of advice is offered in a reasonable way, these clients do not react with the same degree of negativism that compulsive neurotics do. Often they feel relieved when the caseworker gives advice that is at least partially in line with what they want; usually they can carry out the advice with the sanction and support of the worker. The worker must, of course, guard against becoming an omnipotent figure; the best safeguard is to base his activity on the conflicts and discomforts described by the client.

2. Emotional Release

The skilful use of guilt-relieving techniques usually brings about a cessation of acute anxiety in these clients. Symptoms subside or become less disturbing. Since the neurotic has introjected the ambivalently held love object, the conflict continues in the superego. The conflict can be modified through identification in the course of a meaningful relationship with a parental surrogate. The new introjection can reinforce the positive side of the ambivalence and effectively overpower the negative. A continuing warm relationship gives added strength to the positive identification.

In some cases, the power of the superego may be further reduced by the development of new ego defense mechanisms. Interpretations can be made that result in depersonalization of anger and in new displacements and rationalizations. The client can also gain substantial relief from anxiety if he is permitted to discuss his current sexual inhibitions and fears, as well as his memories of adolescent sexual conflicts that are conscious or near conscious. Being given permission to talk about these problems, in itself, reduces their danger. Guilt can also be reduced if the caseworker universalizes the problem; many of these clients have never discussed sexual matters with their own age group, either as children or adults. The superego of the hysteric is harsh, but it is not as implacable as the superego of the compulsive neurotic.

3. Clarification

Clarification techniques, ranging from simple educational discussions to the more elaborate process of separating reality and fantasy, should be utilized. Specifically, these clients need to be helped to make a new appraisal of their reality situations, which are usually relatively good, and to find new opportunities for enjoyment. Even when reality difficulties are present, they are usually not as serious as the hysteric fears them to be. The caseworker must recognize that these clients have been trying to escape internal danger by attaching the danger to reality situations. In many instances, the caseworker is drawn into handling the reality problems only to find that the client produces a new set. Sometimes, of course, help can be given only with each adverse reality problem as it appears. However, in situations where the ego is relatively strong and the neurosis not too pervasive, the client can develop some degree of awareness as he is helped to see his repetitious behavior patterns and to make connections between childhood feelings and current adaptations.

155

4. Selected Interpretations

Certain interpretations of the meaning of the client's behavior can be made in the later stages of treatment. These interpretations should be of the kind that will help the client realize the undue influence of his parental ties and his childhood feelings on his current functioning. The connection between his typical ways of reacting to situations and his need to work against his own best interests can be pointed out. Further discussion of his sexual problems and the way they interfere with his personal relationships may also be helpful. Some modification of sexual conflicts often takes place under the influence of the transference. Also, hysterical clients can be helped to gain useful insights through discussion of conscious and preconscious feelings and experiences; the deeper oedipal material, of course, is not touched. By working with the social components of the instinctual conflicts, the caseworker can help the client achieve considerable emotional relief. For example, a man's fear of sexual intercourse is frequently lessened after he has discussed his fear of being dominated by his wife. A discussion of the client's feeling of personal and social inadequacy can carry deeper meanings, thereby relieving the underlying feeling of sexual inadequacy.

In the case of the mother and son mentioned previously, the mother became angry because the boy's caseworker gave him a present. She expressed her anger to her caseworker after the latter had talked with the father and advised him to associate himself more actively with his son. The worker raised the question of jealousy and the mother, in this interview, admitted her jealous feelings and then talked freely about her close relationship with the boy during his first four years while her husband was in service. She was able to see that she had subtly kept him from developing a good relationship with his father during the subsequent years. She brought out feelings of anger against her husband for leaving her alone during these years, although realistically she knew he had been drafted and had no choice. She also reported that she never had a satisfactory sexual relationship with her husband. The caseworker suggested that she might be withholding in the sexual relationship to punish her husband for leaving her and that she accused him of being unloving, whereas this might be her problem. The woman in subsequent interviews was able to make connections between her

anger at her husband and her childhood feelings of being insufficiently loved by her father, who preferred her brother. Her
relationship with her husband improved during contact and
she gained considerable self-confidence.

In another situation, a married woman, who had been in
treatment for some time, started an interview by saying that she
should never have married. Her mother had told her that men
cannot be trusted. Her mother, even now, would like to take
care of her and her children, and put Mr. R, her husband, out
of the house. She made these statements in a half joking way.
When the caseworker asked whether the mother knew that things
had been going a little better, Mrs. R looked startled and said
she had not discussed her affairs with her mother recently. She
then asked whether she would be disloyal to her mother if she
allowed herself to be more fond of her husband. The caseworker
commented on the incongruity of the question, and soon after
Mrs. R began to report about the good times she was having with
her husband. Later she started to look for a new apartment,
stating that they needed a pleasant place to entertain friends.
She also said that she knew it is important for a father and
children to be close to each other. In one interview she said that,
if her husband would be patient with her, she believed their
sexual problems could be straightened out.

In general, clients with anxiety hysteria are relatively well on
their way to adult adjustment. Their capacity for a certain degree
of love for the marital partner and for the children, and their
ability to be partially satisfied and successful in work, can be
considered positive indications for treatment. The strong urge to
equal their parents, even on a neurotic basis, is an active conflict
which can be used to motivate treatment. Usually the material
about their parental relationships comes early in the contact and
is accompanied by deep feeling. Their overinvolvement with their
parents and the influence of the parents in their current reality
situation make the central problem readily available for discussion. Also, their current relationship problems with the marital
partner and the children provide many opportunities for fruitful
discussion.

Conclusion

It is important to conclude this discussion of treatment with the
note that sometimes casework treatment should be viewed as

157

preliminary to psychoanalytic treatment. Although casework treatment may be the method of choice in some cases, in others such treatment can only bring partial or temporary relief. Psychoanalysis is a specific treatment for this neurosis and offers possibility of resolution of the basic conflict. Analysis should be considered, if possible, for young persons, particularly young adults, who have such pervasive anxiety and symptoms as to prevent marriage, disturb a marriage, or interfere with their successful functioning in parental and work roles. It should also be considered for young women who are fearful of childbirth or have been traumatized by the birth of their first child. It should be considered also for all clients who are symptom ridden to the point where the only avenue to treatment is to work with the unconscious content of the problem.

The adults who suffer from anxiety hysteria are handicapped in the performance of their social and sexual roles. Since this neurosis is rooted in an unresolved oedipal conflict, its resolution often requires analytic treatment. Casework treatment, however, can serve to reduce the client's anxiety and to restrict the influence of the neurosis on the client's functioning. If the caseworker identifies the neurosis and understands it dynamically, he can help many of these persons live satisfying and productive lives.

11. The Balanced Expression of Oedipal Remnants*

George E. Gardner, M.D.

SPEAKING AS A CHILD PSYCHIATRIST, I shall consider the topic of the anxiety hysterias, whether in a child or an adult patient; with special emphasis, first, on the level of development in childhood at which the crucial factors in the *genesis* of the neurosis seem to have had their traumatic impact upon the patient; and, second, on the persistence and periodic reactivation in later years in the thus vulnerable adolescent or adult.

In respect to genesis I would emphasize that, in general, (1) there are certain definite tasks in personality development that the child has to solve at certain chronological age-levels from birth to adulthood; (2) the proper and orderly initial solution of these tasks will alone render the solution of later tasks possible; (3) there are definite categories of trauma, crises, or threats, which, in short, are variations in extreme of the basic fears of death (total destruction) or of mutilation (partial destruction) to which children may be exposed, which can result in a nonsolution or malsolution of these tasks just because these threats assail them in fairly specific forms and contexts at that particular level of development; and, finally, (4) the reactivation of the disabilities engendered will be primarily related to stresses and strains in the interpersonal relationships of one milieu, that one milieu being the family.

* Reprinted from *Smith College Studies in Social Work*, Vol. XXVII, No. 3, (1957).

159

Not forgetting for a moment the basic importance of the tasks for solution presented to the child in the preoedipal years, and certainly not minimizing the serious effects of malsolution of these tasks upon the later years of child development, I have always thought of anxiety hysteria as the adult replica of the task solutions posited for the oedipal, immediately postoedipal, and early latency child, and particularly the task solution of the latter age level.

The child at this stage of development—the latency period—is faced with (among others) the following critical tasks: (1) the satisfactory resolution of fear of annihilation through abandonment; (2) the resolution of castration or mutilation fears for sexual activities and fantasies; (3) the control and sublimation (through play and fantasy) of the aggressive drives, and even more specifically, the impersonalization of aggression; (4) the satisfactory consolidation, as it were, of the superego; (5) socialization in the family and with the peer group beyond the family; (6) security in a bisexual identification; and (7) the struggle to differentiate for later effective living the sexual and the aggressive-sadistic drives.

Each item in the typical symptomatology of the anxiety-hysteric state is referable to faults in development, loci of fixation through unsatisfactory solution of these seven tasks of the postoedipal or latency period in childhood. These tasks of the latency period are not entirely distinguishable from those of the preoedipal period save in one crucial respect, and that is that they are the remnants of those problems of the earlier levels—a galaxy of diffuse remnants—which present themselves for final solution, synthesis, and nonconflictive integration.

For emphasis of this point, the title of my discussion might be, "Anxiety Hysteria: The Persistent Disabling Expression of Oedipal Remnants." The healthful organization for subsequent balance in sublimated expression of these oedipal remnants constitutes the over-all task of the latency period. The failure to complete these separate and disparate tasks will present, as a clinical picture, any one—or any constellated arrangement—of those diffuse symptoms which we find in any anxiety-hysteric patient. It is worth emphasizing that these thrusts in development or these tasks for solution for the latency-period child are normally accompanied by great initial fear; and that the hallmark in symptomatology in the adult anxiety-hysteric is fear—fear of death, of mutilation, of defeat, of loss of prestige, and so on.

I should now like to turn to another emphasis, the significance of which we cannot escape—the crucial importance of the intra-familial milieu in the reactivation of this disabling response of the anxiety hysteria. It is not merely that the childhood origins of these responses are in the family-membership-role relationships, but also it is important to note that the stresses and strains relative to roles to be played within the immediate present family (of the later adult) disable the patient (that is, the vulnerable member) repeat-edly. And although Mrs. Austin categorizes her cases of anxiety hysteria into those that relate primarily to parent-child relationships and those that relate primarily to marital relationships,[1] I should like to associate them as a unit-group and comment upon them in a broader framework of "family cases," whether the particular anxiety-hysteric patient is married or unmarried, or, if married, whether a parent or nonparent.

I hope that a brief discussion, at this point, of the family as an institution as I see it clinically will not be considered a digression. It is intended to be in direct line with my previous comments upon latency-period task solutions and the symptom expressions of anxiety hysteria. My thesis is, in short, that the sublimated expression (satisfactory and satisfying expression) of these diverse oedipal remnants is possible for the adult only—or, at least, with the greatest possibility for expression—within the family setting. By the same token, the failure of the family setting to admit such expression can lead to symptom formation; and, in turn, the symptom expression may well be critically causal in relation to eventual serious family dislocation or breakdown.

In this light I shall be general in my remarks about the family as an institution, and then specific about it as I refer to the etiology of anxiety hysteria in one of its members.

The family, as an institution, was not, to my mind, set up by man in the first instance, decades of centuries ago, primarily or solely to care for children (as is so often stressed); nor was the helplessness of the child the single or sole impulsion to its founding. Like all behavior, the emergence of all social institutions is multiply deter-

[1] See Chapter 10 of the present volume.

mined. In this instance, in respect to the institution, the family, the multiple determinants were the multiple biological drives and needs, including and over and above the needs for sexual expression and sustenance. There are neo- or para-biological needs closely allied to, and founded upon, these two primary needs that it is necessary for man to satisfy; and these needs are those that are demonstrable in the tasks of the latency period and the expression of which is largely dependent upon the existence of a family setting. The family is potentially the finest instrument that could be devised for their acceptable expression. And I am sure, had we been an omniscient, detached observer of man's development through eons of time, we would in all objectivity declare the family to be the cleverest device of his creativity, even though at times it seems a frail and uncertain institution.

To be specific, and thus return to our patients, these multiple biological determinants and needs are translated for expression, in the case of the individual family member, into multiple roles. They are needs that must be satisfactorily and satisfyingly expressed, and the expression of them should have been made anxiety-free through the proper solution of the tasks that I have emphasized.

If we take, as an example of all this, the American housewife, bearing in mind the ever-present remnants of needs and the introjected persons in childhood with whom she is in part—"remnant-wise," one might say—identified, there are at least three different need expressions which she must have: (1) the need to be a wife, which includes the expression of her heterosexual needs and is associated with the segmental needs expressed as a homemaker; (2) the need to be a mother; and (3) the partial-need expression of a daughter—the latter including the need for some expression of the sibling-need role. To my mind it is not clinically correct to assume that the expressions of some of these persistent needs—all closely allied to biological needs—are correct and healthy and that some of them are incorrect, neurotic, or pathological. All must in some part be expressed, and gratification in the expression must exist. It is the imbalance or lack of fluidity and flexibility in these need expressions—the fixation-determined overexpression of one, or the guilt-laden underexpression of another—that results in anxiety and in the various defenses against anxiety in symptom formation and neuroticism. And not only must the housewife herself gain expression of these diverse needs. She must be able to tolerate and indeed to meet the comparable diverse needs of her husband and those of each of her children—and, again, to accept, tolerate, and fulfil them without guilt or fear.

To take but one example of multiple need expression, that is, bisexuality, I feel that in clinical thinking we have, with good reason, in theory and in practice, modified our recent position that the adult male must be all male, the adult female all female; that, otherwise, personality fragility, or even pathology, exists or is bound to occur. In the light of our clinical impressions and observations we should have recognized that segmental biological needs make such a personality structure impossible, and that it is not the bisexual needs in themselves that make for pathology, but rather the cultural insistence that all expressions of such needs are errors, thus inducing unnecessary guilt, fear of, and need for, punishment. In like manner the other partial or remnant multiple needs that I outlined could be commented upon (in their total prohibition) as potential foci for anxiety-hysteric symptoms.

12. The Conscious Use of Relationship with the Neurotic Client*

Sylvia Perry

THE CENTRAL SOURCE OF TROUBLE for the client suffering from anxiety hysteria is his inability to master completely the oedipal conflict. The oedipal period has been fraught with trauma for him and the traumatic events of this phase have prevented, to a greater or less extent, his using ego strengths to achieve satisfactory personal relationships and a stable social adjustment. The task of the social worker is to free the client's ego so that it is able to function to the fullest extent possible. In order to do this, the caseworker must have dynamic understanding of the sources of the ego's discomfort so that he may both recognize the client's difficulties and know the appropriate techniques of casework treatment.

In order to work with the anxiety hysteric, the caseworker must answer two related questions. First, why was the oedipal period so troublesome that the client remained fixated at this stage of development while most persons are able to move beyond it? Second, how does the worker's understanding of the causal factors influence the client-worker relationship—the cornerstone of all casework diagnosis and treatment?

* Reprinted from *Smith College Studies in Social Work*, Vol. XXVII, No. 3 (1957).

Significance of the Oedipal Conflict

The first question cannot be answered, I believe, without considering in some detail the parent-child relationship during the oedipal period. Since psychiatric study has shown that many anxiety hysterics fantasy that they were sexually assaulted, although they did not have such experiences, we must look to their relationships with their parents for an explanation of the events that played an important part in causing the disturbance. A mother or father who has had a warm, loving relationship with the child prior to the oedipal period can become anxious and upset by the child's attempts at mastering the conflict. At this point such a parent may, in accordance with his own life experience, alter his relationship with the child by becoming overconcerned and curious, or by becoming more hostile toward the child either through open criticism or withdrawal. The child, therefore, must try to resolve the conflict in an atmosphere that has become in some measure less loving and accepting. To the child it appears that it is not wholly safe to identify clearly with his own sex, because directly or indirectly the parents have conveyed that this is not acceptable to them. Not only does the child feel guilty about his own sexual drives, but the parents by their reactions can increase feelings of guilt and hostility to such an extent that the child is immobilized. In other words, the oedipal problem can spark emotional deprivation at the hands of the parents; and the deprivation in turn causes the child to withdraw from resolving the conflict, to feel guilty about his own behavior, and to blame his parents in an exaggerated manner for the situation. The child, rather than take the complete blame for his feelings, projects them, and continues to build the projection so that when he becomes an adult he may relate somewhat fantastic stories of the meanness of his parents, which do not coincide with the client's obvious level of adjustment.

The emotional deprivation of the anxiety hysteric is of a particular kind. It is not that the child is not loved, but that the parent cannot love him to the extent of accepting the fact that he has sexual wishes, or the parent cannot tolerate the child's angry feelings toward him during this period. The child, in response to these parental reactions, feels compelled either to repress his desire to

165

be wholly masculine or feminine as his sex indicates, or to risk losing the parent's love. This also explains why the symptoms of the anxiety hysteric, which are also in some measure defenses, are to be found predominantly in the sexual sphere—frigidity, diffuse anxiety related to sexual problems, and phobias designed to lessen exposure to heterosexual relationships.

Relationship with the Caseworker

I have elaborated on the part parents play in hindering the anxiety hysteric from mastering the oedipal conflict because, in forming and using the relationship with the social worker, this client brings both the positive and negative feelings that he felt toward his parents. He brings the capacity for a warm relationship, because he has experienced it with his parents. He is eager to please because he is fearful that he will lose the worker's affection as he risked losing, or did lose in some measure, that of the parents. He asks to be protected from a repetition of this loss and from his anger about it. Frequently he presents himself initially as more disturbed than he is in order to make sure of getting sympathy, to guard himself against the possible angry feelings he anticipates, and also to point out what a bad child he has really been. His initial attitude toward the worker can create problems which hinder an early diagnosis.

The anxiety hysteric's fears are so overwhelming to him that he often presents a more exaggerated picture of illness than actually exists. For example, a woman came to a psychiatric clinic with the chief complaint that she was afraid of harming her children. She also gave a full, accurate description of grand mal epileptic seizures and was sure that the Virgin Mary had appeared to her, warning her of death. The complicated symptom picture required a lengthy period of neurological study and psychiatric consultation. Subsequently, after she had been seeing a social worker for some time about her problems with her children, she was able to describe her more alarming symptoms as anxiety attacks and bad dreams. In the meantime, the caseworker could not be certain of the nature of the problem. Recognizing that the client seemed to relate with unusual warmth for a person with such severe symptoms, the worker still had to keep in mind the possibility of a more malignant condition than anxiety hysteria. Nor can one always rely, in the initial stages, on hearing that the client has achieved a relatively satisfactory social adjustment as compared with those with more severe disorders. At times, the hysteric can present himself as an isolated person who has good relationships with neither sex. He avoids heterosexual contacts since he has seduction and castration fears. He also avoids contacts with his own sex.

One vital clue to diagnosis of the anxiety hysteric is the fact that he forms a warm relationship with the caseworker although he denies that he has other satisfactory relationships. In this instance, the caseworker can rely on his own feelings toward the client, because this client's warmth and fundamental adequacy arouse an instinctive positive response toward him which is not as likely to occur in relation to the client whose disturbances are on a deeper level.

Caseworkers need to be fully aware of the clinical description of the anxiety hysteric. From the beginning of the contact with him, by means of the client's presenting symptoms, social problems, previous history, current social adjustment, and the quality of his relationship with the caseworker, the worker must be aware of various diagnostic groupings in order to lay the groundwork for a more precise clinical diagnosis and to determine quickly the treatment goal. If the worker can detect, at an early stage, the hysteric's inherent strength and ability to relate in spite of his need to convince the worker otherwise, a more ambitious goal in treatment can be set than is possible with the sicker client. However, because he does exaggerate, distort, and talk of feelings about his adjustment rather than what it is, the caseworker should not be too disappointed if several interviews are required before the worker is certain of the diagnosis.

During the initial stages of treatment, while the worker and the client are exploring the presenting social problem, the worker needs to be constantly aware of the dynamic quality of the client-worker relationship. Through this relationship, the first clues to problems in early parental relationships which have prevented the client from feeling comfortable in his sexual identity can be picked up. Although the client may not talk about his parents during the initial period, he expresses directly and indirectly how he fears or

167

wants the relationship with the caseworker to be; from these clues, the worker can deduce the parental responses that have worried and blocked him in the past. If the worker can identify in what way the client was failed, he can more readily adapt himself to the corrective parental role which is so important to the treatment process. The worker's role is corrective in the sense that the worker can give the client what was missing in the parental relationship. The anxiety hysteric hangs on to his grievances toward his parents which prevent him from enjoying his current life situation. The caseworker must recognize that the grievances are exaggerated and overemphasized by the client in order to protect himself from looking at his own guilt feelings. However, one needs to ask why the client had grievances in the first place and to be aware that there may have been some reality to them although their exact nature and extent only gradually become clear to the client.

Supporting the Sexual Role

The hysteric, because of the stage at which the trauma occurred, is complaining, not that he was totally deprived of love (although he may put it this way), but that in the specific area of being loved for his sexual qualities, he achieved only partial acceptance from the parent. Thus, when the woman client complains that her mother did not want her to marry or pursue feminine interests, it may not be literally true, but the client has correctly felt some reservations or doubts on the mother's part in allowing her girl child to be truly feminine. It is therefore of the utmost importance for the femininity of the woman and the masculinity of the man to be supported by the caseworker so that *restitution can be made for the earlier deprivation.* Through the relationship, the worker "allows" and supports the client's true sexual identification and permits him to grow to maturity in a way that the parents would not permit. Thus, when the anxious or phobic client is allowed to voice his aspirations as well as his despairs, he is often experiencing for the first time a relationship in which his desires for a more normal heterosexual adjustment are approved and encouraged.

Similarly, with the woman client who presents a problem with her child, the worker's emphasis on her role as a mother, and the worker's help in regard to the woman's personal conflicts so that she will be able to be a better mother, serve to point up in terms of her deeper conflict that the worker sees her as an adequate woman and thus she is viewed differently from the way in which she was viewed by her own mother. Similarly, active suggestions in relation to job changes, social activities, or referral for medical advice are most effective when related to the purpose of pointing up the client's ability to function and succeed in the masculine or feminine role, as the case may be.

If the worker's relationship with the anxiety hysteric has been focused on helping him feel more comfortable with his own sex, and if the worker has given him considerable help in this area, there is not much danger that the client will have depressive reactions as he begins to clarify and examine his own part in hanging on to his early fears and grievances. Moreover, if the worker has given support and help to the client in the specific area of his deprivation, there is not much danger that a too dependent relationship will develop.

If the client knows with some degree of certainty that the worker accepts him in the role of his choice, it becomes relatively safe for him to look at the ways in which he is hampering his own adjustment by distorting his current and past relationships. The client-worker relationship is the most fruitful setting in which to help the client sort out what are real and what are unreal grievances toward parents and parental figures. At times the client may complain about the worker. The worker again must sort out for himself and the client the reality of the complaints and must recognize that the client's complaints at times may be about parents rather than the worker.

It is sometimes puzzling to the worker that this type of client is angry when the worker has tried to be helpful. When the true nature of the anger is understood, it is easier to handle than is the anger of the sicker client. The latter must learn that although he has suffered a great deal of deprivation, the worker cannot, at this late date, completely make up for these lacks. This realization can be a severe disappointment. The deprivation of the anxiety hysteric is slight in comparison. The worker can more easily make up for it, and the hysteric can gain real relief from seeing that he was not as rejected and deprived as he feels that he was. Nor does he have to go on adding to his guilt by blaming his parents or the worker for hostile acts that have not actually occurred.

The worker should anticipate the possibility that the hysteric will act out at certain stages in treatment. At points at which the client feels some relief from symptoms, or when he begins to see himself as a man or woman who has something to offer, he may test out these gains in inappropriate ways. The girl who has been scared to have dates will accept a date with a boy who is known to be unreliable. She does this partly to test her new-felt strengths and partly to prove to herself and the worker that heterosexual relationships are bound to be disastrous for her. This type of client can benefit from the worker's intervention in the management of his affairs; he can be helped to see realistic dangers perhaps for the first time.

When the worker is clear about the role he needs to assume in supporting the anxiety hysteric, the actual sex of the worker need not become a vital factor in determining the successful outcome of treatment. However, in certain cases it can make a difference. An unusually painful experience or relationship with parents can make it extremely difficult or impossible for the client to use a constructive relationship with a worker of one particular sex. For instance, if a woman client's relationship with her father has been complicated by seductive behavior on his part, it may be extremely hard for the client to relate to a male worker in any but a flirtatious, seductive manner.

Discussing Sexual Problems

The discussion of sexual problems should be handled by the worker in the same way as other material brought by the client. Just as the worker recognizes that when a client talks about feelings about the casework relationship, he may be talking about parental attitudes, so must he be aware that the client discusses sexual matters in many disguised forms. He may talk at great length about his guilt and misconceptions concerning sexual matters by telling the worker about conversations his friends have had—the unnecessary pain his friends have suffered—from mis-

170

understanding about such matters, and so forth. As he becomes more secure he may tell the worker about his own part in such conversations.

One should remember, however, in relation to this subject, that the sexual problem is the primary symptom of the hysteric, and for this reason sex tends to be a more emotionally charged subject than it is for clients in other diagnostic groups. The decision as to whether to discuss or not discuss sexual material directly with this client needs to be made in the light of this fact and in the light of the relationship the worker wishes to establish and foster with the particular client. For example, if the client, seeing the worker in the guise of his parents, expects and fears that the worker will be forbidding and inhibiting as his parents were, it would be a serious mistake for the worker to block the client from talking about sexual problems. On the other hand, there are clients whose parental figures handled the ambivalent feelings about the child's oedipal strivings by becoming actively overconcerned and overcurious about sex interests and behavior. Such a client is likely to see inquiries and discussion by the worker as prying and an invasion of privacy. In so far as the worker departs from his role as the "good parent" who trusts the client and is not worried if he has his own secrets, he blocks the client and does not make use of the corrective and restitutional aspects of the relationship. To put it another way, the client must look upon the discussions of sexual material as non-seductive and non-hostile, or they will not be helpful. Even when the worker has no unconscious desire to sexualize the relationship or attack the client, certain clients will see the discussion in this light and, depending upon the degree and kind of trauma experienced during the oedipal period, refuse to see it in any other.

Although workers are often overcautious in discussing sexual material, they also have been known to be carried away by the knowledge that the client's problems stem from conflicts about sex, and they feel that they are not really treating the client until such matters have been verbalized. In this situation the worker may be overlooking the dynamic nature of the relationship and forgetting to evaluate whether the material is raised directly or indirectly because the client is seeking relief of guilt and clarifica-

171

tion of misinformation from a good and objective parent figure, or whether he is testing the relationship to discover whether the worker is "safe" and will let him talk without prodding, and will allow him to make his own discoveries at his own pace. In any event, the opening up of problems by the caseworker, whether they be in relation to guilt, angry feelings, or sexuality, must be done on the basis of how the particular client sees the relationship with reference to earlier relationships, and the value of the discussion at that specific point in treatment.

As treatment progresses into its final stages, particularly with the client who is able to sort out and relate past experiences and relationships to present adjustment in a meaningful way, the role of the caseworker changes. The corrective or restitutional aspects of the parent figure gradually fade into the background, and the kindly reality figure on an object relationship level becomes more actively the role of the social worker. Just as these clients distort other relationships, so they may be unclear about the casework relationship, even with constant clarification. Frequently one sees the client beginning to look at the worker as a reality figure at about the same time that his fears and anxieties about others in his environment are clearing away.

Treatment Goals

The general goals and expectations of casework treatment are to relieve anxiety and, with certain clients, to bring about a better social adjustment. It seems to me that we can be somewhat more specific in defining our goals with the anxiety hysteric. Caseworkers attempt, through the use of the relationship, to help this client feel more comfortable within himself, particularly with reference to his sexual identity. In doing this, they also try to help him improve his over-all adjustment in relation to feeling comfortable with members of his own sex. A number of such clients are thereby freed to make more realistic relationships with persons of the opposite sex. The man who has gained new confidence in his masculinity no longer needs to blame his wife for her shortcomings, and the marital relationship improves. The girl in her twenties who chose to confide in older women now has warm relationships with girls who go with boys and who introduce her to them.

There are, however, a certain number of hysterics who, even with the gains made in casework treatment, such as enjoying active social lives, still fail to make rewarding adjustments to the opposite sex; or severe symptoms again arise when they attempt to form these relationships. It is for this group that referral for psychiatric help must be seriously considered.

For example, the single man who has been referred to a social worker because of difficulties he experienced in his work may feel perfectly comfortable in his job and with his male colleagues as a result of treatment. He has even been freed to have a girl friend and contemplates marriage, but such contemplations lead either to renewed symptoms or to his behaving in such a manner that a stable relationship with his partner is jeopardized. In such a situation further exploration of the oedipal problem is indicated, and through the preparation he has received in casework treatment, the client is more capable of making use of psychiatric treatment.

Or, to take another example, a mother in a child guidance clinic, in her work with the caseworker may have shown marked improvement in her relationship to her child and an improved social adjustment, but may have begun to have problems in the marital relationship. Whereas previously, because of her feelings of unworthiness, she was satisfied with her obviously inadequate sexual partner, she now feels she wants more and, in looking for ways out, has further emotional difficulties. Again, referral for psychiatric treatment should be considered. When the client wants changes of this nature and is prepared through the casework treatment to look at himself with less anxiety, referral to a psychiatrist for further insight into his problems is indicated.

The caseworker needs to recognize the point at which the client has gone as far as he can with the casework relationship; he must then evaluate whether the particular nature of the client's problem lends itself to psychiatric help, as well as assess whether the client has enough security within himself to examine other aspects of his neurosis constructively.

13. Initial Treatment of a Client with Anxiety Hysteria: A Case Presentation*

Flora M. Hunt

EARLY IN JUNE Mrs. L was referred to the family service agency by a psychiatric clinic in which she had been interviewed once. The doctor who had seen her felt that she was facing many reality problems and needed a continuing relationship with a caseworker. When she first came to the office Mrs. L was extremely tense and frightened. She was an attractive woman in her late 30's, neatly dressed but very thin and pale. The family agency was the latest of a long series of places to which she had gone in search for some kind of help. Her symptoms were a feeling of tension and panic which particularly became acute at times, a fear that she was "going to crack up," and phobic reactions when she was away from the house, particularly on public transportation. When she had the nervous spells—which she could describe only as a terrible feeling—she became very frightened that something awful was going to happen to her and that she could not continue to carry on.

The previous February Mrs. L had gone, in a panic, to a general physician who had sent her to a small private hospital for observation. Since no organic basis could be found for her disturbance, it was suggested that she go to a private mental hospital for shock treatments. Mrs. L had gone as far as the hospital admitting office but became very frightened and refused to admit herself. It was then suggested that she go to a general hospital with a psychiatric

* Reprinted from *Smith College Studies in Social Work*, Vol. XXVII, No. 3 (1957).

174

ward, but no bed was available. On her own initiative she then went to still another medical clinic where she was referred to the psychiatric clinic which, in turn, referred her to the family agency. Mrs. L felt that the doctor who had seen her at the psychiatric clinic had been understanding; and she was considerably reassured by his statement that she did not need shock treatments. I agreed with his judgment, and subsequently, when she expressed fear of a "break," I recalled and reinforced the doctor's opinion.

As Mrs. L described her situation it seemed clear that she was facing many reality pressures. Mr. L was her second husband and the father of her two younger children, Betty, 5, and Anne, 3. There were also three children by her first marriage, Richard, 16, Donald, 13, and John, 8. For a year and a half Mr. L had been ill with cancer, although he had not been told this. After a series of X-ray treatments he had been able to return to his job as a government clerk but he had not felt well and had been exceedingly irritable and increasingly dependent on Mrs. L. As he became sicker there was increasing friction between him and the children, especially the two oldest boys. Mrs. L was also disturbed by the uncertainty about the future because of the nature of her husband's illness.

In the first interview I recognized with Mrs. L her increasing panic as her symptoms had frightened her more and she had gone from one place to another looking for some kind of help. She had been very much afraid that I would also send her away. I told her immediately that I would plan to see her regularly and offered a second appointment later in the same week. Subsequently I have seen her twice a week. In the second interview, in response to her concern about how she could possibly manage during the summer with all the children at home, I offered help in making camp plans for Donald, about whom she was particularly concerned, and for John who wanted to go to Scout Camp.

Mrs. L was at first quite guarded in talking about her first marriage and divorce. She described her first huband as immature and irresponsible. The family had had to move several times and each time she had been left with the entire responsibility of finding a new apartment and making arrangements. Finally, she and the children had moved by themselves. Within two weeks after I began

175

to see Mrs. L, Mr. L was readmitted to the hospital because of acute pain. Both Mr. and Mrs. L were Catholic and at this point Mrs. L showed increasing upset and guilt about her irregular status with the church. In response to this increased anxiety and her growing confidence in our relationship, she was able to tell me about her second marriage.

She had met Mr. L while she was still married to her first husband and there was an instantaneous and strong attraction between them. Mrs. L had never experienced this kind of feeling before and she struggled with it for over two years. For part of this time Mr. L was away in military service. When he returned she tried not to see him but could not help herself. She would often meet him for a cup of coffee. Just to see him and be with him, even for a few moments, was the most important thing in the world to her. She expressed a great deal of guilt about this relationship, saying she had always "lived by the book" until she met Bill. She had never wanted anything in her life as much as she wanted him and she just had to have him. She now felt that her husband's illness was a punishment for their wrongdoing and that she should have known that such a marriage could not work out happily. At the same time she felt that the first few years of this marriage, prior to her husband's illness, had been happier than any other period in her life and under the same circumstances she would do the same thing over again. At this point it seemed important neither so to minimize her guilt and concern that I would seem allied with her feelings of badness, nor yet to seem in any way to share her self-condemnation. I recognized and accepted the importance of Mrs. L's relationship with her husband as the most meaningful one in her life and their very real need for each other, but also accepted her conflict with the church as important.

It was very difficult to clarify the prognosis in Mr. L's illness and throughout the contact this has been a complicating and disturbing reality. During the summer when Mr. L was in the hospital I talked with his doctor, who confirmed the diagnosis of cancer but said that the recent tests had been negative and as far as he could tell it had been arrested. However, the prognosis was uncertain so that there might be a return at any time. In spite of the negative tests, however, the pains continued and Mr. L lost a good deal of weight. At this point it seemed that there might be a crisis

176

at any moment, and I told Mrs. L that she might feel free to call me if she did get into a panic; I gave her my home telephone number. It is interesting that although my ready availability meant a good deal to her, she has never called me. However, the fact that she could carry the number on a piece of paper in her wallet seemed important and reassuring to her. Also, during the period of Mr. L's hospitalization we made arrangements for a homemaker so that Mrs. L could go to the hospital every day to see her husband.

In talking about her marriage, Mrs. L spontaneously brought out a good deal of background material. She felt that she had never had much in her early life and, except for the few brief happy years before her husband's illness, it looked as if she never would. She was the oldest of three children and had two younger brothers. She described her childhood as upset and deprived. Her father was alcoholic and very abusive toward her mother although he worked steadily. She remembered being very much frightened for her mother and trying to protect her. From the time Mrs. L was 8 or 9, her mother would sometimes leave the home for several days after a particularly violent upset with the father because she could not take it any longer. Mrs. L would manage as best she could to care for herself and the two younger children. Sometimes the father would take them to the paternal grandmother's home. Mrs. L recalled her grandmother as kindly and warm but she did not give the impression that the grandmother was a very important figure in her early life. She could express no hostility toward her own mother for these periodic desertions, but only identification with her suffering. She felt that her mother had never been a strong person but did not say this in a critical manner. Rather, she herself had assumed a protective role on behalf of her mother. It was interesting that, although Mrs. L's mother was now living in the home with her, she did not regard her as any sort of help. Mrs. L did not want her mother to stop working because, if her mother were at home all the time, Mrs. L thought she would just sink into a state of apathy and become dependent.

When Mrs. L was 17 she went to live with a friend. However, she worried about what was happening to her mother at home and could not sleep at night, feeling that she was comfortable

177

while her family was not. It was at this time that she first had experienced symptoms of panic and a feeling that something dreadful was going to happen. At 18 she married her first husband whom she had known since her junior high school days. She described him as quiet and "clean thinking." She thought that it was these qualities that had attracted her since they represented something quite different from her home life and she had determined that she would never bring up children in the kind of situation she had lived in. She felt somewhat maternal toward her first husband whom she thought of as rather frail physically. She had felt little sexual attraction to him, in contrast to her later feeling toward Mr. L. She now felt that her relationship with her first husband was a lukewarm one, in which there were seldom quarrels, but with no very strong positive feelings either. She remarked that she had felt about her first husband much as she now felt about Richard, her oldest boy. The first husband apparently was quite passive and did not assume active responsibility in planning for the family. However, he was still supporting the older children and was seeing them.

As Mrs. L brought out both her current feelings about her husband's illness and some of the earlier material, her strong feelings about dependency were evident. As a child she had felt very much on her own and actively responsible for her younger brothers. She had great feeling about the brother next to her who had had a head injury as the result of an automobile accident at the age of 4 and, according to her, had thereafter been retarded. It was exceedingly difficult for Mrs. L to talk about this brother who was now alcoholic and, although living in the same vicinity, was not in regular touch with any members of the family. Even after she had left home, Mrs. L felt responsible for her mother and her brother. She did not see her first husband as an adequate man, but rather as boyish. When she met her present husband she felt that, for the first time in her life, she had found "strength." He was tall and nice-looking and very proud of his physique and his athletic ability. Both Mr. and Mrs. L had great feeling about his illness in terms of the decline in his physical assets, his athletic ability, his good looks, and most recently in the loss of his teeth which had to be removed. Mr. L had become increasingly dependent on his wife, wanting her never out of his sight while he was at home and evidencing jealousy of any attention shown the children. Mrs. L had the feeling that he was "drowning" and trying to pull her down with him.

Throughout the contact I have tried to work with Mrs. L's feelings about dependency in two ways: through the implicit and continuing support offered by my relationship with her; and by discussing with her the meaning of her husband's increasing dependency on her owing to his illness as this related to her earlier feelings that she could never depend on anyone. In this discussion I tried to help her express and accept her feeling of disappointment and loss because Mr. L no longer seemed "the strength" she married, and at the same time to emphasize what strength he still had. For example, Mr. and Mrs. L had always had arguments; when she felt that he was being unreasonable, she was always able to stand up for herself and to work things out with him. Although she still was considerably irritated with him at times, she felt that she should not express any anger because he was sick. I questioned whether it was necessary to treat him in a completely different way because of his illness, and wondered whether he could not still respond as he had before and might not actually feel better if he were not always handled with kid gloves. Mrs. L was able to be more realistic in some of the subsequent disagreements, with the result that Mr. L responded more as he formerly had.

In July, after Mr. L returned from the hospital, Mrs. L began to express concern about their sexual relationship. This had been a very important part of the marriage for both of them and, in the early years, they could always patch up quarrels with love making. However, as Mr. L became ill and irritable and angry with her, Mrs. L felt increasingly less physical attraction for him. This, too, represented a tremendous loss to her. At this point Mrs. L told me, with some difficulty, that she would feel more comfortable with me if she could tell me something that no one else knew. Prior to her divorce and marriage to Mr. L she had a sexual relationship with him and she was certain that her third child was actually his. This story was told with great emotion and guilt. Mr. L also thought that this child was his, but Mrs. L had never been able to admit it even to him. At the time that she was pregnant with this child, Mrs. L had had a recurrence of the symptoms of panic and the feeling that something dreadful was going to happen which had first occurred when she had left home at 17, and which had brought her to the agency recently.

During the discussion about her changed feelings toward her husband, Mrs. L said that her husband, when he was difficult and quarrelsome, now reminded her of her father. Although she had at first expressed no feeling about her father except resentment at his behavior, when I now asked further about this relationship, Mrs. L said that actually he had been proud of her and had bragged about her on the outside although at home he had been critical. He felt that the mother favored her and he was jealous of any attention the mother gave her. As she grew into her teens he had accused her of having sexual relationships with boys. She recalled an episode when a drinking friend of her father's came to the house. He had asked her if she had had anything to do with men and then chased her around the table. She was only 8 or 9 at the time and had not really known what this was all about except that she was frightened and ran away from him. She also compared her husband with her father in that her father, when he was sober and penitent, would prepare a meal for the mother which he insisted she eat alone with him. The children were excluded and nothing was given them to eat. The mother was so frightened of the father that she dared not intervene in their behalf. Mrs. L felt that Mr. L now wanted this kind of exclusive relationship with her. She felt torn between his demands and the needs of the children.

It seemed that Mrs. L's first marriage had been essentially a reaction against her unresolved oedipal feelings for her father. She had been able to handle this conflict much more satisfactorily in the second marriage until her guilt was reactivated by the fact that Mr. L, in response to his illness, became more hostile and aggressive but with increased underlying passivity—in other words, more like her father. Mrs. L herself began to recognize and point out this similarity. I agreed that because of his discouragement and resentment about his illness, Mr. L did seem to her more like her father and pointed out that some of the resentment which she

180

was now feeling toward her husband was similar to the resentment she had felt toward her father. I did not explicitly carry the similarity in feeling further since Mrs. L herself volunteered no material that would make it appropriate to do so. However, I consistently pointed out that Mr. L was still the same man whom she had loved and married, that he was not her father, and that we could see that his recent behavior was in direct response to the progress of his disease.

We also talked about how the difficulty in real communication between Mrs. L and her husband made it harder for both of them. If they could be more comfortable with each other, he might be less irritable and unpleasant. Mrs. L wanted very much to feel about her husband more as she used to and could see this as one of the ways in which she hoped I could help her. It seemed clear that Mr. L's increasing sense of inadequacy had been aggravated by Mrs. L's changed feelings toward him. Whenever Mrs. L brought up her fear that Mr. L's sickness was a punishment for their sexual attraction and subsequent marriage, I accepted this as her feeling but I pointed out that actually we both knew that cancer is not a retribution for sin. In connection with Mrs. L's guilt and confusion about her sexuality it is interesting to note that she suffered a phobic reaction whenever she attempted a shopping trip although she was very much interested in clothes and previously had taken great pleasure in buying things for herself. Both she and Mr. L had enjoyed dressing up and going out. I encouraged her to try a window-shopping trip in connection with the hospital visits and suggested that if she felt panicky she could telephone me. Subsequently Mrs. L was able to carry out the suggestion and, although somewhat uneasy, she was not in a panic and did get some enjoyment from the venture. She did not call me.

I was careful to tell Mrs. L that I would be taking a vacation toward the end of the summer but I had assumed she would know how long it would be. She seemed to accept the prospect calmly but it developed that she had thought I would be gone only for a week or ten days. Mr. L at this point was at home but continued to complain of pain in spite of the fact that the doctor could find no definite cause for the symptom. He was depressed and irritable and Mrs. L was very much concerned about what might

181

develop. She was markedly taken aback when, she found I was to be gone for four weeks. Both because of the uncertainties involved in her husband's illness and because of her strong fear of loss and desertion, I suggested that it would be possible for me to telephone her once a week. With this slight contact and the knowledge that I was available she managed very well.

At present Mrs. L is handling her many reality problems amazingly well. She takes very good care of the home and the children and manages all the contacts with the doctors at the hospital, and with the insurance companies in regard to hospitalization and the complicated compensation forms. Although she expresses fear that she will not have strength to carry through, she has always been able to handle her situation competently. I have pointed this out to her, at the same time recognizing the importance of her feelings to the contrary.

Recently the family has been able to move to much more adequate housing and Mrs. L is hoping that some of the tensions may be eased when the five children, her mother, a sick husband and herself are not all congregated in a small four-room apartment. Although she dreaded the move and feared that she might not be able to carry on, she was able to do a very good job and to turn to Mr. L for what help he could realistically give. We planned for a homemaker for two days to help with some of the work and the care of the children during the moving process.

In presenting this beginning phase of treatment, I am very very much aware that Mrs. L's emotional disturbance is greatly complicated by the uncertainty that she and her husband are facing and I anticipate that my contact with her will be a long one for this reason. Several efforts have been made to see Mr. L on a regular basis but he has not kept appointments because of his feeling that there is no point in talking. Mrs. L herself was active in initiating his coming to see me, feeling that it helped her to know that she could discuss her feelings every week and hoping that he could have similar help in facing his illness. She is able to understand and sympathize with some of his reactions, and I feel that in spite of the neurotic complications, there are real strengths in their relationship. Thus far, in spite of the many difficulties, Mrs. L has not had a recurrence of the acute panic symptoms.

14. Casework Intervention in a School*

Cornelia T. Biddle

THE FIELD OF CASEWORK in schools presents tremendous possibilities and challenges. As schools throughout the country recognize the need for special help for troubled children, the question inevitably arises as to who is best suited to give this special help. Various plans are tried, in many of which teachers with extra training are used. Unfortunately, in some areas, strong feelings have been aroused against caseworkers' working with school children and rigid standards have been set, with emphasis placed on actual teaching training and experience. Where the feeling has been strongest, it is possible that caseworkers themselves must bear some of the blame, not because they have needed special teaching training, but because they may have neglected to use the very skills that are an intrinsic part of their own professional training.

Caseworkers are trained to think of and to sympathize with the individual. They recognize and deeply understand the many vicissitudes with which he is faced because of the impact of a strict and depriving environment on his personal wishes and drives. In their daily work, they see individual suffering that may have resulted from early unmet emotional needs and from aggressive energies that had been too rigidly controlled. Perhaps because of this understanding of and this experience with unhappy adults, it is difficult for caseworkers really to appreciate the positive contribution that the early school experience can make toward the individual's total development; too often the school experience is associated in their thinking with the repression, rigidity, deprivation, and author-

* Reprinted from *Smith College Studies in Social Work*, Vol. XXVI, No. 1 (1955).

183

itarianism which they decry. And yet, the first requirement for satisfactory work in the schools is that the caseworker must have a sincere and positive conviction of the positive values of the school experience for children. She must have a real understanding of the true meaning of education and must understand how the school experience contributes toward this education.

Education does not begin when the 5- or 6-year-old enters kindergarten or first grade. It begins when the child first draws breath. From then on, in varying degrees and with varying methods, the child is being led, pushed, cajoled, and encouraged toward socially acceptable participation in adult society. The best education is the one that does not overindulge the child in his many intense wishes and needs or frighten and block him; but rather that which helps him to channel them into acceptable outlets or to come to terms with them or control them of his own volition.

The school does not begin the educational process; it furthers it. The school helps the individual child by supplying him with tools with which to master, channel, and come to terms with his emotional strivings. In other words, it helps to develop ego strengths which are such an essential part of healthy functioning. The person who develops the satisfactions of being able to say "This is what I can do; I can master this skill," is the person who is developing a sense of himself as an adequately performing individual. The more sense of mastery an individual has, the better able he is to deal with the inevitable tensions and conflicts that will arise throughout his life. In helping the child toward mastery of skills, the school also provides an acceptable outlet for aggressive drives. All learning does this. A tremendous amount of free, unrepressed energy is needed to learn.

The school helps in many ways other than in encouraging the development of skills. It sanctions and encourages curiosity. It provides opportunity for the first real separation from the family setting. (It is an accepted fact by kindergarten and first-grade teachers that they will be called "mommy" and will share many of the child's feelings for the real mother in the early months of his school life; one of the teacher's major tasks in this period is to help the child to differentiate between home and school—to evaluate reality.) The school provides competitive situations, both scholastic

184

and athletic, in which, through competition with his peers, the child can channel and master his jealousies and resentments of siblings. Conversely, his guilty feelings because of his hostility toward parents and siblings can be evaluated and tolerated through his recognition that he is not unique in having hostile feelings since other children have them too. His need for security and belonging can be satisfied as he moves on in school; first, through his growing sense of loyalty to the teacher, then to his class, and finally to his school. These are but a few of the broader values for the child of the early school experience. Caseworkers, if they are to work constructively with schools in any capacity, must have a genuine appreciation of them. They must recognize, too, that the schools, in the main, are always working toward a better service to children and to the community. If they were not, they would not show increasing evidence of concern for the individual child who is unable to take advantage of the values mentioned above. They would not seek the services of specially trained teacher-counselors or caseworkers to help these children.

Children with flagrant difficulties, such as truants who have become involved in delinquencies or who show other evidences of deep emotional disturbance, will become known to the proper community agencies. The children for whom the school will ask the help of the school caseworkers would probably not come to the attention of any professional person. They would slide through somehow or be left behind, and would never realize their capabilities. Or they would become snowed under by an increasing succession of frustrations and failures plus the various mechanisms that each child would employ to deny to himself and to the world that he was a failure.

The Caseworker's Relationships in the School

The school caseworker is just as much a part of the school staff as are the principal, the teachers, nurses, dietitians, and so on. It is essential that she be in harmonious accord with the rest of the staff and she cannot be in accord unless she has a genuine understanding and appreciation of their roles and goals. It is essential also that they have understanding of and trust in her contributions. One of her first tasks is to build a base of mutual

185

trust, recognizing that in the beginning the staff will have little real understanding of her work and will either expect her to perform miracles or will be apprehensive about this representative from an unknown and possibly threatening field.

The principal is the head of the school; in the last analysis he or she is responsible for each individual pupil and for each member of the staff. This includes, of course, the caseworker. Just as the principal must know of the work that each teacher is doing, so must he have some understanding of the caseworker's contribution. It is perfectly natural and understandable for him in the beginning to want to know what the caseworker does and how she does it. He will want to know what she has "found out." In the beginning it is not at all unusual for a principal to drop in while the caseworker is having an interview, just as he will drop in to any classroom. This can be disconcerting, but if the caseworker understands the principal's position she will not feel threatened or antagonistic. There are times when this "dropping-in" can be valuable.

One time, for instance, a very shy and fearful little boy had just got up the courage to paint a gaudy picture and, in the process, had spilled a lot of water on the floor, with mixed feelings of delight and apprehension. Just at that moment, the principal dropped in. The worker immediately remarked that John had had a lot of fun painting, but that he was concerned now about the mess. The principal looked at the picture, admired it, and then said that it looked as though nothing had been spilled that could not be cleaned up. Needless to say, John was relieved. Later, the principal confided to the worker that perhaps he had dropped in at the wrong time. John had looked scared and embarrassed. The worker agreed that John had been scared, but she added that the principal had said the very thing that had the greatest value for him, that expression of feelings was not dangerous and bad, and that he himself could exert the required controls over them. The principal said he supposed it was fear of being naughty that made some kids timid and shy. He added that it might be better if he did not drop in unannounced.

More usually, in the beginning of the contact, the principal will want to have joint conferences with the worker and parents, just as he has conferences with teachers and parents. Here again, great steps can be made in establishing the base of confidence and co-operation.

186

Jimmy, a first-grader, was having extreme difficulty in school (constantly fighting, needling the teacher, tense, excitable, completely unable and unwilling to learn). Special help had been requested for Jimmy by the teacher, but first the parents had to be interviewed and given some explanation of why this help was deemed advisable. The father arrived, carrying a magazine article titled "What Is Wrong with Our Schools?" He proceeded to discourse on this subject for some time, finally stating that he knew the teacher was having trouble with Jimmy. He wondered if she was not using the wrong methods with him. He himself wondered about these new methods of teaching, and said that things weren't done that way in his day. He wondered if the children didn't pick on Jimmy because they knew of the teacher's irritation with him, since it seemed there was always some kind of a fight going on, with Jimmy in the midst of it. In a way Jimmy was like himself, he said. He didn't like to be taken advantage of, and if he thought somebody was being unfair he fought back.

During this tirade, the principal started to speak several times, but each time desisted. Finally the worker said that it seemed that Mr. D had had a great deal of feeling about coming in to this interview; perhaps he felt it was only because of Jimmy's fighting that he had been called in. She assured him that this was not the case at all but that the school recognized that Jimmy was intensely unhappy for some reason, and at the present time was unable to use his good intellectual abilities; it was hoped that in some way they could all work together to help him. The father immediately relaxed and thereafter the interview proceeded entirely differently. It was an enlightening one for all parties concerned. For the parents, it provided proof of the school's positive interest in their child; for the caseworker, it provided clues for understanding Jimmy but, beyond that, it provided a graphic example of the sort of pressures to which the head of a school is always subjected. For the principal, it provided an example of a caseworker's activity which had more meaning for him than any amount of theoretical explanations. As he himself expressed it, "He came all ready for a fight, didn't he? And I was all ready to let him have one. But I decided to let you handle it. Did you notice the change when you said we didn't want to punish Jimmy? I'm going to try your method sometime myself; let them talk first and get it off their chest."

As the caseworker becomes more and more an accepted member of the school team, the principal will refer parents to her to talk about their own concern about their child even though the child may be adjusting satisfactorily in the school setting. This is a very

187

important part of the program. Thus, a principal suggested that one young father talk with the caseworker about his concern over his first-grade son's lack of interest in competitive sports. The worker could talk with him realistically about the developmental stage of six-year-olds and could suggest some further talks with the first-grade teacher. A mother was eager to know if she should take her daughter to a clinic in order to help her avoid the unhappiness in adolescence which the mother herself had suffered. In cases such as these, the children are not seen although there may be several talks with parents, in which their personal apprehensions can be realistically evaluated.

Sometimes referral to another agency is indicated. This was the case with a mother who was deeply concerned because her 5-year-old daughter sucked her fingers. In fact, she was so disturbed that she had already gone to the family doctor to ask that he put a splint on the child's hand; the mother had heard that this would cause an infection and discourage sucking the fingers. The caseworker already knew from talking with the kindergarten teacher that the little girl was quite happy in school and that she did not suck her fingers more than many other young children who were finding themselves in the first months of school in a new and rather "scarey" situation. In further talks with the mother, however, she became aware of many other conflicts between her and her little girl. Consequently, since one of the essentials for healthy development is that the individual must learn the difference between family people and people in the outside world, and since the school itself provides a prime opportunity to make this differentiation, it seemed unwise for the school to enter into what was primarily a family problem. This was talked over with the mother, and referral to a family service agency was suggested and eagerly accepted.

It is, of course, the teacher who first becomes aware of the child's need for help. It seems that the teacher-caseworker relationship has the most pitfalls; and yet, if there is to be any help for the child, the two must work as partners. It is true in every school that there are teachers who never ask for help with individual children; others wait for a long time. There are many reasons for this, but one that caseworkers must fully appreciate is the teacher's feeling that she is somehow failing the child. This feeling may be present even with those teachers who do refer children; as it is recognized and handled by the caseworker, the good working relationship between the two will be strengthened. It is usual for a teacher to say deprecatingly, "Janey looks forward so to seeing you; she never gives me a smile like that," or "I guess Henry tells you a lot about me; did he tell you I kept him in from recess yesterday?" or "I guess you think I don't give Joe enough attention." Agency and clinic caseworkers are quite accustomed to remarks of this sort. They recognize the guilts, fears, and resentments that lie behind them and they handle them accordingly in a casework relationship. But it must always be remembered that the relation between the caseworker and the teacher is a partnership and not a caseworker-client relationship.

Remarks of the sort quoted indicate that the teacher has become somehow emotionally involved with a particular child. Whenever possible the caseworker wants to alleviate this involvement just as she would hope to bring about a change in parental attitudes which contributed to or aggravated a child's difficulties. The methods she will use to bring about this change without establishing too close a relationship require considerable skill on the worker's part. Of course, they will vary with different situations. First of all, the worker must convince the teacher of her non-critical attitude and of her need of the teacher's help in working with the child. She will find many times that the teacher is eager to talk about the child and from this talking the worker may gain valuable insight. Teachers know a great deal about children. It is very helpful if the worker can enable them to appreciate how much they do know. This means helping them to a different point of view about a child and, above all, to an understanding that all behavior is not under conscious control. Teachers are used to working with the logical and rational side of human nature; they have taken a great step when they can say, "I used to think Mary purposely did things to annoy me because she didn't like me; but now I don't believe that's true. She just doesn't know why she behaves that way herself."

If a worker, either consciously or unconsciously, feels critical of the teacher because she considers her too strict, harsh, and dictatorial, her unexpressed condemnation will be felt and will naturally block a good relationship. When such criticisms arise

189

in the worker's thinking, it is well to check the child's record first to ascertain how he did with other teachers. Then it is well to ascertain how other children have got along with this teacher and to visit her classroom to get the "feel" of the group. This latter step is always an enlightening experience to caseworkers who are accustomed to working with individuals and who have little experience with groups. Most important of all, the worker must always bear in mind that, just as the teacher is not a client, she also is not an individual therapist. She is a group leader.

It is very rare indeed to find a situation in which the emotional difficulties of child and teacher have become so intertwined that a change of teachers seems advisable. An exceptional situation of this sort arose in the case of the aforementioned Jimmy, whose father had been antagonistic to the principal and worker.

When the first-grade teacher first talked with the worker about Jimmy, she admitted that he was driving her to distraction. He had no interest in learning; actually he seemed determined not to learn and to have put up a wall against even allowing himself to be aware of school subjects. He seemed to go out of his way to precipitate a battle with her. A dozen times during the morning he would drop the lid of his desk or spill his crayons, or dump the children's coats off the rack, or tear and spit on the children's books. If she reprimanded him, he cringed and trembled which made her feel terrible; if she spoke to him gently, he had a hard and deadpan expression which was infuriating. He was disrupting the class so that nobody was learning. It was already past the middle of the year which meant there was not much time left for all the work which had to be done. The teacher's voice was harsh and angry as she talked with the worker. She went on to say that she had talked with Jimmy's mother who was on the verge of a nervous breakdown, probably because of Jimmy. The teacher could not forget how the mother had looked as she talked about the boy.

In the early grades, a good warm relationship between child and teacher is an absolute "must." It is through fondness for the teacher and a wish to please her that the child is first encouraged to master skills; pleasure in himself for his accomplishment comes a little later. If there is emotional strife between the two in the early years, and particularly if this strife approximates conflicts with the child's mother, the child's learning may be permanently harmed. Certainly there was emotional strife in the case of Jimmy.

190

When the worker talked with the mother for the first time, she learned that Jimmy's behavior in school was identical with his behavior at home; and that the mother and the teacher reacted to it in much the same way. But the worker did not suggest changing teachers at this point. Instead, there were several conversations between the worker and the teacher. In the first of these, the teacher expressed considerable anger at the worker because Jimmy seemed so loving and outgoing with her. Then she brought out her intense dislike of the boy and again spoke of the fact that he was driving his mother to a nervous breakdown. She then blamed herself for not liking him but the worker casually said that nobody could be expected to like all thirty children in a classroom and reminded her that the previous year she had been of tremendous help with a little boy who was also having intense difficulties. (The worker did not add, however, that that little boy had aroused the teacher's sympathies because of an alcoholic mother whereas it was the mother of Jimmy who had aroused her sympathies this time.) The teacher agreed that she had helped the other child and then confided to the worker that things were different for her this year. She was having difficulties of her own revolving around her mother's placement in a sanitarium. Yet, she felt that if Jimmy were not in her class, she would be able to carry through adequately. She wondered if the worker felt it would be all right if she asked to have him changed; it just seemed that they were neither of them good for the other. Without waiting for the worker's reply, she decided to make the request.

After the change had been made and Jimmy had been in the other class for several weeks, his first teacher talked with the worker about him again. She was gratified to learn that all of Jimmy's troubles did not stem primarily from the relationship with her. She added, however, "I can't help thinking that I may have complicated them, but I guess that does happen sometimes." She then went on to talk about another child.

As the teachers' confidence in the school caseworker grows, they will use her more and more, not only to refer specific children to her, but just to talk about situations which may concern them. Thus, one teacher talked several times with the worker about an outburst of sexual curiosity which was openly evidencing itself in her fifth grade class. Other teachers will frequently talk over prospective interviews which they must have with parents. These are very often ordeals for the teacher although they are an essential part of her job.

191

Perhaps one of the chief difficulties caseworkers have in working with schools lies in the inability to find a common means of communication. Caseworkers are quite used to talking with each other and they understand each other because they have a common vocabulary. But explaining their understanding of a child to a teacher who does not have the same vocabulary poses handicaps. Many a time, a little incident related to the teacher will have great meaning. For instance, a very tough 9-year-old bully who was always using arrogant and abusive methods to prove to the other kids that he was a big-shot told the caseworker, the fourth time she saw him, of a movie he had just seen in school about the salmon industry. The thing that had impressed him most was the fight that the mother salmon put up to get upstream to "lay her babies," only to die afterwards. There were actually tears in his eyes when he told this, although of course, he immediately demanded to know why he was coming to see the caseworker anyway. When the caseworker related this incident to the teacher, the latter was completely amazed and exclaimed, "Whoever would have thought that he would feel anything like that? He certainly never shows it. Do you suppose he's afraid people will think he is a sissy?" It was not necessary to talk with her about his fear of passivity or femininity. The example was enough to help her in a new insight.

Another time a teacher related the peculiar behavior of a 10-year-old girl in the lunchroom who had dropped her lunch tray, cleaned it up, gone back for another and dropped that also, to the amusement of all the other children in the cafeteria. When the teacher had gone to help the girl, she had been angrily pushed aside, although the child was crying to herself. It just happened that that morning, this little girl had told the worker of her mother who was in a psychiatric hospital. She had said, "I think it is a very nervous breakdown. She doesn't know what she is saying." She had gone on to tell the worker that her mother had been getting sick for a long time. When she was little, she had had St. Vitus's dance and, even now, she was always "dropping things." The worker, having previously secured the father's consent to tell the teacher of the nature of the mother's illness, could now relate to the teacher what the girl had told her that morning. The teacher could immediately see the tie-up and it was not at all necessary to go into theoretical discussions on identification with the mother or anger and guilty feelings about the mother. All the teacher had to understand was that it would be necessary to go out of her way with the girl to help prove that she was a good and healthy child who did not have to "drop things."

In the writer's experience, most of the caseworker's time in the schools goes into direct work with the children. From the beginning, she uses the same evaluative methods she would use in any other casework situation. Her primary question is always, "Is this difficulty arising from external factors or does it arise within the child himself? If it arises from environmental causes, is the child's behavior then logical and appropriate?" If the child is unable to learn, as are so many of the children referred, the worker naturally wants to know about his natural abilities; even though he is of average intelligence, it would be helpful to know about the group average of his class. If it is exceptionally high or low, the child may be having difficulty keeping up with his peers or be bored at their slow pace. In such a situation, a change in specific educational methods may be of immediate help. The worker also wants to know something of the parents' attitude toward the child's school life. Is it over-pushing, overprotective, too disinterested?

Contact with the parents must, of course, be an integral part of helping the child. In some situations the worker may concentrate almost exclusively on working with them. Usually, however, in the writer's experience, parents whose emotional involvement with the child's school experience is so intense as to affect his school performance are referred elsewhere. This is generally merely a matter of expediency since the worker seldom has time for many hour-long interviews on a weekly basis.

The Caseworker's Relationship with the Child

The above material is related to environmental causes of the child's troubles. The worker must know the child himself to ascertain how much of his difficulties arises from within.

It is usually advisable that the teacher introduce the child and the worker. This introduction immediately allies the teacher and the worker, and as the child becomes comfortable in the relationship, he cannot help but recognize that the teacher must be interested in him to send him to somebody who is to be his special friend. At first he does not know what is going to happen, and questions like "What did I do?" "Are you a nurse or a dentist?" are very common. One 11-year-old girl asked the worker, "Are you a psychiatrist?" When the worker asked what she knew about psychiatrists, she answered indirectly, "I am a Catholic; I am not allowed to see the movie 'Red Shoes' because it's about suicide and that's against my religion." Through these early questions the worker can recognize the child's apprehension and can find ways of handling it. She can also get clues as to how the child himself deals with his fears.

The general procedure, in the writer's experience, is to have regular weekly appointments with the children in the school. It seems best to have the time of these appointments approximate regular school periods. This is most easily accepted by the children and interferes least with the rest of their school curriculum. The worker plans with the teacher to find a time that is suitable to her. If the teacher feels that the child should not miss one class or another, or should not miss recess, the period is adjusted to this whenever possible. There is also considerable flexibility in the keeping of the appointments. If a shy child, for instance, has with great effort decided to be in a school play and if the time of rehearsals coincides with his appointment, adjustments are made. The worker must always keep in mind that the ultimate goal is to help the child find a satisfactory place in the school. Of course, it is often possible for the worker to attend the rehearsal or to visit the classroom or to go to the hobby show.

Adjustment of the time is not always advisable, however. Thus, a 10-year-old boy suddenly began to put pressure on the worker to change his period to the last one in the afternoon to avoid art class, a usually popular period. On inquiry, it developed that he felt some of the boys were picking on him; they took his paints and laughed at his pictures; he got mad and then got in trouble with the teacher. The worker knew this boy pretty well. His pattern of behavior had been one of retreat into babyishness in the face of any difficulty. He had already made great strides in facing up to his classwork and had begun to derive satisfaction from that. The worker now agreed with him that avoiding this new trouble might be the easiest way, but she pointed out to him that she knew he was a boy who could work things out without running from them and so, since she was awfully anxious that he should know this too, she wasn't going to change his time.

The school caseworker usually carries with her a kit of simple toys. About these toys there are always many questions in the beginning. It has great meaning to the children to be told that the school has given the money for the purchase of the toys. The idea of a school's buying toys is an entirely new and enlightening one for them. So, too, is the idea that there are other children who come and play with the toys. This must mean that there are other children who are having difficulties, and the school wants to help them. One little boy said to his mother, "You know, I think I go to the best school in the world. We have a teacher there who cares that children are worried and nervous." Mention was made in the beginning of the fact that one of the values of the school experience lies in the opportunity it provides the child to recognize that others besides himself have good and bad feelings. Troubled children are sometimes so involved with themselves that they cannot recognize this. They feel alone and different. The realization that the caseworker helps many children can be very reassuring.

At this point, it may be helpful to consider excerpts from a specific case, continuing with the case of Jimmy, the first-grader who was raising such trouble in school.

The teacher introduced the worker to Jimmy, who came readily to her room. He moved stiffly and his expression was closed and dead pan. He made no response when the worker said that the school knew he was having a miserable time and that perhaps in some way she could help. His only question was about the toys but he made no response when the worker explained that the school had given her the money with which to buy them. He did, however, pick them up gingerly, one by one, saying each time, "Donald has one of these." The worker learned that Donald was his 12-year-old brother but Jimmy froze at any other questions. When the worker asked, "And what does Jimmy have?" he stared and asked "Who is Jimmy?" He then told her, "My name is James C——." He went on to say, "I used to have a truck like this but I gave it to Donald." Then he noticed that one of the trucks was broken but when the worker explained that some other child had broken it, he only stared and then volunteered to fix it. He did this for the rest of the period and at the end the worker congratulated him on being a little boy who was able to put things back together. He asked if she would be in the school tomorrow but accepted the fact that she was in school only once a week and that she would see him the next week at the same time.

The following week, when the worker went for him, he threw his arms around her. This was the episode that angered the teacher. He again went through all the toys, pointing out again what Donald had, but again he froze when encouraged to tell what he had or more about Donald. He did volunteer several personal things about his family but he tightened up and became silent whenever the worker tried to follow any lead in the things he said. One thing he talked about was the Siamese twins whose picture he had once seen. He emphasized that their heads were together and added that he wondered a lot about it. But again, when the worker agreed that things like this were very puzzling to understand and remarked that this was one of the wonderful things about learning in school—so many of our questions could be answered there—he fell silent. Yet when he left, he again hugged the worker.

At about this time the worker had the second interview with the mother and learned that the older brother, Donald, was feeble-minded and was attending a special class for subnormal children. The mother talked primarily about this boy, emphasizing the many things they had done for him, and her determined philosophy about him. She brought out that the main source of contention with Jimmy at home was that he constantly disturbed Donald. With much feeling she enlarged on the conflict between her and Jimmy. It seemed that all of the trouble with him was during the daytime. At night, he seemed to soften. He loved to sleep with her and was very affectionate. He had great trouble getting to sleep and frequently had to be given sedatives. She confided that he also still wet the bed, and added that he had begged her not to tell the caseworker. The caseworker could certainly understand that the mother was having a very hard time with her two sons; she emphasized her wish to help Jimmy. Perhaps if he could find some success in school, his satisfaction would carry back home. She asked the mother specifically to assure Jimmy that the worker knew many grown-ups and children and did not consider their troubling behavior and habits as bad. She also made some concrete suggestions for a change in sleeping arrangements.

In the next few weeks, the change to the new teacher was made. Jimmy had never complained about his first teacher, but his cringing or hostile manner toward her was very apparent,

196

as was her resentment of him. As a matter of fact, Jimmy never talked connectedly during these weeks on any one subject. The subject most often repeated was that of the Siamese twins. Once or twice he tried the worker out by being naughty and was gratified by her non-retaliation although she did explain to him that she always let children know if there were things they absolutely could not do. [This technique is necessary in any work with children, not only when it is done in the school setting. Children would be frightened if they thought there would be no limitations put on any behavior.] Jimmy continued to refuse to learn. This was in spite of the fact that the new teacher used every encouragement she could think of. And he continued to fight with the other children. The only difference now was that, environmentally, everything possible at this point had been done.

The third interview with the mother gave her an opportunity to express tremendous feelings about the older boy, along with her recognition that Jimmy had really been lost sight of because her whole life had revolved around Donald. It developed that she had never told Jimmy about Donald, except that he must be quiet with Donald; he must be good to him; he must love him. When she was asked how she would feel about telling Jimmy something about Donald's differences now, she still hesitated. Then she expressed the many guilty feelings that mothers of handicapped children so often have. Finally she said that Jimmy really should know that Donald was different from other children. She would try to tell him sometime.

Shortly after this, in an interview with the worker, Jimmy started to draw a circus animal. He told the worker that he had never been to a circus. He had never even been to the zoo. At Donald's school they went to the zoo almost every week. The worker said it sounded as though this was again something Donald had which Jimmy didn't have, just like all the toys and things Jimmy talked about. With the first real feeling, Jimmy burst out that at Donald's school they only played; they never worked. Donald didn't have to read, to spell, to sit still. Why should Jimmy? The worker said she believed Jimmy had been angry about this all the time. Maybe he felt that, since Donald didn't have to do those things, he wouldn't either. Jimmy enlarged on this with great feeling and when he had quieted down, the worker asked if he knew that Donald really couldn't learn the way Jimmy himself could? Everybody in the world was different and Jimmy happened to be a lucky one who could really learn very easily when he wanted to; Donald couldn't learn in the same way. Jimmy looked at the worker very straightforwardly for a minute, and then suddenly got up and sat in her lap. He said then that his mother had told him that something

197

was the matter with Donald's head. When he was a baby, he had fallen on it. He then said that he had seen another picture of those twins with their heads together. Now the worker could say that this must be why he wondered so about them; he wondered if Donald's head could have been hurt like theirs. Jimmy gave the worker a quick hug at the end of the interview. The next week, for the first time, he brought a school paper with him and spent the whole time giving the worker spelling lessons.

Shortly after, he came in one day, proudly showing that most of his front teeth had fallen out and assuring the worker that this was a sign he was growing up. He added, "Donald eats faster than I do now, but I do other things faster than he does. I can learn to read." He then went on, "You know that picture of those twins? They weren't born that way. They slept in bed together, and their heads were too close and they grew together. Once I saw a picture of some other twins. They were fastened together at their bellies. I wondered a lot about that. How do they go to the bathroom, do you suppose, without getting hurt?" He added, "I guess they figured something out." The worker agreed and added that Jimmy was a little boy who thought and wondered about so many things, she was glad he could say now what he wondered about. Jimmy then told her he was going to get promoted. He would be tutored over the summer and, next year, be in second grade. [This was true and was based on the rapid strides he had made in the latter weeks.]

When his mother was seen for the last time, she was feeling very proud of Jimmy's accomplishment and admitted that in the beginning she and her husband had been afraid there might be something the matter with Jimmy, just as there was with Donald. She was much gratified to know of his real ability to learn; she was grateful to the school and to the worker. She added that Jimmy was more communicative than he had ever been. He was talking a blue streak nowadays and was asking questions about every conceivable subject. She then confided that he still wet the bed and his insomnia was still cause for concern. It was then possible to talk these things over with her realistically. The worker could talk about bed-wetting as being not too unusual in a boy Jimmy's age and as something that, with time and with his mother's reassurance, he might be able to overcome. She could point out that Jimmy had made great strides in a short time and that his achievement in school and the satisfaction he derived from that might carry over into other areas. She suggested, however, another interview in the fall at which time Jimmy's needs could be talked over further.

Jimmy's case has been chosen because it contains so many facets that are typical of school casework. When he was first referred, Jimmy was unable to differentiate between home and school. This had been further complicated by the teacher's sympathies with the mother and by their identical reactions. Jimmy was unable to channel his aggressions into the mastery of skills which would have been so beneficial in helping him to develop a sense of pride and satisfaction in himself. In these areas, the worker helped, with the co-operation of the school and the parents. The worker recognized indications of possible deep neurotic disturbance but, fascinating as these were to her, she did not endeavor to handle them. If, in the future, more intensive work seemed needed, the worker's good relationship with the mother would make it possible to discuss this.

It is children like Jimmy who are referred to the school case-worker, children who carry too many emotional tones from home to school and who are unable to form realistic relationships with adults or with their peers; children who are unable to use their energies in socially acceptable and personally satisfying ways. Naturally, the teachers do not give such reasons for referral. Their reasons sound more like—"Always looking for a fight, with me or the children"; "unable to accept rules of work or play"; "always needs my praise and encouragement"; "unable to learn."

The school caseworker must know a good deal about normal child development. As indicated, she can learn a great deal from teachers. The more she is able to recognize the appropriateness of a child's behavior, either in relation to the environment or as typical of his particular stage of development, the better. This means that she must have a sense of timing. She must be able to evaluate when the child's behavior is no longer appropriate, and to determine whether his difficulties arise from external or internal pressures. She must have a good knowledge of basic casework procedure. Finally, she must have an understanding and appreciation of the people with whom she works and a conviction that their mutual goal is the same although it may be viewed from divergent angles. If this partnership is a successful one, it usually ends with the worker having a better appreciation of the forest and with the school personnel having a greater awareness of the trees.

Part III

Toward New Knowledge
For Practice

15. Learning Through Recorded Material*

Yonata Feldman

THE STUDENT WHO is learning the practice of social casework must be taught how to understand the client's total needs and what casework methods are most useful in helping the client to master reality and to make a satisfactory social and emotional adjustment. It sounds relatively simple to say that the client states his needs to the worker, and that the worker then uses the method appropriate to meeting these needs. The real problem lies in the fact that the client does not really know what his needs are. The client often has emotional needs of which he is unaware, although his specific request may be stated in concrete terms. He may unconsciously distort the request in such a way that its real meaning is difficult for the worker to determine. In addition, the problem each client presents must be viewed in relation to the particular client, since each individual has a specific way in which he presents his problem and a specific pattern of distorting the meaning of his request.

The social work student is placed in the position of having to face the client alone while he is still only partially trained. Only he listens to the client's story and observes his gestures and facial expressions. He must remember the sequence of the conversation and pick out of the mass of the client's production those details that are important. Since we do not expect the beginning student to understand the full meaning of the client's recital, it

* Reprinted from *Smith College Studies in Social Work*, Vol. XXVII, No. 2 (1957).

is logical to assume that he may not even observe much that is taking place; he may not hear some of the things that are said, and may forget others. Under these circumstances the student is even less capable of recording his own reactions and activity. It is logical, therefore, to expect that what the student records of his interview is at best so fragmentary that it is impossible for the supervisor, who has not been present during the interview, either to know what really took place, or to be able to determine what the student's training needs are.

That this problem in student training is of concern to many supervisors is seen in the fact that occasionally a supervisor expresses the wish that interviews could be recorded verbatim through the use of a mechanical device such as a tape recorder. I hope that the reason this practice has not been adopted to any large extent is not entirely a financial one. The use of a recorder would only serve to expose the student to an anxiety-provoking experience. The knowledge that every word said by him and his client would be recorded mechanically, and then analyzed, could result in the student's centering all his attention on himself; thus his capacity for listening to and observing the client would be lessened. It would also rob the student of his spontaneity and his creativity. His anxiety would unconsciously be transmitted to his client and would restrain a free interchange between them.

The remarkable thing is that the student *does* transmit in his recorded material important information about the client and about the role he himself played. It is remarkable that, although he usually does not understand the meaning of the client's production, he does record important material. Of course he does grasp some of the meaning, but in a peripheral way. The student understands even less the role he plays in the interview. It is remarkable, too, that without having full understanding of what the client's emotional needs are, he often seems to meet these needs in the proper way, and that his activity is reflected in his recording. It is perhaps even more remarkable that if the student does not meet the client's needs or even acts in a way that is contrary to those needs, he still records this fact.

It is only because the student records much more than he is aware of that it is possible for the supervisor, although she herself has not been present during the interview, to understand the client far beyond the student's own comprehension. The supervisor is thereby enabled to watch the student's spontaneous responses, to understand these responses, to help him develop the proper casework attitudes toward his clients, and to help him develop casework techniques and skills that harmonize with his own personality structure—techniques and skills that he can make his own.

Student Recording

Let us now consider how it is possible for a student to select and record important material without understanding it or being aware of its meaning.

When a person comes to an agency to seek help (and I am speaking here only of the person who really needs casework help, through a casework relationship, regardless of how he presents his problem), he has usually tried to help himself in every possible way, but has failed. Thus, he is in a position of utter helplessness. The person who listens to his problem and offers to help him then becomes symbolically the powerful person who can and is willing to help him. This situation recreates an early childhood situation in which he had to seek help from his parents and had full confidence that they were willing and able to help him. It is thus that a casework relationship is established. It is this situation that tends to make the client not only communicate to the caseworker (in this case, the student-worker) all the facts around the specific problem that brought him to the agency but also tell the worker symbolically about the unmet emotional needs of his early childhood. These unmet needs are usually the important barrier that stood in the way of his early personality development and now stands in the way of his ability to solve his present problem—the problem that brought him to the agency.

A very interesting phenomenon which occurs during casework treatment and which often baffles both worker and client is worth noting. The client tells the story of his difficulties in the first interview; then, as time goes on, he keeps repeating the same story over and over again. Sometimes the client brings in some new material, and sometimes the worker finds it necessary to ask questions to get additional information. On the whole, however, if the client is permitted to be spontaneous he continues to repeat the old story. It is through these repetitions and their elaborations that the client, unknown to himself, is trying to transmit to the worker his unconscious, unmet early childhood needs and his not completely sublimated childhood strivings. These emotional needs of childhood must be understood and, in the beginning, met symbolically through the casework relationship.[1] The client then uses the casework relationship to help himself gradually learn to control and to find avenues of sublimation for his inappropriate strivings and thus is enabled to meet his present-day problem.

The client's repetition of the same material over and over again can be compared to a record on a record-player. The melody goes smoothly until suddenly it begins to be repeated endlessly and the melody is interrupted. We all know that this means there is a crack in the record; the record is broken. The repetitions of the client have the same meaning. Through them the client wishes to give the worker a message, to tell him about the particular phase in his emotional development during which something went wrong. They point to a traumatic experience in the client's life. This is the phase of development in which growth stopped and the personality could not develop further even though the mind and body grew and life took its course. With the repetitions the client tells the worker, "Unless you understand what I am saying, and help me, I cannot proceed with my emotional growth and with the solution of my problem."

It is interesting to note that often, when we look at an interview, it seems to us at first glance as if the client had spoken about many unrelated subjects, sometimes subjects that seem to have nothing to do with the problem he brought to us, that seem irrelevant and a waste of time. Yet when we look at the interview more closely, we see that everything mentioned by the client during the interview has a common denominator and conveys a message to the worker, a message that expresses the client's emotional needs in a disguised way. In fact, if we pay attention to the client's behavior during the interview, we see that even the client's behavior reflects this message.

[1] Marguerite A. Sechehaye, *Symbolic Realization*, International Universities Press, New York, 1951.

206

It is the client's message that has a forceful impact on the student or the beginning caseworker. He cannot help recording it, whether he understands the message or not. Thus he brings the client's message to his supervisor who is then able to enrich the student's understanding and to teach him ways of helping the client. Often, because of the client's emphasis and the student's intuitive perception, the student-worker finds the proper casework response, even though he himself does not know that this is the proper response. This student response is possible because the student is human, has gone through the same growth process as his client, has a sound wish to help, and thus intuitively steps into the role of the helper and spontaneously finds a medium by which he transmits to the client his desire to help.

Yet the student himself is often not aware of the contribution he made to the client. It is very important for the supervisor to explain to the student the meaning of the material that he has already perceived intuitively, since this serves to connect in a positive way the new knowledge with knowledge that was already part of the student's personality. It is particularly important to point out and explain the meaning of the student's proper responses, since creativity is thereby encouraged. Casework treatment is a complicated process, and often the intuitive person, if he is not made aware of what goes on in the casework process, may lose courage because he does not recognize gains; he may become inconsistent in his attitude and sometimes destructive, even though he started in the right way.

A careful study of the student's recorded material clearly indicates what weight he gave to the client's production—what he understood fully, what he perceived only intuitively. A study of the student's reaction to the client's material reveals his training needs. These training needs are, of course, tested and better understood through discussing the material with the student in the supervisory conference.

An Example of Student Performance

The following is an example of a student's performance as it was revealed through the study of her recorded material. It illustrates how a student does good work intuitively but does not

207

understand what is going on between herself and the client. It also illustrates the student's attitude toward her own achievement.

The student is in her second year of training. The case centers on a 5-year-old girl who cannot tolerate separation from her mother. The mother must stay with her in kindergarten. The child weeps constantly, vomits when she stands in the line and in the classroom; she is restless and withdrawn. The teacher blames the mother for the child's behavior. Indeed, the clinic psychologist finds the child charming, friendly, outgoing. Little Mary says "the test is fun" and wishes she could come more often. Her I.Q. is 120. The projective test indicates that she is "fearful of her mother."

The mother, Mrs. B, is assigned to the student. The student has obtained some information about the mother before the mother is seen by her. In the first interviews with the student, Mrs. B keeps on complaining repeatedly that she is ashamed of her child. The child disgraces her in front of her own parents and in front of the teacher. At home she gives in to all of Mary's demands and never disciplines her. She bribes Mary because she does not wish to "raise issues." She fears Mary will cry and disgrace her before neighbors.

The student, when she begins to see Mrs. B, has a concrete aim in mind. She wishes to get more information about Mary and about the parents' handling of her. The psychiatrist will treat the child and he will need this information. The student knows that the mother has had something to do with the child's difficulties. She hopes that after she has obtained all the information from the mother, she will then be helped by her supervisor and the psychiatrist to devise a proper treatment plan for the mother.

In the interviews with the mother, the student finds that it is not so easy to get the information she planned to get. The student says, "The mother cried; I could not stop her." The mother repeats the old story of the child's trouble; relatives look upon her child as queer; her sister-in-law is sarcastic about her ways of bringing up a child. She knows it is her own fault. She is too weepy—too nervous to care for the child. She asks, "What did I do wrong?" Social workers and doctors only confuse her. The student says she is not here to judge; she only wishes to understand so she can help Mrs. B.

From interview to interview one theme of the mother's repeats itself over and over again—that she is disgraced by the child, and the child dominates her; her child is queer, abnormal. The student made some attempts to get the information she wanted and needed, such as developmental and background history; but each time she added a bit apologetically, "I did not think it was right to interrupt Mrs. B at this point." Perhaps the student does not get all the necessary information to fill in the outline, although she gets quite a bit. What she does get is the mother's increased revelation of her deep feeling of inadequacy—"She wants another child, but thinks she is too slow to care for two children." It is interesting to observe how consistent the student is in permitting the mother freedom of expression and in refraining from giving advice. When the mother blames herself, the student says she is not here to judge, but to understand and help. Finally, the mother tells the worker her own deep-seated problems, her own frustrations in regard to eating and toileting, and her emotional reactions to feeding her infant daughter.

From the way in which the student permits the mother to speak freely, volubly, and without interruption, one would think that the student understood the mother's frustrated oral needs and thus, by permitting her to talk, met them symbolically. The student's consistent, non-critical attitude relieved this mother's feeling of unworthiness. She could now tell the student most damaging things about herself without fear of being disgraced. Did the student know that she was helping the mother develop a healthier attitude toward herself and the child? At first it would seem as if she did, but the following interview will show that she did not understand what the mother was trying to tell her, and because she did not, she was no longer attuned to the mother's needs. Instead of playing the role of the constructive, permissive, and understanding mother, as she had done in the past, the student-worker has now, unbeknown to herself, assumed the same attitude the client's mother had in her childhood.

Today Mrs. B came in on time for the first time. *She wondered if I had noticed that she was on time.* I told her that I had, and that this must have meant that she did not have so much trouble getting Mary to school today. Mrs. B said that Mary did not "gag" today and that she was able to put her right in line at kindergarten. She had told Mary that she was coming down here today. I wondered how Mary felt about this. Mrs. B had explained to Mary that she was coming here in order to understand why Mary had so much trouble in going to school. Mary had not objected to her coming here.

I asked Mrs. B if she had anything that she would especially like to talk about today. Mrs. B said things were still the same. I wondered if she would like to tell me what a day with Mary was like. Mrs. B picked a difficult day with Mary, and related in detail what had happened.

We see here that Mrs. B came in like a small child to her mother. She came early for the first time and wanted the worker to notice her good behavior. She was able to achieve, as a good mother, putting the child in line. She was able also, for the first time, to tell the child the truth, that she would leave the home while Mary would be in school. She was proud that she could do it; and the child, in reaction to her mother's courage, had lost her fear of going to school. She had gone without protest and had permitted her mother to come on time. The student did not seem to see the mother's great need for her to make a bit of a fuss about this achievement. The mother had to call the student's attention to the fact that she had come on time. After she told her about the other, more important achievement, the worker asked if she had anything she would especially like to talk about that day, thus indicating that she had not understood that what she especially wished to talk about then was her achievement, and what she needed was praise. That the worker did not understand the mother's need was further confirmed by her asking that Mrs. B tell her what a day with Mary was like. The mother picked a difficult day, as if to say, "You do not wish to see my achievement so I will tell you about my failures." The student did not realize what was going on in the interview. She was apparently still motivated by her aim to gather descriptive material to write a summary for the psychiatrist.

When Mary gets up in the morning, her mother has her clothes laid out for her. Occasionally Mary will choose her dress. Mrs. B has to dress Mary most of the time. Mrs. B stands over her as she washes and helps her brush her teeth. Then Mary's chocolate milk for her thermos is made. Mary may go to the window once or twice to see if the lines have formed at the school. (They live across the street from the school.) Sometimes Mary will start gagging before going to school. *Mrs. B used to remind Mary to gag or burp before they left,* but lately she tries not to remind Mary. Lately Mary has not needed to gag.

Mrs. B picks Mary up from school at lunch time. On this day Mary asked if she could watch TV. Mrs. B told her that she could watch until lunch was ready. When Mrs. B called her she would not come. Mrs. B reminded her of their agreement, but Mary still would not come. She wanted to make an agreement with her mother that she would eat in front of the TV or run in and out of the kitchen to the living room in order to watch the program. Mrs. B said that they had argued for about forty-five minutes. Mrs. B feels that since she allows Mary to eat supper by the TV, "that is enough."

Like an obedient child, trying to please her mother, Mrs. B tried to tell the student-worker what she wished to hear. What she told her was only a repetition of what she had told her before. The new element, however, put the finger on the core of the whole problem. Before, Mrs. B used to remind Mary to gag or burp before they left for school. One could just picture Mrs. B, full of anxiety, certain that something would go wrong with her child, pushing her to gag or burp, thus flooding Mary with anxiety, which made her vomit and made going to school impossible. This was the situation that had started the pernicious process. But Mrs. B said that lately she had tried not to remind Mary—lately Mary had not needed to gag. Again we see that the mother told the worker of her achievement; she felt less anxious; she was in better control; she merited a little approval.

After lunch Mrs. B does some school work with Mary. I asked if Mary is getting homework. *Mrs. B said that she is not but she and Mary practice Mary's writing. Mary has not gotten a star a few times,* and she and another girl *were the only ones* who did not get a star. Mrs. B feels that this is silly since Mary can do well. Mary has been able to write for a year, but printing is difficult for her. I asked how long Mary has been having writing at school. She has only had writing for two weeks. Mrs. B seemed quite concerned about Mary's not getting a star. She wondered if this difficulty in learning might be related to her fears. I said that I was not sure, but that it was a possibility.

This shows particularly how Mrs. B relates herself to the worker like a child. She does not say, "I help Mary do her school work,"

211

but "After lunch I do some school work with Mary." She and Mary practice writing. Mrs. B was quite concerned about Mary's not getting a star. Is it possible that it was Mrs. B who had craved to get a star and who had not gotten it? She wondered if Mary's difficulties might be related to her fears. Did not Mrs. B just describe her anxiety in the morning when she pushed the child to gag, to burp? The worker's saying "This is a possibility" shows again her intuitive power to perceive that she must not give a definite answer of yes or no, but must create an atmosphere in which Mrs. B can tell where she had gained the wisdom that fears interfere with the ability to function.

Mrs. B tried to have Mary play with a friend, but she would not go because there was a dog in the house. Mrs. B said that Mary had never been hurt by a dog. *Mrs. B does not like dogs but she has tried not to let Mary know about this and has never kept her away from dogs.* Mrs. B took Mary to visit her mother and then came home for dinner. Mrs. B started to tell me how Mary would not stay alone at her mother's. *I think that this was discussed outside of our discussion of a day with Mary.* Mrs. B feels badly that she cannot leave Mary because her mother becomes insulted and remarks that another grandchild will stay. Mrs. B becomes disgusted when Mary won't even stay there to watch TV.
Mrs. B said that Mary was somewhat difficult at dinner that night. I asked if the family ate together or if Mary ate alone. Mrs. B said that she cannot eat with Mary, because she runs around, won't sit at the table, and cuts out paper or colors. *However, Mrs. B said Mary likes her to be at the table.* Mrs. B said that *she likes to try to please Mary's tastes* and makes her the things she likes. *Mrs. B said that she is always trying to bribe Mary. She knows that this isn't right, but does not know what to do about it. I told her that this is something we will be helping her with.*

And indeed, in response to the worker's intuitive understanding of the limiting forces of fear and anxiety, the mother revealed her own fear of dogs which was transmitted to the child. It is now easy to see how, by association of ideas, Mrs. B told of Mary's fears of her grandmother; Mrs. B told the worker that her mother prefers the other grandchildren to her child. This reveals the grandmother's lack of acceptance of her, and Mrs. B's disgust with herself and her child that they do not seem to find a way to her mother's heart—that both do not seem to find a way to gain approval.

Mrs. B here gave the student a most profound revelation as to the dynamics in this case. Because the student did not understand it, she did not appreciate it, which is seen in her remark: "I think that this was discussed outside of our discussion of a day with Mary." Because the student-worker did not understand the value of the material, she was displeased with her client. She could not make her do what she wanted her to do; thus she repeated, unconsciously, the pattern of Mrs. B's mother, whom Mrs. B could never please. It is obvious that the student did not verbalize her thoughts, which she however recorded; but we know that our attitudes and feelings are usually transmitted to the client unconsciously. We also see here how the student-worker did not give herself credit for her own achievement; she did not realize that it was her own attitude that helped the woman reduce her anxiety and be more patient with her child; that it was her attitude of permissiveness that enabled Mrs. B to reveal herself more and more; and that it was to her credit that even before the child had a chance to start treatment she was already much improved through improved maternal handling. We see the worker's lack of full appreciation of her contribution by her constant refrain: "I told her that this is something we will be helping her with."

Mrs. B became tearful. After dinner she and Mary had gone to visit her aunt. The aunt talked about her daughter-in-law who has four children and handles them more easily than a woman with only one. *She told her how the children knew when they were bad and went to their room on their own. Mrs. B was very hurt by this.* I asked her a little about her aunt. Mrs. B has never been close to her, and they really never had a good relationship. I wondered if Mrs. B then could look at what her aunt said in a different light. Mrs. B said that her husband felt that maybe she was just sensitive. I said that I could understand Mrs. B's sensitivity in this area. *Mrs. B was able to go on to tell me* that Mary started to punch her and indicated that she wanted to go home. At home Mrs. B read to Mary and she went to sleep. The father is home three nights a week and has taken to reading to Mary. I asked if Mary likes to be with her father. Mrs. B said she does and that *Mary only seems to have trouble with her.* Last week she and her husband wanted to go and

213

buy a hat and Mary would not let them. Mrs. B began to cry and said, "Imagine that, a five-year-old can control me!" They had to wait until Mary fell asleep and then "sneaked out on her." *I said this was another problem we could help her with.* Mrs. B complained that Mary was not hanging up her sweater in school. She has told Mary that she would get her a ballet book if she hung it up. Maybe she did the *wrong thing* for she was bribing. Again I told Mrs. B that *we would help her with this.*

I told Mrs. B that she seemed quite unhappy today and *was there something she wished to talk about.* Mrs. B had been drying tears from her eyes throughout the interview; she said there was nothing. I said that it is difficult when your family does not know what you are going through. Mrs. B said that the incident with her aunt had bothered her, but that it was probably not important. I said that I thought it made her unhappy and that we could talk about it the next time if she liked.

Mrs. B then asked me if I had seen a TV show about a delinquent and an attendance officer. The story implied that it was all the parents' fault. I said that TV sometimes makes things awfully simple. I told Mrs. B that all of us act the way we do because of our life experiences and that parents are not the only people who are involved in our lives. I suggested that possibly the next time we could talk about the incident that had come up with her aunt, and the family in general.

We see that to the very end the student-worker did not appreciate the important revealing material Mrs. B gave her. She ended the interview by saying: "I told Mrs. B that she seemed quite unhappy today and was there something she wished to talk about" —as if what Mrs. B was talking about today was nothing; as if it had no importance to the worker.

To sum up: in the beginning the student-worker, in this case unbeknown to herself, assumed the therapeutic role of a good mother toward Mrs. B. She permitted her to talk, to express feelings in any form she wished, thus gratifying Mrs. B's need to be accepted, good or bad. She gave Mrs. B the feeling that she was understood, which means loved, that she was not there to judge her—whether she was bad or good—but she conveyed to Mrs. B that she understood that Mrs. B was entangled in a mesh of unconscious conflicting forces that created anxiety and made her transmit her fears and her lack of confidence in herself to her child. We see that the student-worker recorded important material, the importance of which she herself was not aware of.

An error that supervisors often make is that when they read a well-done interview by a student or a young worker, they draw the conclusion that the good recording was based on the worker's full understanding of the dynamic process. This is not always the case, but such work is good material on which to start training.[2] When half-perceived understanding and reactions of client and worker are brought into conscious understanding by the supervisor, the worker is enabled to develop deeper intuitive perception.

[2] See Yonata Feldman, "The Teaching Aspect of Casework Supervision," from *Principles and Techniques in Social Casework—Selected Articles, 1940–1950,* Cora Kasius (ed.), Family Service Association of America, New York, 1950, pp. 222–232.

16. The Responsibility of School and Agency in Student Research*

Sophie T. Cambria

IT HAS BECOME an established tradition that candidates for professional degrees—liberal arts and professional—be required to demonstrate capacity to undertake individual research. In the development of the professional social work curriculum, research has come to play a conspicuous and often very time-consuming part. It is one of the eight basic areas required by the former American Association of Schools of Social Work [1] for accrediting a course of study. In adapting this long-honored university tradition to social work education, however, very little consideration has been given to the contribution that research can make to the training of the professional person. The result has been a rather general lack of clarity as to what the research requirement is intended to achieve; the by-product has tended to be the detachment of research from other phases of professional education.

Research in social work and, in turn, the teaching of it ought to follow from a conviction that it is inextricably related to the skills for which the student is training. If the following three assumptions are correct (and only a few skeptics will challenge them!), then training in research attitudes and methods is central to both the present and the future of social work. These assumptions are: (1) social work is a profession; (2) it possesses a body of

* Reprinted from *Smith College Studies in Social Work*, Vol. XXI, No. 2 (1952).
[1] The accrediting organization is now the Council on Social Work Education.

knowledge and theory uniquely its own; and (3) this body of knowledge and theory is researchable.

Whitehead, in his *Adventure of Ideas*, states, ". . . foresight based upon theory, and theory based upon an understanding of the nature of things, are essential to a profession. . . . The antithesis to a profession is an avocation based upon customary activities and modified by the trial and error of individual practice. Such an avocation is a craft." [2] If this concept applies to social work, theory based upon things as they actually are, and not simply as we would have them be or believe them to be, is essential to the practice of the profession. Modern man, in his efforts to learn the nature of things, has come to rely heavily upon the scientific method in contrast to the earlier methods of magic and alchemy, intuition, dogma, and empiricism. The last mentioned combined with the method of logic (which now, as always, remains indispensable) have been fruitful sources of hypotheses in all the sciences and professions. It remains for the scientific method, however, to weld these into the knowledge and fact out of which sound theory can be made.

Much of the theory on which social work practice is based has been derived from related professions and scholarly disciplines: psychiatry (particularly psychoanalysis), anthropology, sociology, psychology, and other social sciences. Large portions of this adapted theory are in the course of being scrutinized and verified by researchers within their respective disciplines. The social work profession retains the responsibility, however, for examining and testing that part of its theoretical foundation which was derived from its own unique experiences and development. Up to the present, social work has produced very little that can be rightly termed scientific research. The vigorous program of research that we need and talk much about awaits the emergence of a research-oriented profession. There has been a tendency in social work to depend upon the research specialist, frequently borrowed from other disciplines, to do the job. Again, the result has been detachment between research and the tasks at hand.

As the recognition of the need for research grows, social work will require not only its own research specialists well-versed in the technical aspects of the scientific method, but, even more

2 Alfred N. Whitehead, *Adventure of Ideas*, Macmillan Co., New York, 1933, pp. 72–73.

than this, practitioners who are able to understand, appreciate, and participate in the conduct of research. This means simply social workers who will be able to distinguish between a fact and an assumption, a truth and a belief, the known and the unknown; who take a lively interest in discovering new facts appropriate to their skill; and who recognize a research problem when they come upon it. The research specialist can carry on from there. Then, and only then, will social work research move out of the realm of pious wishes into reality.

The first step in developing a research-oriented profession is to teach research in such a way that it relates to all other aspects of the curriculum. If the precious hours and vast quantities of anxiety and energy put into research by students are to bear fruit, it must somehow be integrated into all aspects of the professional program; the compartmentalizing of research has yielded only tedium, remoteness, and sterility. The remarks that follow do not approach the problems of research teaching on all fronts but, rather, are focused on the integration of research teaching in school and field as one possible means for eliminating the barriers that separate research from other phases of professional study.

The Goals of Research in the Curriculum

At this point in the development of social work, research is rarely taught as an end in itself. The preparation of specialists in social work research remains a need of the future. Despite this, research training holds a significant place in the course of study and is completely justified when directed toward the following ends: (1) the development of research-mindedness; (2) the deepening of knowledge and understanding of social work theory and practice; and (3) the development of ability to consume research.

An understanding of what the scientific method is and what it may contribute to professional knowledge is basic equipment for all social workers—basic in the sense that it is the foundation of an attitude that can be applied to all aspects of the social worker's day-by-day job. Such an attitude is characterized by healthy questioning as distinguished from unhealthy skepticism. As a condition of professional growth, the practitioner finds it necessary to examine and re-examine continually the assumptions

218

behind theory. In contrast to taking things for granted, the research-oriented worker is able and willing to look at what he is doing critically, analytically, and objectively. Such an attitude holds a large potential for the development of skill and knowledge. In a recent paper on research teaching, Gordon refers to this attitude as "the spirit of searching or seeking, the spirit of carrying through until something is found." [3]

The research attitude is compounded of other useful ingredients. It includes the capacity to accept new answers to old questions when the facts so indicate. Orthodoxy is the antithesis to the spirit of discovery. The latter requires that one be able to accept all knowledge as partial and tentative. The history of the sciences proves this to be true. Although it is not anticipated that all students will develop sufficient interest or skill to apply later the scientific method to questions that intrigue them, it is hoped that out of a sound research attitude will emerge an appreciation for the scientific method as the best means to date for testing, establishing, and verifying hypotheses and assumptions.

As consumers of research, social workers are being called upon increasingly to read, understand, analyze, and sometimes apply the findings of research in social work and related fields. The more recent research product in our field demonstrates that sound preparation is needed for its intelligent and critical consumption. As research on the agency level expands, staff will be called upon more and more to co-operate and participate in the planning and conduct of studies.

As a method for discovering and ascertaining fact, research must be taught through doing. For this reason, the schools of social work have come to rely heavily on the thesis, project, or study, both individual and group, as a medium for teaching, implemented by formal courses in research concepts and methods along with elementary statistics. In the opinion of the writer, the thesis provides the student with the best opportunity for experiencing the scientific method in its totality, embracing as it does all the essential elements of the research process: (1) asking a question about some limited aspect of theory or practice; (2) gathering appropriate data from

[3] William E. Gordon, "The Research Project in Social Work Education," *Social Work Journal*, Vol. XXXI, No. 3 (1950), p. 111.

primary and secondary sources; (3) analyzing the data; (4) interpreting and drawing inferences therefrom; and (5) publication as a medium for sharing findings and for verification by other researchers. The individual project in the form of a thesis permits the student to select an area of interest—interest and curiosity being the motive power on which all research must run. It also encourages the sense of personal accountability for method and findings which is so often lacking in group research projects. Although the remarks that follow are based on experience with supervising theses, there is no reason to assume that they do not also apply to other methods for fulfilling research requirements in social work education.

Teaching Research in the Field

Social work has made a unique contribution to educational theory and practice by use of the field placement and supervision in teaching casework, group work, and other social work skills. Rarely do the same integration and co-ordination exist between class and field in providing the research experience. The same student who is given meticulous supervision in casework by the agency may be put off when problems relating to the research requirement arise. In teaching casework or the other social work skills, the agency assumes a large portion of the responsibility for giving the student an experience of educational worth; research, on the other hand, even when closely related to the agency's interest, is frequently considered "academic" and, therefore, the responsibility of the school. And so a wide chasm comes to separate training for the practitioner skills and research. Closer co-ordination between school and agency in teaching research may be one big step toward bridging the distance between the two and, thereby, injecting vitality and reality into student research.

There are at least three points in the process of doing a thesis at which the agency can and should become an active participant in the student's research endeavors: (1) selecting a topic, (2) securing the data, and (3) ascertaining the accuracy of the material collected.

In regard to the selection of a topic, the student's own interest and curiosity should be respected. Many students approach the research assignment with quite well-defined plans as to what they want to do and, when possible, these should serve as the source out of which the study flows. Many other students, however, require close supervision and stimulation in the choice of a topic, and at this point both research faculty and agency personnel play a role. The fact that agency staff are in the best possible position to suggest useful and interesting questions for study is frequently overlooked. As one social work researcher has put it, ". . . in social work the inspiration of research must proceed from the tasks in hand." [4] In the article by Gordon previously referred to, he says, "First of all the identification of major questions to which we need answers . . . is the task of the unquestioned leaders, the statesmen of the social work profession. They alone are in the position to have the perspective and vision to perform this key task. And they are the ones whose sanction is essential to the full development of a spirit of discovery that can reach the social work student." [5]

Research topics that develop out of practical experience are more likely to have a realistic ring than those conjured up out of mid-air. Participation by the agency also serves to convey to the student a sense of its interest in and awareness of research as a part of the professional curriculum. For this reason, it is suggested that administrators and supervisors maintain resource files of interesting research ideas to be used as needed in assisting students in the choice of research topics.

The final responsibility for approving or shaping the question ought to rest with the school's research adviser. Although co-operative planning usually yields a topic satisfactory to student, agency, and school, the thesis remains essentially an educational responsibility with specific goals and standards to be met. There are other reasons beyond this. As a research specialist, the thesis adviser is able to judge which topics lend themselves to research activity and which do not. The relationship between research faculty and agency is similar to that which is coming to prevail

[4] John S. Morgan, "Research in Social Work: A Frame of Reference," *Social Work Journal*, Vol. XXX, No. 4 (1949), p. 151.
[5] Gordon, *op. cit.*, p. 115.

generally in social work research between research specialist and practitioner. Even though the questions requiring research arise only through intimate contact with practice, the task of reducing these to terms that permit scientific scrutiny belongs to the research specialist. In a paper given at the National Conference of Social Work in 1948, Philip Klein stated: "Ideas for research may come, and I suspect most often do come, not from research people, but from others: practitioners or even just innocents. To somebody's curiosity, ingenuousness, or ingenuity, should then be added the research technician's competence, boldness, caution, and methodological ingenuity." [6] The same relationship between practitioner and technician has more recently been outlined by Gordon. "The recognition of the basic questions on the one hand, and finding ways to answer them on the other, are two distinct tasks requiring different talents and approaches." [7] The application of this principle to the teaching of research should go far to define the relationship between school and agency in student research.

There are additional considerations which support the belief that the school should have final responsibility in the selection of a research topic. Teaching experience is bound to yield knowledge as to what students may generally be expected to undertake within the limits of their time and previous background. As to the individual student, the research faculty, through classroom association and interchange of information with other faculty members, is likely to possess a reasonably good knowledge of the student's intellectual and emotional assets and liabilities. It is well to take these into account in helping the student to choose and shape a research topic.

In effecting the integration of research with other curriculum content, topics that are related to the area of social work practice for which the student is training are useful. In addition to providing a research experience in the student's area of interest, such studies serve to enrich and deepen theoretical and practical learning. Studies too far removed from the student's major interest, or too far removed from social work in general, can scarcely meet the

6 Philip Klein, "The Contribution of Research to the Progress of Social Work," in *The Contribution of Research to Social Work*, American Association of Social Workers, New York, 1948, p. 22.
7 Gordon, *op. cit.*, p. 115.

requirements of a unified learning experience. Further, going too far afield may require an orientation which the student lacks, or the use of research techniques for which he is unprepared. Beyond these, few limits in content seem necessary. In the choice of a thesis or project topic, the main criterion ought to be that a subject lend itself to research activity. Studies intended to prove or demonstrate an established belief or conviction, rather than to discover or learn, fail to meet the first requisite of the scientific method.

Once the topic has been decided upon and shaped into research terms, the student needs direction in obtaining the appropriate data. It is obviously the function of the faculty research adviser to provide continuing supervision as to the kinds of data needed to answer the question around which the topic revolves. The agency, however, plays a role in assisting the student to locate these. Such help should go far toward eliminating many of the hours that students must sometimes spend floundering through the files in search of the needed material. The typical study involves the examination of a series of instances which, in turn, means locating a number of cases displaying the variable in question or otherwise meeting the criteria for selection. Although the examination of a single instance or case may be an enormously useful process, this scarcely meets the standards of the scientific method. For this reason, numbers are usually involved. In addition, students will frequently need data on the historical development of the agency, clientele served, aspects of its policy and function, and the like. Obviously, only the agency can provide adequate direction in locating material of this sort.

The quality and validity of the student's end product depend on the objectivity and the accuracy of the material obtained. The educational value of the entire research project is lost if the student is permitted to be careless or biased in securing evidence. Not infrequently the novice researcher will read into the source material his own subjective bias and meanings, unconsciously distorting the facts to yield the desired rather than the actual answer to the question. The control of bias is a problem of which even the most experienced research must remain constantly aware. In research teaching, then, it becomes necessary to set up a system of checks

223

and controls for ascertaining accuracy—a long-established procedure in scientific research.

There are a variety of available methods for checking on the accuracy, or reliability as the technician will term it, of the material abstracted from the agency's files. Since the data are usually the possession of the agency, part of the responsibility for verifying belongs to the agency. While it is the faculty adviser's task to check on the suitability of the material and to emphasize the need for objectivity and accuracy, the agency, because of familiarity with its own material, should establish some procedure for verification. The supervisor or some other staff member may review all or a sample of the records abstracted by the student, and compare these with the original. Another device that some agencies have found useful is a verbal review of the abstracted data with the worker and/or psychiatrist in charge of the case, a method that can be used only when the case is of more or less recent origin. Whatever the method of review, it is important that the review never appear as a censorship device, for this is not the intent.

Once the data have been obtained and verified, the job of analysis and interpretation remains. Under the guidance of the faculty research adviser, the student will manipulate the raw material in such a way that order may be brought out of chaos. This becomes the end for which all the earlier steps were designed. Undoubtedly, this phase of the thesis process presents the greatest intellectual challenge. The extent to which students are able to make constructive use of supervision at this point differs markedly, as do the final results in the form of the written reports.

The responsibility of the agency terminates with the verification of the data. Final responsibility for conclusions, inferences, and implications belongs to the author of the thesis. Assuming that the method was sound and the data reliable, the answer arrived at must be accepted pending further investigation. Very often the answer to the question is what might have been anticipated, and sometimes not. In writing of social work research in general, Philip Klein says: "In the first place research must be conducted on a basis of absolute and unconditional academic freedom. There must be no censoring of findings or procedure. To this end there must be no administrative participation or review, except as expert

224

advice may be sought by the researcher and accepted or rejected in his discretion. There must be no interference with the scientific method." [8] The same applies to student research.

Summary

The purpose of these remarks has been to suggest a few ways for integrating research into the curriculum. As is true of all learning, research must be taught in an atmosphere conducive to it. Undoubtedly the first step in creating such an atmosphere is to bring the thesis into closer alignment with the fields of practice, thereby lessening the distance that has tended to exist between them. The time, physical and psychic enegry, and funds that go into the research project cannot be justified on the grounds of its being an academic exercise—a term sometimes used to describe the thesis. Rather, it must be oriented in terms of the broader educational and professional objectives discussed at the beginning of this paper.

Close association between school and agency in teaching research has a potential for opening up vast, untapped research resources. The school of social work, like the school of medicine, holds responsibility for leadership in professional research. In order to effect this, however, it will be necessary for the schools to maintain close working relationships with social agencies. This may be envisioned as much the same type of relationship as exists between medical school and hospital for training and research. The sharing of responsibility for student research by school and agency brings us closer to that goal.

[8] Klein, *op. cit.*, p. 23.

17. Social Science in Social Work Practice and Education*

Herman D. Stein

SOCIAL WORK IN recent years has recognized the need for an increasing investment in the social sciences. The purpose of this paper is to examine this relationship—to identify its values and its risks and to discuss some means for developing a more fruitful, reciprocal relationship between social work and the social sciences.

In the early days of organized social work in this country, the two fields were closely related. The first national conferences of social work, in the 1870's, were sponsored by the then "American Social Science Association." Although the Conference was established independently in 1879, social work continued until about 1920 to draw heavily on sociology, economics, and political science. Since the early twenties, however, while social work has never lost interest in or contact with the social sciences, we have been largely concerned with incorporating the insights of dynamic psychology into our theory and practice. As one effect of our close alliance with the behavioral sciences—particularly Freudian psychology—the problem of defining our role as practitioners loomed large for many years. Today, however, the issues related to function are no longer uppermost. Although questions continue to arise, we have succeeded to a large extent in establishing our role and have developed security in it. We know the kind of material that is relevant to our purposes and have had extensive experience in working with psychiatrists, psy-

* Reprinted, with permission, from *Social Casework*, Vol. XXXVI, No. 4 (1955). This article is based on a paper presented at the Massachusetts Conference of Social Work, Boston, December, 1954.

choanalysts, and psychologists. We are now in a position to assimilate, without great commotion, the research findings and the new insights that emerge from the behavioral sciences.

The social work profession has not, however, developed the same close relationship with the social sciences. We have not kept abreast with the marked technical and theoretical advances made during the past thirty years by the various fields, particularly those of cultural anthropology, sociology, and social psychology. We can no longer afford to ignore these contributions, but we are in the position of trying to restore a relationship that has been weakened by neglect.

A trained social worker, for example, can read with understanding a highly technical psychoanalytic paper, but would probably encounter difficulty in comprehending the average article in a journal of sociology; the issues, the concepts, or even the very language itself may not be understood by him. To some extent, the social worker's lack of interest in, and unfamiliarity with, social science literature are related to the nature of its content. Unlike psychoanalytic writing, which is directly applicable to clinical practice, the subject matter of social science is not generally oriented to application. Social science is concerned with demonstrating what is true—why it is true and to what extent—and with raising hypothetical questions for theory and research. Social workers, on the other hand, tend to seek answers to the problems of practice and therefore are disappointed when the social sciences fail to provide answers in such terms.

Nevertheless, with the current emphasis on putting the "social" back into social work, we are turning naturally to the social sciences for help in providing knowledge on which to base our theory and practice. The social sciences can contribute to the development of this base in three main areas: (1) substantive knowledge, (2) theoretical contributions, and (3) research methods.

Substantive knowledge includes information about the nature of a particular society, an ethnic group, or a social class sub-culture; it also includes facts about the social structure of specific communities, the significance of distributions of incomes and occupations, the behavior of groups under stress, and an endless variety of data which can be drawn upon for social work use. The large-scale study of the relationship between social stratification and psychiatric disorders which is being conducted at Yale University is an illustration of such efforts to discover new knowledge.[1] Indeed, the tie-up of social science and psychiatry may quicken the interest of social work in social science.[2]

Theoretical contributions include concepts with which social work is becoming increasingly familiar, such as the relationship between culture and personality; and explorations which are less familiar, such as the nature and implications of bureaucratic structure and reference group theory.

Research methods for studying social and behavioral phenomena have been developed largely in the social sciences. Social work has drawn on these methods for its own research purposes. The growing interest in research should bring social work in closer alliance with the social sciences.

In this connection it may be noted that the scientific skepticism characteristic of the social science researcher may touch our sensibilities as we move closer to the social sciences. Doubtless we shall encounter a questioning attitude about many of our basic assumptions. Our most cherished notions are likely to come under the chilly-eyed scrutiny of the scientist who maintains his inalienable right to ask, "How do you know?" In our attempt to answer, we may be able to enlist the help of the social scientists themselves. Out of such joint scrutiny we may gain a better perspective of our own theoretical position through distinguishing between (1) knowledge that has been arrived at empirically, (2) premises that are provable but have not been properly tested, (3) assumptions that we accept on faith but have no way, as yet, of proving or disproving, and (4) values that we simply affirm.

[1] August B. Hollingshead and Frederick C. Redlich: "Social Stratification and Psychiatric Disorders," *American Sociological Review*, Vol. XVIII, No. 2 (1953), pp. 163–169; "Social Stratification and Schizophrenia," Vol. XIX, No. 3 (1954), pp. 302–306; A. B. Hollingshead, R. Ellis, and E. Kirby, "Social Mobility and Mental Illness," Vol. XIX, No. 5 (1954), pp. 577–584.

[2] An example of cultural knowledge put directly to social work use is the book, *Socio-Cultural Elements in Casework: A Case Book of Seven Ethnic Studies*, Council on Social Work Education, New York, 1953. This work is the product of a group of cultural anthropologists and social workers who met together as the New York Cultural Project, under the leadership of Katherine Spencer, an anthropologist. This publication summarizes relevant material about different ethnic groups, applying the data to case records. The Russell Sage Foundation co-operated in this Council project.

Differences in Functions

Twenty-five years ago, Robert M. MacIver said: "The relation of sociology to social work is that of a science to an art. . . . An art manipulates, controls, and changes the materials with which it deals; a science seeks only to understand them. An art individualizes, a science generalizes. . . . Social work can never call on social science to justify its aims. The justification of these lies not in the logic of science but in the hearts of men." [3]

Here we have a statement of the fundamental element in the relationship. It follows that social work is not applied social science; it is not even applied social, psychological, and biological science. Social work derives its knowledge from science but its spirit from philosophy, religion, ethics, moral values; and its method is derived, at least in part, from unexplored—or unexplorable—subtleties of human relationships. There is art in social work method precisely because it is not all science, and while we must strive constantly to enhance the scientific base of our work, we would not wish to, even if we could, eliminate the aesthetic or the ethical components.

The heart of the distinction between social science and social work lies in the difference between the function of an academic discipline and the function of a professional discipline. The underlying function of the academic discipline is to acquire and to disseminate knowledge—even if it is knowledge only for its own sake. This is the overriding purpose of all science. The professions have as their major function the application of knowledge for the rendering of services. The central objective of social work is to help people—through social planning and through preventive and direct services. In order to further this objective, knowledge is necessary and much of that knowledge comes from the social sciences. But the task of developing knowledge for its own sake belongs properly to the academic, and not to the professional, disciplines.

It would be false, of course, to state that social scientists are not concerned with applying what they learn. Today it is perhaps the rule, rather than the exception, that social scientists are concerned about values which they wish to strengthen through their scientific

[3] Robert M. MacIver, *The Contribution of Sociology to Social Work*, Columbia University Press, New York, 1931, pp. 1–3.

efforts. The ivory tower has been invaded by the headlines of the world we live in, by the bread-and-butter problems of daily life, by issues of good and evil, and by the force of the scientist's own convictions about promoting what he believes is good.

In this country, for example, cultural anthropologists have contributed to governmental deliberations on the problems of war and peace. Social psychologists have pooled their knowledge and utilized it effectively in such instances as the recent Supreme Court ruling on school segregation, by submitting supplementary briefs. Sociologists have studied the problems of interracial housing with little ambiguity about their position on the social issues at stake. Economists have used their skills in policy formation in the field of social security.

At no time has all of social science been wholly "pure" or unentangled with social reform. Social scientists have frequently translated their knowledge into social action, but we should not confuse these activities with the essential function of social science—which is *science*. The fact that many scientists have interest in a wide range of human affairs and a concern about social values brings them in close harmony with the objectives of social work. We should not assume, however, that the productions of the various branches of social science will be consistently oriented to human betterment, nor should we expect that the individual social scientist will be interested in the *social work* application of his findings.

A relevant question has been asked by Henry Maas: "Is it essential that social scientists compartmentalize research and service, knowing and helping?" [4] His answer was in the negative, with which I agree. It is not essential that the functions of "knowing" and "helping" be rigidly separated. I also agree with Mr. Maas's suggestion of establishing service-linked research—where a service is rendered in conjunction with research, largely in the interest of accumulating knowledge. I should like to stress, however, that social work should retain a firm hold on its own function, which is to render service. The search for knowledge in social work, in contrast to that in the academic field, must always be a means to an end.

[4] Henry Maas, "Collaboration Between Social Work and the Social Sciences," *Social Work Journal*, Vol. XXXI, No. 3 (1950), p. 106.

Negative and Positive Implications

The social sciences can contribute knowledge on which social work may draw for its purposes, but the social scientists cannot teach social workers how to accomplish their ends, or even what findings to use. This is an obvious point, but it is an important one to remember. If we forget it, and follow social science as a shining new lodestar, we are likely to repeat the mistakes of the past generation when social work developed its alliance with psychoanalysis. A hierarchy of status developed, based on the proximity of the social worker to the psychiatrist. This prestige stratification in our profession is only now being dissolved and its marks on the field remain. We should be careful not to let the same thing happen in relation to social science. It should not become necessary for a social worker to become a "little social scientist" or for an agency to jump on an esoteric "band wagon" of social science research, for example, in order to achieve recognition in the profession. We may decide to do research in our schools and in our social agencies on straight social science subject matter. There is nothing necessarily wrong with this, provided we are clear about what we are doing. We must be clear that research is not *social work research* unless it is oriented to the development of social work theory or practice.

Another risk in the new relationship is that social workers may accept everything that appears under the name of social science as sacrosanct. We should remind ourselves that the social sciences are still groping for answers to their major problems, and there are at least as many schools of thought in social science as there are in social work. Let us not assume that there is any less chaff among the kernels in social science literature than there is in social work literature. We should develop the capacity to pick and choose for our purposes—not only what is relevant but what has worth. We may not all make the same selection but we should have some basis for making a discriminating choice. We do not all have to belong to one school of social science thought, but we should be able to distinguish between the schools.

Moreover, the elaborate and necessary specializations within the total social science field should caution us against assuming that any one scientist can speak authoritatively on all aspects of social science, any more than a social worker can be expert in all areas of social work. Therefore, in seeking the resources and skills of any given social scientist, we should be prepared to appraise his areas of special technical competence, as well as his more general social science perspective. It is fair to assume that social scientists themselves would be the first to want us to do so.

These admonitions imply that social workers need a high level of sophistication and this requirement, in turn, means that we cannot expect the whole body of social workers, already hard-pressed in doing their daily tasks, to encompass and evaluate the staggering amount of social science knowledge that is available. It seems likely that we shall develop "specialists" within our own field, that is, social workers in particular areas of practice with sufficient grasp of relevant social science subject matter to be able to feed in and relate data to their area of practice. The advanced educational programs, particularly the doctoral programs, should help provide us with social workers who can exercise this essential middle-man function. Interpreting social science findings for social work use is a task that we cannot assign to the social scientists, for it is we who will use, or not use, the knowledge. We, therefore, must be responsible for the choice of what is significant.

But such an essentially one-sided relationship—where social work is the "taker" and social science the "giver"—is bound to change. Because of its basic role of meeting the needs of people, social work has much to contribute to social science. Social workers, in both the governmental and voluntary fields, are constantly exposed to human distress and are in a strategic position to see the effects of changing social conditions, even if the conditions themselves are not clear. Social work, therefore, should be able to offer to the social sciences help in the following ways: (1) identifying significant problems, (2) presenting evidence from social work experience related to hypotheses developed by social science, (3) expanding social work research that utilizes and tests concepts developed by social science and applies them in relation to problems of social work, and (4) making available the raw data of our experience for social science research purposes, in as organized a form as possible and with due protection of the client.

These potential contributions of social work to social science will be increasingly realized as we continue to involve the social scientists in collaborative study of our problems. Already, after only limited experience in working with us, many social scientists have come to sense the richness of our resources—in data, ideas, and approach. With further experience we should gradually overcome both our diffidence in asserting our knowledge and our other problems of communication. We shall learn both how to frame questions for study and how to organize our information for appropriate use by the social sciences. This closer relationship will develop as the social scientists interest themselves in our problems and in our data, and seek better communication with us, just as we now seek it from them. It will develop particularly as more social workers become informed on the subject matter of the social sciences.

Patterns of Collaboration

Appropriate channels are required to make the contributions of social science available to social workers. If we recall our premise that we should start with the needs of social work, and apply this principle to an agency, we can envision the following steps. For example, an agency in a suburb—either a casework or group work agency or a community council—may decide that it is important to know something about changing family patterns in suburban life in different social class groupings. If the interested group explores the sociological literature, it will learn that some sociologists who have examined "the urban fringe" are of the opinion that a new family form is emerging in this setting. Among other trends they have found: a tendency toward fixed social stratification, with higher education and membership in a profession becoming a badge of acceptance; a prominent functioning of the kinship system with a strengthening of parental roles, the associated roles of siblings, and particularly the role of the father; increased control by parents over the courtship process, which represents a compromise between arranged marriages and the, theoretically, completely free choice implied in the dating pattern of urban youth; a higher rate of family participation in social institutions; more solidarity in the family role of the aged. In brief, what is suggested is that the historical functions of the family—including the economic, educational, recreational, religious, and protective functions—are becoming reconstituted and better retained in these "urban fringe" areas.[5]

The agency may then ask: How do these trends, if true, affect our clientele? What do these findings suggest for our program? What do they suggest for over-all community planning of services? The agency may feel that the information from current social science literature is insufficient to help answer the questions, and may wish to call on an expert who knows the trends and who can relate his knowledge to the problems of the specific community. Or the agency may question the trends and hypotheses suggested in the literature and may decide to embark on research of its own, with or without the help of a social scientist.

In such instances, we can see that each field may make reciprocal contributions to the other. Social work agencies—through appropriate participation of board and staff—are in the position of raising problems that are of interest to social scientists: they can react to hypotheses, undertake research of their own with the help of the scientists, engage in independent research, and make data available for the use of the social scientists.

To use another illustration, cultural anthropology has a good deal to offer agencies that have sizable numbers of clients belonging to ethnic groups about which the staff members have little knowledge. An agency may gather whatever information it has on a particular group and have it discussed in board or staff meetings. Some agencies have done this. The Puerto Rican migration, for example, into New York and other cities on the eastern seaboard, has stimulated study of the Puerto Rican culture, its internal variations, and the strains placed on these families as they are exposed to our way of life.

Social workers may feel the need, however, for more information than they can obtain from their own sources. A series of questions may be raised: What are the best ways of preventing family disorganization in those Puerto Rican families where the position of wife and mother is affected by her going out to work; where control over the social life of young women in terms of Puerto Rican standards becomes difficult; where the man of the family cannot maintain the

[5] E. Gartly Jaco and Ivan Belknap, "Is a New Family Form Emerging in the Urban Fringe?" *American Sociological Review*, Vol. XVIII, No. 5 (1953), pp. 551–557.

traditional patriarchal role? What strains are placed on interpersonal relations when members of this group are exposed to racial or cultural prejudices? How do these clients visualize the functions of the various social agencies? Is it true, for example, that they tend to want only practical and concrete services? The social scientists, obviously, cannot change the social environment or provide the resources needed to cope with such problems, but they can provide us with certain important information if we raise the questions and they also can help us develop methods for dealing with these problems.

An agency may be concerned about a specific group of clients or it may raise more general, and therefore more difficult, questions such as: What is our clientele like in terms of significant social and cultural factors? The question, when answered, leads to the more significant one: Does this information indicate the need for changes in policy or program? The development of a sociocultural profile of a caseload may not be an easy task, but it offers real possibilities for improvement of services.

What does this task involve? It means identifying a current caseload in terms of such factors as occupation, social class position, residence, nationality, generation in this country, and comparing the caseload and the total community with respect to the distribution of these factors. This analysis should serve as a basis for inquiry along two lines: (1) What is already known in social science about the ways of life, attitudes, and values of the groups represented in the clientele which will be of help in diagnosis and in treatment? (2) What may be learned about the differences and similarities between the caseload and the population of the community being served which will enable the agency to identify needs of particular groups, as an aid in agency planning and interpretation, and also to generalize about the problems being faced in the community as a whole? These questions may lead the agency to social science source materials and may also motivate it to seek the co-operation of social scientists in analyzing and interpreting the materials. New questions of special interest to social scientists themselves may also arise which, if explored by them, will further illuminate the problem and thus enable us to serve our clients and our communities better.

Whether the questions are simple or complex, they cannot be studied unless people are interested in the task and are given time to do the work. Conviction about the value and importance of developing such information must be present, not only among the practitioners, but among administrators and supervisors. The conviction must be translated into assignment of the personnel and the time for staff meetings; that is, concern for such study should have a measure of priority in an agency program. Since it is at the agency level that integration of social science subject matter takes place, social work agencies have a particular responsibility to initiate inquiries. Obviously some questions are of mutual concern to several agencies in a community, or to agencies in a particular field on a national basis. Some problems "cut across the board" and require the resources of many agencies for proper exploration.

Current Studies

It may be relevant to make brief note of a few of the current social science studies that have particular relevance to social agencies, councils, and professional and national associations.

The work being done on sociocultural approaches to medical care in many settings, giving rise to an expanding stream of publications,[6] should be of direct interest to social workers. The studies cover such subjects as the response of different cultural groups to pain, to medical care, to problems of rehabilitation; the effects of the social organization of the hospital on personnel and on patient reactions; and role interaction among the professions in medical settings. The findings of these investigations are becoming increasingly familiar to certain segments of our profession, particularly to workers in medical settings.

Reports of studies of the attitudes of foreign students to the United States and to their educational experiences in this country are also now available. This research project is sponsored by

[6] Otto Pollak, "Cultural Factors in Medical Social Work Practice," *Medical Social Work*, Part I, Vol. III, No. 3 (1954), pp. 81–89; Part II, Vol. III, No. 4 (1954), pp. 139–152.

Lyle Saunders, *Cultural Difference and Medical Care*, Russell Sage Foundation, New York, 1954.

Leo W. Simmons and Harold G. Wolff, *Social Science in Medicine*, Russell Sage Foundation, New York, 1954.

"Sociocultural Approaches to Medical Care" (special issue), *Journal of Social Issues*, Vol. VIII, No. 4 (1952).

the Social Science Research Council with the assistance of the Rockefeller and Ford Foundations and the Carnegie Corporation.[7] The material published has considerable bearing on problems encountered by schools of social work in planning training for their foreign students. The reports still to come of these studies of cross-cultural education will undoubtedly be as relevant.

Studies of national character, several of which have been sponsored by Columbia University Research in Contemporary Cultures and by UNESCO, have direct relevance to the understanding of social work in other countries and have particular value to those who take on social work assignments abroad. The study of national character—a field that now engages the attention of psychoanalysts and anthropologists as well as tourists—is yielding illuminating insights about the characteristics of many societies, including our own.

The research that has been done in the field of mass communication and public opinion has also produced information useful to social work in its public relations program. Such subjects as the suitability of various media for particular audiences, evaluation techniques, the relative effectiveness of different methods in influencing public opinion have all received attention. Often even our public relations specialists are not aware of the extent of the social science information available for our use. Some effort, of course, may be required on our part to translate the material into a form suitable for social work purposes.[8]

The study of social stratification—the field in American sociology in which there has been extensive research and reporting—has produced considerable material of direct relevance to social workers. Between 1945 and 1952, some 333 articles and books on social class were published.[9] Of this total, at least 17 are of direct interest to social workers, and perhaps twice as many are of peripheral interest. This selected list deals mainly with questions of child rearing, family life, and mental illness in relation to social class.

[7] Reported in part in *The Annals*, "America through Foreign Eyes," Vol. 295, September (1954), *passim*.

[8] Herman D. Stein, *Measuring Your Public Relations*, National Publicity Council, New York, 1952, pp. 36–45.

[9] Harold W. Pfautz, "The Current Literature on Social Stratification: Critique and Bibliography," *American Journal of Sociology*, Vol. LVIII, No. 4 (1953), pp. 391–418.

The work of Robert Merton and others [10] in analyzing bureaucratic structure should be of help to us, not only in increasing our understanding of social organization in general, but in applying sound organizational principles to various social work processes, including administration and casework. Also, reference group theory is adding new dimensions to the understanding of human behavior. Much of the research in the field of group dynamics is, as group workers know, directly applicable to group work practice. The work of Talcott Parsons [11] and others, in analyzing American family structure, provides many new insights which should be of value in diagnosis and treatment, as well as in social planning.

Implications for Schools

Schools of social work have an important function in establishing a closer relationship between social work and the social sciences. They should take leadership in developing a conviction, in the whole field, about the usefulness and relevance of social science materials. They should be in a position to help agencies translate the academic material into suitable form for use in their professional activities. The schools, however, cannot meet the objective of bringing social science back into social work simply by accumulating social science information, or even by engaging in research. Somehow the social work practitioner must be given the impulse to keep abreast of these developments and must be trained in the capacity to use the knowledge. The scientific outlook must be incorporated into the profession as a whole.

A single specific course in the application of social science to social work, which now is given in some schools, has certain merits but it should be considered only a supplement to the basic educational responsibility of integrating pertinent social science material into all parts of the curriculum. However, such a specific course [12] can be a vital influence in promoting positive identification on the part of the students with a social science point of view. The

[10] Robert K. Merton and others (eds.), *Reader in Bureaucracy*, Free Press, Chicago, Ill., 1952.

[11] Talcott Parsons, "The Kinship System of the Contemporary United States," in *Essays in Sociological Theory*, Free Press, Chicago, Ill., 1949, pp. 250–274.

[12] The writer is familiar with two of these courses, given at the New York School of Social Work, Columbia University; and Smith College School for Social Work.

objectives of such a course are: (1) to develop in the student an awareness that certain concepts and findings from the social sciences are important to social work practice and theory; (2) to broaden the student's understanding of the social and cultural aspects of human behavior; and (3) to help the student be selective and judicious in his future use of social science material and of social scientists.

The emphasis in these courses is on applying relevant content, from cultural anthropology, sociology, and social psychology, to social work purposes rather than on delineating theoretical subject matter for its own sake. Considerable attention is focused on "group membership determinants"—ethnic, religious, social class, and so forth—and their use: in casework, as an aid in diagnosis and treatment; in group work, as an aid in defining objectives for particular groups and in clarifying the group worker's role; in community organization, as a way of examining community structure in order to define need and to plan services. The instructor, naturally, can assume that full-time students have a basic minimum grounding in the social sciences and can refer to content taught in other parts of the curriculum. Some allowance must be made, however, for students whose previous school experience dates back several years and for those who come from other countries and therefore are not abreast of the social science concepts or vocabulary of this country. Throughout the course the instructor must help the students maintain a balanced point of view, avoiding the temptation to ride the hobby-horse of social science to the neglect of social work learning.

It is important, also, not to have such a course focused entirely on cultural differences of ethnic groups. It is true that social workers have a particular interest in this area and want to learn more about the cultural differences of Italians, Jews, the Irish, Puerto Ricans, Negroes, and so forth. Although this is an important content area and one in which social workers are responsive because of social work's emphasis on accepting differences, the course should not be limited to this one theme. In this connection, note should be made of the dangers of developing stereotypes, particularly in the discussion of ethnic materials. Although the value of generalizing about cultural patterns, on sound evidence, should be recognized, we must take care not to exaggerate the usefulness of these generalizations and forget the individual and his uniqueness.

It is not possible to predict at this time how this part of a school curriculum will ultimately develop. The current objective, however, is to instil in the student a social science point of view, with full awareness that we are training him to be a social worker. Gradually, we should succeed in strengthening the intellectual and scientific content of our teaching, both in class and field, with the help of the social sciences, and give the student a sound conceptual grounding in social work theory, practice, and research.

Summary

Social work is rapidly strengthening its ties with the social sciences. We have much to gain from this relationship. To make the most of it, however, we must be careful to retain a firm grip on our professional function, which is a helping one. It must be distinguished from the academic function of the scientist. We can do this best by utilizing the social sciences in relation to our needs for theory and for collaboration in developing new knowledge and improving social work methods. The relationship between the two fields should be developed by professional associations, agencies, and schools. We shall have to develop increasing sophistication in order to make the best use of social science materials and of social scientists themselves. Such sophistication can most logically be achieved by working on special problems related to areas of service of social agencies, and by developing social science competence in certain practitioners—by means of basic courses and advanced programs. Social work has its own contributions to make to social science. These can be specified; they will grow out of interaction based on the needs of each field requiring the help of the other, rather than by social work seeking to aid social science without reference to its own purposes. The schools of social work have a vital stake in strengthening the social science content of their curricula, in class and field, in order to aid in the further development of social work practice and theory in the whole field.

240

18. Clinical Research in a Child Psychiatry Setting*

George E. Gardner, M.D.

IN THIS PAPER I am attempting to answer four principal questions most frequently asked of me and my associates at the Judge Baker Guidance Clinic by staffs and trustees of other clinics who are considering the establishment of research programs. These questions are as follows:

What is the need for clinical research in child psychiatry?

Why now this newer emphasis upon research? Child guidance clinics were established primarily for the treatment of children. What happens to the treatment program when research is emphasized, especially in the face of long waiting lists?

What types of needed studies should be carried out in a child psychiatric clinic?

What about the availability of competent personnel in child guidance clinics to do research? And costs? And space?

Do We Need to Have Research in Child Psychiatry?

As a general answer, I would state that the body of fact and knowledge from which we draw in the psychiatric treatment of children, both in its theoretical aspects and in its technical aspects of treatment techniques, is woefully meager, and much of what we do hold to be true perforce of our impressions and intuitions—

* Reprinted, with permission, from the *American Journal of Orthopsychiatry*, Vol. XXVI, No. 2 (1956). This paper was presented at the Annual Meeting of the American Association of Psychiatric Clinics for Children, New York, March 14, 1956.

and which seems to have been demonstrated at times in clinical practice—has never been really tested out. By "really tested out" I mean that the alleged cause or effect has never been studied in such a controlled fashion that we are sure that it—and not some concomitant fortuitous factor or variable, rather than the one which we have concentrated upon as being of primary and exclusive importance—is truly the cause or the effect.

Of equal importance in considering the needs for research in our field are the numerous conflicts of opinion which exist and which receive, or have received, varying degrees of emphasis as one decade follows another. A simple example of such conflict is one which is known to you and which still needs resolution through research, and hence at least requires an open mind until further research helps us to more definite conclusions. I refer to conflicts in notions concerning basic child-rearing practices and attitudes on the part of mothers which have had three definite and opposite emphases during the past thirty years. For example, in the late 1920's and the early 1930's the mother was supposed to place her baby on a rigid schedule—a schedule relative to feeding, toilet training, bedtime, time of contact with people, including with *what* people. This was really an era of "maternal distance," that is, distance from the child. In the late thirties and early forties, an opposite emphasis supervened and the emotional and physical distance between child and mother was to be as small as possible if the child's mental health was to be assured. Mothers—that is, good mothers—were instructed to hold their children often, to cuddle them, to feed them not on schedule but when they demanded it, and always to bear in mind that training should not be forced. The mother, in short, was to be as close to the child as possible. However, just after the middle forties, a minor revolt set in when some Philadelphia colleagues of ours decried this as "momism," and attributed to the child's alleged overclose relationship with, and dependency upon, the mother the marked instability among adult males—or at least among those adult males in the armed forces. Mothers were again urged to embrace the "maternal distance" principle if they ever wished to see their children become mature or independent. I have characterized this revolt as a minor revolt. And it was minor because the data available for the research did not

242

bear out the hypothesis when examined widely enough; and, probably, the data did not bear it out, nor would we expect them to, for the simple reason that the researchers in their enthusiasm failed to recall that the very cases under study, the 20-year-olds of the forties, had been brought up precisely at the moment on the American scene when scheduling, rigidity, and "psychological distance" —the very opposite of "momism"—were at their height.

But finally—to end this example of the need for more research on this conflict regarding the deleterious effect of overprotection and warmth versus scheduled care and needful frustration—we are now entering a fourth reversal, and this time from unquestionably competent child psychoanalysts, wherein it is suggested that the nuclear prerequisite for basic ego growth and development is some degree of frustration in earliest infancy.

Such conflicts in principles of child care—this particular one being basic to our practice—can be resolved only by good research by competent people. In this area and in many others, numerous allied plausible assumptions can be formulated, assumptions that can be tested by methods that should give us answers and predictions—at least negative answers if not positive ones.

I do not think that this state of affairs is peculiar to psychiatry or child psychiatry alone, or that we as a special group are notoriously ill equipped to treat children or have no body of knowledge upon which we can with reasonable surety rely—or worse, that we quarrel endlessly with one another. Yet it is only just fair to state, I suppose, that as a medical discipline we did come upon the research scene relatively late, and that the problems with which we deal—problems of behavior and development—are enormously complex. And our very lateness and the nature of our problems require added emphasis upon research. So, as in all fields of science, basic as well as applied, we are ever in need of *new* knowledge, and we have in our field the personnel who are highly motivated toward unearthing this new knowledge if conditions are such that they can.

Why Turn to Research?

The second set of questions usually centers around the fact that child guidance clinics were set up to be *treatment* centers for

243

children. Would not a research program alter the primary aim of the clinic—treatment—or in fact would it not curtail the amount of treatment facilities available? Moreover, the waiting list of patients needing treatment is usually stressed, a state of affairs—even an "institution," I might add—which is more than vaguely familiar to all in the field of child psychiatry!

There is implied here—or at least one makes the implication of—a generally held and popular notion that research, *real* research, is an activity that is to be carried out—can only be carried out, in fact—in an elaborately equipped laboratory crammed with mysterious gadgets of measurement that are applied mechanically and rigorously to none too willing, or to unsuspecting, research subjects, or in a pristinely immaculate hospital ward adjacent to this laboratory.

I think—if this inference of mine is correct—that I should state immediately that research in child psychiatry would be for the most part (1) clinical research (applied research) as distinguished from basic research, and that it must be carried out in a clinical setting; and (2) that the essential features of the psychiatrist-patient relationship, so very important in treatment, must be maintained in the only type of research that we might do in child psychiatry which really would have much relevance or significance.

But to turn back to the question and its direct significance, namely: Will not a research program, or a single research project, tend to lessen the treatment potential of the clinic? Will not fewer children be seen than heretofore? Will you not in your research concentrate so much upon the types of cases you need as research material that you no longer exist as a general child psychiatric clinic with a valuable diversification of caseload—at least valuable and even crucial for an adequate program for training of students? These questions are important and are asked by many staff members and even board members when research projects are contemplated. They were raised by both in the clinic in which I myself work. But the treatment potential is not materially affected, as you will see from an example from my own clinic.

At the Judge Baker over two years ago, we became interested in the school phobic child, the child who exhibits a fear of going to school and demonstrates this fear with accompanying severe

244

physical symptoms in the morning, nausea, vomiting, abdominal pains, and so on. It was ascertained that in each year for a period of many years we usually had had from fifteen to twenty-five such cases, with clear-cut symptomatology. They and their parents were treated by various psychiatrists, social workers, and psychologists. We designed a research project; our request for funds was granted; and a special clinic team, all members of which had signified their great interest in and aptitude for the study, was selected. Since that time, all school phobic cases have been referred to those clinic team members for diagnosis and treatment in accordance with the methods stated in the research plan.

But the treatment potential of the clinic was not lowered by this maneuver at all, because those staff members who throughout the year customarily had received school phobias on assignment rotation as they appeared at the clinic now were assigned other types of cases. As a matter of fact, because of the assistance given to the clinic in the form of the research grant, it was possible to appoint to the staff and pay additional psychiatric, social work, and clinical psychological personnel as substitutes for those now devoting half time to the research project, thus increasing the over-all treatment load of the clinic.

Naturally, all the research that a particular clinic wishes to do may not fit so easily into its treatment aims, but a great deal of it will, and should. It should because the topics and areas that are really—and perhaps exclusively—open to research in a child psychiatry clinical setting are of the nature of my school phobic example; and second, they should be of this nature for a moral reason, if you will, if the clinic is in large part a *community*-supported child guidance clinic. By this I mean that I feel that it is ethically incorrect to divert community fund money allotted for treatment of the greatest number of children possible to the support of research projects if the treatment needs of the community were to suffer—just as I think we could question, too, and used to question before federal grants were available, the use of community chest funds for the postgraduate training of professional groups who would presumably leave that community before returning in service to the community the investment that had been made in them.

245

At any rate, I think it is apparent that the child psychiatry clinic that embarks on research with thoughtful foresight as to treatment needs can do so without altering its primary function in, and obligation to, the community which supports it. Nor would it abrogate or nullify the specific intentions of bequests or endowments given to such a clinic for treatment programs.

Before I leave this particular question, may I add that I think that the greatest care and precaution should always be exercised to see to it that monies given to research are *used* for research and not diverted to supplying strictly service needs, that is, to increasing staff personnel; and by the same token, that training grants also not be confused with either of the other two.

Suitable Studies for a Clinic

What types of needed studies should be carried out in a child psychiatric clinic, with some assurance beforehand that adequate data, if sought for, will be available for the study, and that significant results may be obtained? This is an extremely important question because many types of studies just cannot be done in a clinical setting devoted to treatment. Studies, for example, that involve experimentation, experiments applied as extra studies simply for data gathering by personnel outside of and beyond those actually involved in the treatment relationship, usually are not feasible just because of their effect on that relationship. This problem arises frequently; for example, when a competent research social scientist in the university community wishes to "come in," as he states it, to do studies or gather control (or comparative) data by using the child patients or their parents for some particular project on which he is working—let us say, for example, on perception—or for the validation of some new testing device. Many times it is difficult for scientists to appreciate the inadvisability of turning over to them this research resource, patients in treatment. The refusal is based not solely on the ethical aspect of making research subjects out of patients who come to us for help, but also on the fact that helping them thereafter might easily become impossible.

In this connection it should be noted also that sometimes our clinical psychologists in training have great difficulty in designing studies to be carried out in a clinical setting which will be acceptable by their preceptors in the university as doctoral theses. It is demanded by the university that these studies be extremely rigorous, and many of our university colleagues seem to find it incomprehensible that such scientific rigor is not possible in clinical research, or, more to the point, that such rigor will make the attempted clinical research almost meaningless in significance and application. I am not, of course, saying that research in the clinical setting does not demand adherence to the accepted tenets of scientific research in the applied field, but I would emphasize that in the light of our present knowledge about—and the complexities involved in—the study of human behavior, one cannot be disappointed or condemnatory if the usual rigor cannot be exercised.

There are additional limitations, set to the type of research feasible in child psychiatry, which are in large part determined by the nature of the clinic itself, and each clinic should examine itself carefully in regard to certain limitations and differences before embarking on a research program. For example, in a general community child guidance clinic nonaffiliated with other types of psychiatric centers, such as a residence or hospital, certain investigations—notably large program research as distinguished from definite discrete project research on a single symptom or syndrome—cannot be carried out, principally because of its relatively small caseload. By contrast, however, because of the *diversified* caseload that it does have, it is in a much better position to get wider sampling and comparative data than is the second type of child psychiatric clinic, the specialized clinic—that is, specialized as to *age* of cases accepted (for example, preschool children, adolescents, latency period—5 to 12 years); specialized as to *type of treatment* (residence versus outpatient treatment, group versus individual); or specialized as to *clinical condition* (for example, delinquents only, autistic children only, or only children suffering from psychosomatic disabilities). Each type of clinic admits certain kinds of needed research and definitely does not admit others, and much thought and planning are indicated to determine precisely what should or should not be attempted.

Our concern for the clinic setting to be used leads us immediately to the two general types of research that are to be followed by any particular research groups. I refer here to *program* research

247

as differentiated from *project* research. The selection of one type of approach rather than the other will in large part be determined by the differences in clinics that I just mentioned. An example of the research *project* is the study of school phobias which I referred to previously, wherein there was selected a single well-distinguishable case entity for intensive study in enough numbers to make generalizations and predictions possible later regarding all cases exhibiting these particular symptoms. To be sure, some of the findings may have significance for child behavior in general, but the primary aim and intent is to gain more knowledge—that is, more exact and certain knowledge—concerning this disability. And we shall be content if we do.

A *program* of research, by comparison, is the study of a rather large area of human behavior, or the study of a behavioral expression which is in evidence in a variety of closely related activities or disabilities. An example of a program of the first type would be the area of juvenile delinquency; and of the second, a program designed to study the origins, types of expression, and control of aggression in children. Program research does not usually require the rigor expected in project research, and it may be quite justly and rightly preliminary and exploratory in nature, with the sensible expectation that from it, or on the basis of it, definite testable hunches, notions, or assumptions will be derived which can then be put in a number of discrete project forms. A program is usually formulated by a fairly large group of investigators, or in fact a complete clinical institution may be devoted to it for a period of time. And, finally, if financial support is given to a project, those who give that support are betting most heavily on adequate design of the project—its clear and concise assumptions to be tested and the unquestioned value in applicability of the tests to be used to gather data. On the other hand, when they give support to a large research program they wager most heavily on the integrity, the research motivation, and the research competence of the principal investigator and his allied colleagues, plus the reputation and adequacy of the research institution in which they work.

Research projects—single studies—can be carried out in every type of child psychiatry setting, whereas the ideal setting for long-term program research, to my mind, is the child psychiatric clinic that is allied by formal affiliation with (1) a teaching hospital with psychiatric, pediatric, and neurological departments, (2) a residence center for the psychiatric treatment of children suffering from disabilities of varying degrees of severity, and (3) a university by means of which co-operation and consultation with competent medical and social scientists are possible.

I shall not attempt, of course, to discuss at length the exact and definite nature of the studies that we need in child psychiatry at the present time or the specific methods to be employed in doing them. Presumably there is no aspect of—or concern relating to—human behavior, and certainly no clinical syndrome or disease, that does not need further investigation through more exact testing and measurement. I shall discuss this topic in a general fashion, however, and give a few examples of our needs. They involve, of course, investigation aimed primarily at either our theoretical concepts or our treatment techniques.

1. I have already mentioned our need for further studies relating to all aspects of maternal attitudes and child-rearing practices. We need these, and particularly do we need them with an added and proper evaluation and differentiation of them in respect to parents in different ethnic and socio-economic groups.

2. Further studies of the theoretical concepts that we use daily, such as (a) repression, (b) regression, (c) aggression, (d) mutilation and castration fears, are badly needed, with emphasis not only upon the appearance of these mental mechanisms, but particularly upon their expected alterations, vicissitudes, and extinction.

3. In the area of diagnosis, at this moment we need (a) more exact tests and measures rather than our impressions to enable us to differentiate more accurately, and at the earliest possible point in child existence, the autistic child from the symbiotically related child—and to differentiate both from the feebleminded child. (b) We need, too, devices to diagnose differentially, at later age levels, the feebleminded child from the child whose potential for learning in general or for learning specific types of material is blocked by earlier traumatic events. (c) Also badly needed are studies aimed at differentiating the delinquent whose antisocial behavior indicates a demand for intensive psychiatric treatment from the delinquent whose acts arise primarily from the effects of

249

a sociopathological or psychopathological family setting or neighborhood milieu.

4. In the field of child psychosomatic medicine we would like answers to the question of "personality type" or "personality pattern" versus nonspecificity as to type as the background from which the selection is made of systems of the body for the expression of insecurity and emotional disturbance, and also for an attack upon the problem of symptom choice, which is still one of the most baffling problems confronting the psychiatrist and one which seems at the present time to defy us in our attempts to formulate any sensible methods for solving it. I myself feel quite confident that it can most profitably be approached through the study of children —not adults—but I am still waiting for some inkling as to the methods to be employed.

5. In respect to treatment, it goes without saying that we need studies concerned with the effectiveness of present techniques for exposing the unconscious motivations of child behavior and the creation of *new* techniques. Particularly do we need studies aimed at determining treatment progress and well-designed (and they are difficult to design!) follow-up studies that will show us the results, or lack of results, of our treatment, and the probable reasons for one or the other result.

6. Finally, in this brief summary of examples of some of our research needs, I should add that we still need more of the studies (good ones!) that have been, for the most part, the most significant contributions of child psychiatrists and child analysts to our literature. I refer here to case studies—or the case-study method— wherein intensive study and accurate reporting have been made of a *single case* exemplary of a particular childhood emotional disability. Kanner's studies of the autistic child, those of Mahler on the symbiotically related child, the case studies on the atypical child by the group at the Putnam Children's Center, and others by Anna Freud and all of the earlier analysts are examples of what I mean. We need more of these case studies, not only (and perhaps even less significantly, from a research point of view) because they illuminate so clearly and impressionistically a particular entity, but because they give us that initial exploration, about which I commented before, which is so important for further detailed research.

250

And such studies are possible in practically all child psychiatry settings if staff members are present who are competent (preferably artists!) in therapy.

Availability of Personnel and Facilities

The fourth and last question relates to needed personnel and facilities, such as space, and to anticipated costs if the child psychiatry clinic is seriously to undertake programs of research and make them a vital part of its over-all function.

In the first place I should state that the desire to do research in any clinic cannot be generated by those other than the ones who eventually are to do it; that is, it cannot be conceived of as a worth-while added function and imposed upon the staff members by either board members or interested professional colleagues from some adjacent division of a department of psychiatry or university. Research must be self-generated by a prospective investigator himself, and the motivation must be of high degree. Furthermore, the complexities and subtleties of motivation in human beings being what they are, the general area of the research selected—involving as it does a whole set of varying values as to what to him is valuable—must be that selected by the research person himself. Others may have different notions of the comparative value of one topic needing investigation as contrasted with another, but this has little weight with the research worker with a stated area or topic preference in which he presumably has considerable emotional investment. Unless it is clearly impossible or extremely impractical to do the research, he probably should be allowed to do it—and not something else. I must add too, in association with this theme, that if one has a highly competent research member on his staff or one highly motivated to do research, and he is denied this opportunity, he will very likely leave and go to a clinic where he can do such research. This happens quite frequently in child psychiatry clinics and constitutes a distinct loss to our field.

But to be more specific in this matter of research personnel, I think the first prerequisite is the presence on the child psychiatry clinic staff of a person who by education and motivation is a well-trained investigator whose primary interest is in the research field. If the clinic does not have such a staff person, it would seem imperative to secure one. This man—or woman—whom I would designate as the research director, will not be hired solely to do research himself, though presumably he will do some, but he will be hired for the primary purpose of assisting others in doing research. Two factors make the presence of this type of person essential; and I will not argue as to what his disciplinary association should be, psychiatrist or clinical psychologist.

The first factor I would emphasize is that clinical research—in this instance, in the *child* psychiatry clinic—will not, and in fact cannot, be done most profitably by one man. Clinical research (certainly in all of those areas that I have listed) requires a *clinic team* approach. It necessitates that data be collected through interviews, testing, experimentation, and psychotherapy, which in the aggregate involve all of the professionals working on any particular case or group of cases under study. Such being the case, one finds that there will be varying degrees of research skill and interest among the team members; and education in research methods and the continuing direction of the research in progress can be, at their best, the functions of a research director with the competence that I mentioned. It was our experience at the Judge Baker Clinic that the first year of our research director was spent in studying the research possibilities and potentialities of staff members and instilling in them in very subtle fashion the desire to take part, within the framework of their usual clinic functions, in a research program. Certain professionals, I should emphasize, have a resistance to—or perhaps a feeling of inadequacy relative to—research even though both may be groundless. Such feelings have to be explored and, if possible, modified.

The second factor that makes it extremely important to have a designated research director is the exactitude and clarity of research formulation that are required—certainly required if financial support of a research program is to be expected. In any piece of research work, (1) aims have to be outlined, (2) hypotheses and assumptions to be studied and tested have to be clearly and systematically stated, (3) methods both inclusive and discriminatory have to be selected which really will test the assumptions made, and (4) procedures and devices for the analysis of the data obtained must be worked out. All these tasks are involved in research in

252

the sociopsychiatric field, and they demand the assistance of and supervision by a person specifically trained and highly skilled in research techniques.

In conclusion I would state that it is my impression that there are many child guidance clinics—or hospital departments or divisions of child psychiatry—in this country that now have well-established and fully accredited programs of treatment, training, and education of an order of unchallenged highest excellence. It is my hope that many of them are now ready and able to formulate and to carry through to completion much needed research programs and projects. My remarks, derived from the experiences within our own clinic, are designed to answer some of the questions and problems that arise when the small but insistent voice of not-to-be-denied motivation to seek desperately needed new knowledge is "heard in the land"!

19. Getting Down to Cases in Casework Research*

Norman A. Polansky

THE CHASM BETWEEN caseworkers and researchers which once stretched so wide has narrowed perceptibly in recent years. The rapprochement has undoubtedly come in large part from the willingness of at least some caseworkers to learn about research. A sizable gap, however, still remains. One reason is that some things that have often been understood to represent "research thinking" simply have not made very much sense to what we as caseworkers know of the world. It is now the turn of those in research to bestir themselves.

The burden of this piece may be simply put: the world is the same whether one views it from the standpoint of casework or of research. Therefore, there must be, at least in principle, a basis on which a collaboration more fruitful than any we yet have known can be founded. Such a basis will be suggested. Explaining the reasoning behind this suggestion requires some background on the present condition and prospects of social work research. As background, I shall discuss three things: (1) the present state of social work research; (2) some significant issues in research on casework; (3) recent research in this field.

The Present State of Social Work Research

Grace Coyle tells a story that seems particularly apropos as a description of the point that social work research, as such, now seems

* Presented at a meeting sponsored by the Philadelphia Chapter of the Smith College School for Social Work Alumnae Association, Philadelphia, May 5, 1957.

254

to be reaching. There was an old Connecticut farmer who, with proper respect for the sumptuary laws, was accustomed to adding a bit of water to his milk before sending it on to the bloated city-dwellers to whom it was consigned. One day, as he dragged his can to the pump, he became aware of something stirring within. And, when he took the lid off, he found a frog. There sat the frog, as big as life, floating about on a pat of butter of his own making. Miss Coyle's point was this: If you kick and struggle long enough in the kind of lifework which engages us all, you may eventually find that you have kicked a little platform into existence on which you can sit and catch your breath. We researchers are definitely kicking, but at this point the rest of the tale is hard to foresee. Something is getting thicker, but whether the reason is that we're starting to churn out some butter, or simply that the milk is getting sour, is still a little hard to tell.

Nevertheless, in general we can be optimistic. The growth of the Social Work Research Group from a little coterie of a few years back to a section of several hundred members of the new National Association of Social Workers is only one reason for this optimism. More and more money is going into research activity, more and more people are directly involved, and we are witnessing the beginning of a stream of productivity of which we should eventually be able to be quite proud. In fact, there seems to be a shortage of personnel, at least of persons who are qualified and imaginative enough to offer leadership to substantial projects. We have been underfinanced, undermanned, and—let's face it—undertalented. However, with the growth of the new doctoral programs, it should soon be possible to meet these shortages. Only in a state of plentiful supply are a few persons with unique talents likely to emerge. Through our doctoral programs we craftsmen of this generation can now hope to put tools into the hands of at least a few of those persons who may be the creative geniuses of the next.

As one sign of the times, I should like to mention the exciting developments in the direction of establishing institutes for research on social work problems. The Institute of Welfare Research of the Community Service Society of New York, a pioneer effort, has now been joined by others, including two under the auspices of schools of social work, one at the University of Chicago, and another at Columbia University. In addition, there are now a fair number of agencies and councils that have persons on their staffs able, and permitted, to devote effort to problems that are related to more fundamental issues than the keeping of routine statistics on services offered, or the identification of areas of need. There are, then, ample reasons to be hopeful about the future, even if we may be quite appropriately dissatisfied about the state of productivity in the present.

A research group takes at least as long to shake down into an optimally functioning organization as does a service agency—or possibly longer. The average number of prima donnas per unit of office space may actually be enough higher to achieve statistical significance. Moreover, there are aggravating problems of theory and method to be solved. The potential contribution of the social and psychological sciences to the types of problems that are of real significance to social work has, in the opinion of some of us, tended to be overestimated by peripheral workers. One cannot dispute the fact that there is a great deal to be incorporated and learned, and that we should get all we can from these sources. But when we come to know the social scientists who work intensively on problems of a complexity comparable to ours, we find them to be puzzled men, struggling quite hard, and certainly not inclined to offer panaceas to the superficial at wholesale prices. We must do what we can, but I, at least, have always in mind a favorite comment of Fritz Redl's: "This theory [or this method] is an insult to the complexity of nature."

It will be no easier, and no quicker, to develop a level of research in social work which tells us things we did not already know than it was to evolve the complicated patterns of organization and skill that presently provide our services for interpersonal helping. There is no doubt, however, that the effort will be worth while, just as there now seems little question that the effort has begun. If, for a time, we succeed only in demonstrating what practitioners already know, or *think* they know, after the fact, they must be patient. The demonstration of the obvious is a necessary first stage in research development; it indicates validity during the tooling-up period. If some of our present results did not appear believable, because they are familiar, we should have reason to worry about them—or about how accurate and sensitive practitioners' observations are.

Some Significant Issues in Research on Casework

Wisdom Research

It has become popular, of late, to emphasize that, to be "scientific," a field of practice should be based on a body of communicable and verifiable theory. The truth of this proposition depends, in part, on what one means by "science." We know that some rather successful methods of treatment which are *not* very easily communicable or verifiable—for example, psychoanalysis—have been developed. Beyond this, there have been highly useful techniques of treatment founded on what were, in fact, misconceptions. The accidental core of effectiveness contained in the method was not understood in principle until many years later. Nowadays, for example, our greater knowledge of ego psychology permits us to see that many of the so-called "spontaneous remissions" occurring in mental hospitals were the result of such things as the very restraint of hospitalization which gave the patient support against his inner feeling of powerlessness to cope with impulses. The fact that the restraints were often imposed simply for the selfish interest of society does not make them less effective as therapeutic agents. I make this point only to demonstrate that there are very few categorical imperatives in the pursuit of knowledge of how to help. Even charlatans may make discoveries. Nevertheless, if we recognize that we are playing the odds, there is no doubt that a theory that correctly reflects natural law is a good thing to have.

It seems worth noting that there is no one way to build theory. For the foreseeable future, it is to be expected that the main source of development of theory for casework will be what it has always been: *wisdom research*. This is a term we have learned from Donald Marquis, and he defines it as "thorough library study combined with firsthand experience and unsystematic observations." [1] Marquis goes on to say that "such studies are valuable

---

[1] Donald G. Marquis, "Research Planning at the Frontiers of Science," *American Psychologist,* Vol. III, No. 10 (1948), p. 435.

guides to immediate understanding and fruitful sources of hypotheses, but the absence of systematic data precludes any verification in the scientific sense." [2] In our field, there has been more emphasis on firsthand observation, of course, than on library study. But there is every reason to believe that progress has been made. A little later I shall discuss more rigorous methods for building theory in our field. When I do so, however, it will be with the attitude that such methods may enable us to force the process of theory-building and theory-testing. The only brief one can hold for such methods is that of long-run efficiency; they are not intrinsically more valuable or more reputable than the considered judgments of honest and reflective practitioners. The choice involves no moral issue.

When we speak hopefully, then, about wisdom research in casework, we may have clearly in mind the superiority of the human being as a recording instrument to most forms of research gadgetry. Such persons as Gordon Hamilton, Annette Garrett, Florence Hollis, Selma Fraiberg, Yonata Feldman, Lucille Austin, and others will continue to have much to teach the rest of us.

Noting that such work is taken seriously, then, I should like to comment as a research worker on some problems looming before us. A major one is the tendency to look to the schools and university settings to provide the intellectual leadership of casework. A high proportion of the writing in our field comes from the schools; major textbooks, as one would expect, are written by teachers. And yet, despite the usefulness for the profession of having its education brought under university auspices, there is cause to wonder if this trend is proper in a *practitioner* field.

For fields of practice the universities tend to be repositories of knowledge, rather than creators of it, until such time as theoretical development has gone far beyond where it now is. The schools are places in which teachers can study, synthesize, and put material into transmittable order. But synthesis of what is known is not an inventive or creative process. It is an energy-conserving one. It seems more likely that new insights and new techniques will develop in situations in which the liveliness of concrete reality provides the goad, stimulus, and confidence to experiment.

Universities are really rather slow-moving and conservative places.

2 *Ibid.*

Dynamic psychology, for example, had to sneak into most of them through the back doors of medical schools, schools of social work, and colleges of education long before it was to be found in psychology departments proper. The same was true of social psychology. Moreover, there is something about the job of being culture-bearer to the young that makes keepers of orthodoxy of us all. And when old techniques and old conceptions are masquerading under new clichés, we have simply neo-orthodoxy. I am concerned, then, that we begin to find some new patterns by which we do our wisdom research. Specifically, we may well soon want a literature that is *not* readily understandable on the pre-master's level, and that *is* written by persons actively engaged in evolving and testing ideas.

Evaluative Research

Some of the current heat under the research boiler was generated with the slogan, "evaluative research." One is grateful that people like David French and others had the energy and the imagination to promote the idea.[3] At the same time, many of us who are closer to practice have always felt resistance toward some implications that might be drawn from the term.

Some persons have hoped that from evaluative research we might discover whether casework, as a total process, "does any good." Others, having listened to the level of discussion prevalent among those proposing to do our evaluating, have shuddered to consider what "research," in such hands, would turn up.

I am grateful to Otto Pollak for pointing out to a group of us that scarcely any other profession would see the whole occupation as under test when results were measured. This is certainly not the issue. It can be taken for granted that nearly all caseworkers help some clients some of the time. Some are more effective, more often; some less, less often. But if casework did not exist we would have to invent something very similar. To imply that the very existence of casework needs "proving" is nonsense.

As a matter of fact, it is doubtful whether "evaluative research" on so gross a level can teach us very much. Even if the results come out "positive," they would offer few leads on how to help

[3] David G. French, *An Approach to Measuring Results in Social Work*, Columbia University Press, New York, 1952.

the next group of clients. What we really need to know is what is the method of choice for helping what specific kind of case. The worst thing that can be said about evaluative research on the global level is that even a successful study may yield no progress. We are left in the position of the golfer who, having made a wild lunge and driven the ball 225 yards, turned to his pro and asked, "Quick, what did I do right?"

Evaluative research on this level, then, can contribute only a kind of reassurance to the field that it is able to help. But are we in this work to reassure ourselves, or to help clients? This is, of course, related to the older question of whether we come into this field to commit ourselves to holy masochism—or to help clients? In this connection, one is reminded of the Movement Scale as a device for evaluation.[4] It was, and is, a major contribution to our limited social work research literature. But, if I am right about gross evaluation, then the tendency to use the scale in a non-discriminative way is certainly wrong.

Another promise held out in association with evaluative research is that we might thereby identify the "treatable" cases. This makes a good deal more sense, since it would mean our discovering which cases we can now succeed in helping with our present—rather loosely defined—battery of techniques, and which not. We might then concentrate our efforts on finding new techniques for helping those now regarded as "untreatable." Unfortunately, the latter idea is often not what the evaluators appear to have in mind at all. Instead, they tend to shift the onus of treatment responsibility from the caseworkers to the clients. Some folks are not able to be helped; theirs, not ours, is the ineptitude!

Psychiatrists may lend themselves to such defensive maneuvers, and they often do, but there really is no escaping who is responsible for the client's treatment—caseworkers are. Quite often, if the client could make himself "ready for treatment," he could go the rest of the way and cure himself. Consequently, the notion that we should simply learn which cases to give up on quickly leaves me rather cold. Similar reasoning applies also to studies of clients'

---

[4] J. McV. Hunt and Leonard S. Kogan, *Measuring Results in Social Casework: A Manual on Judging Movement*, Family Service Association of America, New York, 1950.

motivations for treatment, as predictors of continuance. It would be dreadful to see such studies misused, consciously or unconsciously, as devices for shifting the burden of responsibility for doing our jobs.

During the economic depression, the saying was, "It's no shame to be poor, but it sure is inconvenient." There is no shame in being unable to help everyone who comes to our agencies, but it is inconvenient to us and especially to our clients. Studies of a group that used to be called the morally defective, later hereditary paupers, later the untreatable, and more recently the unmotivated or unreachable, all stop short if they do not probe what different techniques might be tried for helping such persons.

As for efficiency, in the long run the most efficient thing we can do is try to help all who need it. Arguments on so-called business principles are ridiculous as applied, and especially as mis-applied, to agencies whose job it is to serve. My impression is that any businessman who puts his bookkeeper in charge of his sales personnel is likely to go out of business. Efficient business operation often involves what looks like inefficiency but amounts to necessary short-run waste for long-run objectives.

Demonstration Projects

The value of demonstration projects for stimulating the giving of service to clients scarcely needs underlining to any social worker. Neither, of course, is there now any question about the point of view of Helen Witmer, and others, that all such projects ought to have measurements of their effectiveness built into the original plan. There are, however, a few issues with respect to demonstration projects which warrant the same sort of simple-minded clarification-by-return-to-basic-issues implied above.

In the first place, "demonstration" implies that a service is known to be effective, and only needs to be applied in a new setting. If the new setting involves a new staff of people, working under altered conditions, the assumption simply is not true. Measurement of effectiveness then becomes all the more necessary— and all the more exciting. For a true demonstration project should have as its scientific goal the discovery of whether a given set of techniques is actually socially transmittable and can be transplanted. The issue is analogous to the question of whether casework is an art, able to be practiced only by certain "special personalities," or an established way of helping, which can be used by a fairly wide variety of people.

Another fact that tends to be overlooked, or glossed over, is that we often really do not know all the answers when we have to tackle a new problem, or an old problem in a new community. Too often, the current conservatism among the dolers of large grants forces us to be less honest than we would like to be, and hampers the creativity of our approach. We are forced to "play it safe" in order to maintain our financial support, settling for small sure-nesses rather than large potential gains from greater risk. Can you imagine a group work agency board hiring a Moreno to run a settle-ment house? Whatever you think of such adventuresome spirits, you have to recognize that they sometimes leave permanent, solid, and widely-used inventions in their wakes. And they do attract practitioners.

I return to my former theme. When it comes to demonstration projects, the true research fascination lies not so much in the pains-taking measurement of effectiveness as in the chance that something will be discovered about *how* to do things we cannot do *now*. One implication of this, of course, is that demonstration teams should not be required to begin measuring their effectiveness at the very beginning of work. They should be given time to organize into a group, additional time to experiment and see if they are beginning to get results. Then we may have something worth while to measure.

Coincidentally, I would hope that no one in social work would expect such demonstration teams to be "objective" about their own work. It is wonderful to meet young workers who are sure, not only that something can be done, but that they can do it. Often such dreams are fatuous. Some of you, however, will recall Oppen-heimer's wonderful phrasing of a tenet for all research workers: "If we do not dream by night, we shall have nothing to correct by day." A demonstration team that sets out in a mood of, "Well, after all, this is very difficult . . . let us see what can be done if anything . . ." has already tacitly agreed to head for shore at the first sign of stormy weather.

Objectivity is for the wise birds, calculating each investment.

Objectivity is for the social scientist charged with measurements. One notes in passing, therefore, that certain agencies which, as social institutions, have come to value their own dignity and respectability even above their job of helping clients, provide very unpromising places in which to sponsor such projects. In such places, everything we know already will be carefully found out again. The resultant monographs should be subtitled: "Nothing new has been added. . . ." Certainly, nothing new will have been added to casework theory; of this, one can be quite certain.

Current Research on Casework

So much, then, for general issues involved in research on casework. We turn next to a review of some of the studies of casework currently going on. Having indicated the place which "wisdom research" must undoubtedly continue to play in our work, let us turn next to more rigorous studies—those that involve systematic collection and analysis of data by procedures commonly accepted in research work. The latter can be regarded as attempts to force the process of discovery; they are an alliance, if you will, between the superego and the id to facilitate entry of new content into the conscious ego.

Research on casework can be further subdivided, in terms of the direction of development of theory to which it dedicates itself. There has been much talk, in recent years, about our need for theory in social work. I, for one, urge it constantly, having ever in mind Kurt Lewin's wonderful statement: "There is nothing more practical than a good theory." But what sort of theory is needed? And what points of departure are possible?

If one looks at the various professions—psychiatry, psychology, and social work—which emphasize the helping of people by interpersonal influence, one notes that historically, at least, theory has developed from three sources:

1. Theory aimed at understanding the *object to be changed.* In psychoanalysis, this theory consists primarily of the extensive psychological model of the human personality constructed almost entirely by Freud. Unlike the model of "an average expectable environment" assumed by the Freudians, the model for casework is more socially oriented. We are very clear that the social en-

263

vironment also varies. The combined model, now coming to be labeled *person-in-situation*, is so complex that no one has yet come up with a satisfying integrated description of the whole. But, whatever it will look like, what is hoped for is a psychosocial theory of the individual, normal as well as deviant, and happy as well as miserable. General theory of this order constitutes the anatomy and physiology of casework.

2. Theory aimed at understanding *dysfunction*—what is wrong with a person. Why does he behave so oddly, or feel so unhappy? In principle, the theory of what is wrong should be derivable from the general theory of normal functioning indicated above. In practice, it has not worked that way, as we all know. Our generation has had the odd experience of learning that, quite unlike the evolution of physics or chemistry, the more satisfactory theory of normal functioning has been the one elaborated by extensions from observations made on the abnormal. The necessary relationship is clear, nevertheless, and among the many advances Freud made over Kretschmer, for instance, was just this: that he always knew his observations must contribtue to a general theory; that beyond pathology lie anatomy and physiology.

3. Finally, we find efforts to explain the process of *correcting the dysfunction*. Once again we recognize that, logically, if one had an adequate general theory of the organism, and an explanation of its pathology, a knowledge of how to do the repair job would follow naturally. Indeed, if one had an adequate general theory, it certainly would! But we have not had one, and we still do not have one. Instead, we have the contrary experience mentioned earlier. Whole techniques of finding and exploiting leverage for helping have been developed. Only later, and sometimes much later, has it been possible to come along with a much grander system of concepts in order to tell the person who has succeeded what it was that he "did right." This direction of theory one may call the clinical therapeutics of casework.

These, then, are the lines of theoretical development to which one who is interested in casework might dedicate himself: (a) understanding the object to be changed; (b) understanding what has gone wrong; (c) understanding *how* helpful change can be effected successfully.

264

With this framework in mind, I shall now review briefly some of the systematic studies which have recently been made in our field. We still do not have an impressive accumulation, but we do have an important beginning.

Studies of the Dynamics of Casework Clientele as Persons-in-Situations

From the angle of the practicing caseworker, studies of this order have their major relevance if they help us to be aware of the feelings and, particularly, the motivations our clients are experiencing. There is a whole body of psychology, and of social science, for example, largely found in the older literature, which is primarily descriptive, categorizing, and non-dynamic. In psychology, we had such typologies as extroversion-introversion, pyknic, asthenic, athletic, and so forth. In sociology, too, we were taught long lists of definitions, describing, for example, how a hobo differs from a tramp and what each has in common with a migrant worker. I believe I know more about this sociological material than most caseworkers, and the reader may be disappointed—or, more likely, relieved—to learn that I have never found any use for it in any concrete case with which I have worked. There have been, however, a great number of studies that do not permit such easy disposal by exclusion.

Included in very relevant studies of this type is a large part of the Freudian literature, of course. Social workers have made some important contributions to the recognition of complexities in family dynamics.

From the viewpoint of social work research, there have been some contributions to knowledge, although scarcely any to general theory. We have shown where theory was applicable; at times, we have elaborated current theory; we have filled in gaps. But no theory comes to mind for which we can be called responsible. There is no law, principle, or generalization in the behavioral sciences associated with the name of a casework researcher.

General theory, for its own sake, is not for us a likely point of departure, nor has it been. Occasional writings have pretended to deal with general theory, but that was all they did. They were likely to be more pretentious than theoretical. I do not count

265

translations (and mistranslations) of concepts, social philosophy, and glittering generalities as general theory, and neither does this generation of students, coming to us from the more sophisticated undergraduate departments!

Studies of the Nature and Causes of Breakdown

As one would anticipate, the situation becomes very different when the shoemaker stays closer to his last. Social scientists who collaborate with us, with a willingness to learn as well as to teach, are often startled by the amount of knowledge about social pathology current among even rather ordinary practitioners. No one in social work needs to be reminded that ours is quite a "classy" society and a highly competitive one. Indeed, many are often justifiably disturbed that, with all this firsthand knowledge, we seem to make so little use of it. Despite the beautiful phrases about adjusting society to the individual with which our public statements are so inspiringly decorated, it is true we seldom feel either the freedom or the leisure to tackle these grand-scale problems when they become visible in particular cases we see. Instead, it may take two years of meetings before the professional membership associations will let the newspapers know that we are against sin. I should add, however, that, no matter what we *say,* social workers are quite clear about the leverage for helping that they actually have, and where it can most effectively be applied.

In the group of studies having to do with the nature and causes of pathology, one would definitely include all those studies of "factors" which are so dear to the hearts of thesis writers and their advisers. If all such studies of etiology were laid end to end, it is likely we would be very agreeably surprised. A substantial group of such studies were those by which Helen Witmer and her students at Smith College backed up the work of David Levy on child-mother relationships.[5] Other studies have been made on the etiology of mental illness, on the prerequisites for unmarried motherhood, and other critical problems. In recent years, it has become the rule to include one or more caseworkers in research teams concerned with studies of etiology of mental illness.

[5] *Smith College Studies in Social Work,* Vols. VII and VIII (1936–1938).

Other contributions to our knowledge of causes of dysfunction have come from the many social work researches which, in a more or less organized way, surveyed special problems or trouble spots in communities. The distinction made between theory developed concerning pathology and that deriving from work toward healing, is nowhere so visible as here. Such surveys have been regarded as useless if they did not lead to action. Failure to involve the community is given as the main reason for this. A reason we often like to avoid, however, is that we may know pretty well what is wrong and still have no clear image of what to do about it. A colleague of mine has commented that, whereas in medicine this situation would lead to a request for funds to study ways of decreasing our ignorance, in social work we are reluctant to admit the possibility of ignorance.

Studies of the Casework Process

We come, finally, to the realm of theory closest to my heart—clinical therapeutics for casework. The time is certainly long overdue since we should have regarded this as a respectable nucleus of theory, in its own right. Only gradually, it is true, may our knowledge of what is helpful find its relationship to pathology and to general theory. But this *is* our most significant point of attack.

Some people imply that one should be embarrassed to focus on this level, which is one of "mere technology." There is this danger in it, indeed. One can easily appear superficial. But superficiality is not necessarily avoided through a hasty dash up many levels of abstraction to the realm of metaphysics, or, at best, metatheory. We can have four-letter superficiality, or four-syllable superficiality.

If this paper does nothing else, I hope it will encourage at least some caseworkers to take seriously the opportunity their job affords for a mode of research. Even if one thinks about the likelihood of contributing to *general* theory, let me remind you of this: *one of the best ways to find out about the dynamics of man as a psychosocial being is to try to change him.* Misconceptions and errors in prediction are much more quickly visible in the first ten minutes of the next interview than they were, for some social scientists, in a whole lifetime of work.

267

It is disappointing, in view of this conviction, to have now to report the relatively small number of more rigorous studies thus far undertaken by social work researchers to help force the process of discovery. The paucity of research on the processes of interpersonal helping is by no means confined to casework. The whole field of psychotherapy is in substantially the same position. Only the followers of Carl Rogers have made any large-scale attempts to record and measure the effects of a narrowly defined technique. And they themselves have done very little experimentation which would permit comparisons with other techniques. A few dedicated souls, including some Freudian analysts, have gradually evolved new techniques for treatment of hitherto unreachable problems. But, among them, only Paul Bergman, to my knowledge, has used anything like a systematic variation in his approach and looked at its effects. Such research, incidentally, moves consistently against pressure from colleagues who fear that a striking success would make their skills, acquired over a lifetime, occupationally obsolescent.

Much of the empirical work on casework has involved rather global measurements of over-all effectiveness. In the Cambridge-Somerville Youth Study, an attempt was made to determine whether the ready availability of casework service made it any less likely that a boy who was receiving it would become delinquent later in his life.[6] The big advance in this very ambitious project was the use of an experimental design. Some boys, you may recall, were given caseworkers, or friendly visitors. Another group, matched to the first, was not given this special attention—or, at least, not in connection with this study. Because of difficulties in maintaining an appropriate staff over the long number of years involved, both the caliber of service and other experimental conditions could not be adequately maintained, and the findings of this study unfortunately proved rather ambiguous.

A study from the Jewish Board of Guardians by Lehrman and others also moved in the direction of trying to assess the usefulness of casework service.[7] This study employed an *ex post facto* design.

[6] Edwin Powers and Helen L. Witmer, *An Experiment in the Prevention of Delinquency*, Columbia University Press, New York, 1951.
[7] Louis J. Lehrman, *Success and Failure of Treatment of Children in the Child Guidance Clinics of the Jewish Board of Guardians*, Jewish Board of Guardians, New York, 1949.

A group of children who had received treatment were compared by means of a follow-up study, with a group of children who had not had treatment. By choosing the latter group from among those who had gone so far as to have a workup in preparation for treatment, but who had not then followed through, it was hoped that two groups roughly comparable as to the need for treatment were being compared. It is not known whether this can be regarded as a safe assumption, of course. There was, however, some reason to believe that those who had had treatment were in better circumstances at the time of follow-up.

Deservedly famous is the work of Hunt, Kogan, and others at the Institute of Welfare Research.[8] This team identified the concept of "movement" as a major dimension of concern in the casework process. Through the use of clear definitions of terms, and illustrations suggesting "anchor" points on the scale, it was possible to establish that this concept can be applied quite reliably by social workers to the kinds of records available in family agencies.

From the angle of research method, the most significant by-product of the work on the Movement Scale has been the demonstration of the feasibility of reliable judgments by caseworkers about quite complex issues in the casework process. In the field test of the scale [9] three groups of persons were asked to make ratings of the degree of movement of a number of cases. Making the ratings were: district secretaries and experienced caseworkers from the Community Service Society, students from the New York School of Social Work, and some college students. When we note to what degree these people agree on the judgments they give, they rank in the same order as their competence. In a recent doctoral study at Western Reserve University, Roger Miller measured degrees of "understanding" of the client in a filmed interview. Judgments were made (by Q-sort technique) about the client.[10] Second-year students made appraisals of the person which were more similar to those of a group of expert casework judges than did first-year

8 J. McV. Hunt and Leonard S. Kogan, *op. cit.*
9 J. McV. Hunt, Margaret Blenkner, and Leonard S. Kogan, *Testing Results in Social Casework,* Family Service Association of America, New York, 1950.
10 Roger R. Miller, *An Experimental Study of the Observational Process in Casework,* unpublished doctoral dissertation, Western Reserve University, Cleveland, 1957.

students; first-year students, in turn, were superior to a group of people without casework experience. Such studies indicate a growing similarity of judgment associated with additional training and experience in casework. They do not, of course, prove these similar judgments are valid. However, it is a convenience, in handling complex problems, to know that even if we are all getting crazier as we learn, we are at least doing so in a similar direction.

To be sure, agreement as to what the record shows is *not* the same as evidence that the clients involved actually had improved. However, a follow-up study of a group of cases by Kogan, Hunt, and Bartelme [11] showed that clients *judged to have arrived at a certain point in the course of casework service tend to hold such gains as were achieved* at that point in time. Ratings of the clients' later status were made quite independently. Again, an impressive by-product of this beautifully executed follow-up study came from the attempt to account for degrees of positive feeling toward the service given, and the agency. How positively a client expressed himself *did* have relation to how much help he had received, *although this correlation was very low*. That is, a person who had shown a good deal of movement was only somewhat more likely to be enthusiastic about the service than one who had had very little help. On the other hand, workers reading the records were able to predict quite accurately which clients would express positive feelings about this. We all know that testimonials are a poor basis for judging how helpful we have been. But it is satisfying to learn that we do seem to know enough about what is going on with a client to be able to estimate who is going to provide the most glowing testimonial. One would think we would have been sufficiently impressed with the ability of caseworkers to predict to have tried to understand *how* we do it. As you may have gathered, this is what Roger Miller's study has started to do.

A number of studies have been made on the matter of predicting which clients are likely to continue, or to discontinue, treatment under conditions in which the caseworker feels they need help. Several such studies have been done by students at Wayne

[11] Leonard S. Kogan, J. McV. Hunt, and Phyllis F. Bartelme, *A Follow-up Study of the Results of Social Casework,* Family Service Association of America, New York, 1953.

270

University, at Smith College, and elsewhere. Although this seems to be a direct and practical problem (whose results may be misused in a way previously mentioned), such studies have another important slant. In the attempt to predict continuance, the investigators have been led to identify some of the major dimensions of the casework process. Blenkner's study of intake at the Community Service Society was an important move along this line.[12]

The most ambitious undertaking on this theme is currently going on under the leadership of Lilian Ripple, at the University of Chicago. Using a sample of 351 records drawn from United Charities and the Jewish Family and Community Service, she and her colleagues have been studying the degree to which continuance beyond four interviews can, for example, be predicted from the first interview. They are working in this general way: What determines the use a client makes of casework service? Does he establish a treatment relationship at all? If he does establish a relationship, does he get anywhere? Their hypothesis is that the determinants will be found under three headings: (1) the motivation of the client; (2) the capacity of the client; (3) the opportunity afforded by the client's environment and by the agency's service. A report of this careful study recently appeared in *Social Work*.[13] Besides validating the general assumptions of the study, Ripple found that the content involved in making predictions varies in accordance with the nature of the problem. Another major study, *Identifying the Potentially Chronic Case at Intake*, by Ethel G. Harrison, gives further encouragement about the feasibility of early predictions of diagnostic significance.[14]

Finally, we should mention those studies that are concerned with the process of casework, as such, viewed more atomistically. These would certainly include the work by Chance and Atkinson, in which they studied the kinds of perceptions that clients and workers are likely to have of each other.[15] They found, as did

[12] Margaret Blenkner, "Predictive Factors in the Initial Interview in Family Casework," *Social Service Review*, Vol. XXVIII, No. 1 (1954), pp. 65–73.
[13] Lilian Ripple, "Factors Associated with Continuance in Casework Service," *Social Work*, Vol. II, No. 1 (1957), pp. 87–94.
[14] Ethel G. Harrison, *Identifying the Potentially Chronic Case at Intake*, Amherst H. Wilder Foundation, St. Paul, Minn., 1955.
[15] Erika Chance and Stuart E. Atkinson, "Some Interpersonal Characteristics of Individual Treatment," *International Journal of Social Psychiatry*, Vol. I, No. 3 (1955), pp. 5–22.

Kounin and I in Detroit, that most clients tend to have very positive attitudes toward, and expectations of, their caseworkers. Although many of us who offer help are nice people, this phenomenon, too, bears investigation. On the one hand, one suspects a need to magnify the favorable qualities of anyone on whom we find ourselves dependent for important kinds of help. This would fit the general hypothesis that people tend to try to "harmonize" their cognitions of other people, which Heider has advanced, and which Festinger and Hutte have studied further.[16]

The same phenomenon, by the way, is also visible in the study at a marital counseling center by Preston and others.[17] It will be recalled that in couples who were happy with each other, the marital partner was seen as similar to one's self; in unhappy couples, the partner was seen as unlike one's self. This was true despite the fact that self-ratings were no more similar. The operation of benign, or even hopeful, "projection" is as of much interest to casework, I dare say, as the hostile form.

This brings me, now, to my work with Kounin at the Wayne State University School of Social Work. Aware that a fair number of clients are lost because caseworkers are unable to "form a relationship" with them, we undertook a number of researches on the general problem of how relationships form. Originally, our interest was in the question: What determines whether a worker is seen by a client as "warm"? Warmth, we decided, was the client's perception that the worker was interested in him and was motivated to help. We soon became aware that clients had another major interest—whether the worker was competent, or able to help.

In one study, we conducted interviews with a total of 150 people who had just had initial interviews with "helping persons."[18] In these interviews, we got the client's impression of how the initial interview had gone, and of the potentially helpful person. I shall give just a few highlights from that study.

[16] Leon Festinger and Herman A. Hutte, "An Experimental Investigation of the Effect of Unstable Interpersonal Relations in a Group," *Journal of Abnormal Social Psychology,* Vol. XLIX, No. 4 (1954), pp. 513–522.

[17] Malcolm G. Preston and others, "Impressions of Personality as a Function of Marital Conflict," *Journal of Abnormal Social Psychology,* Vol. XLVII, No. 2 (1952), pp. 326–336.

[18] Norman Polansky and Jacob Kounin, "Clients' Reactions to Initial Interviews: A Field Study," *Human Relations,* Vol. IX, No. 3 (1956), pp. 237–264.

Contrary to our expectations, the clients distinguished rather clearly between their perceptions of the worker's motivation to help, and his relative competence. We had expected a sort of "halo effect," but it simply was not there to any significant degree. The difference became very visible, for example, when one considered the nature of the *commitment* experienced by the client at the end of such an interview. Clients who had experienced major satisfactions from the interview out of liking and feeling liked by the helping person tended to want to continue contact with him. But this is only one part of what we hope for in "relationship." We asked also whether the client would be willing *to be influenced* by the helping person. This factor did not correlate significantly with relationship-satisfactions. Rather, those clients who felt they had made progress during their interview toward clarifying the problem for which they came, and who felt the worker was competent, were more likely to be willing to be influenced.

Later experimental studies with simulated interview situations bore out some of the associations we had found in the field study.[19] In addition, some new insights emerged. It appears that clients who are more "central" (that is, spontaneous or "open") are more likely to expect to be favorably impressed by an interview than people who keep their inner selves guarded. Passive-dependent people are quite likely to be more disappointed with the amount of relationship-satisfaction offered in an initial interview. Among other things, we varied interviewing style. One variation related to ways of being "understanding." One can be "understanding" in an intellectual sort of way, or in a feeling way, that is, "empathic." One can also direct his apparent understandingness to different aspects of what the client is presenting. Thus, one can "understand" him as a person, or his "situation." Although our subjects generally preferred an empathic kind of understanding, another side came through which is quite impressive for all of us who do intake. The preference in the first contact was that one be *empathic,* not with the client's feeling toward himself, but with

[19] Jacob Kounin, Norman Polansky, and others, "Experimental Studies of Clients' Reactions to Initial Interviews," *Human Relations,* Vol. IX, No. 3 (1956), pp. 265–293.

his feelings *toward his situation.* Kounin coined the phrase, "inviolacy needs," and it is a fine addition to the vocabulary we have for describing gradual penetration to central affect. We found two papers especially stimulating in preparation for these studies, one by Annette Garrett on transference,[20] and James Mann's article on establishing contact with psychotic patients in an out-patient clinic.[21]

More recently, I have been working with staff members of the Family Service Association of Cleveland. They have a small project, centered in one school, aimed at making contact with the children who need help, and most of whom, under usual conditions, are not brought by their parents for help until it is very late. The caseworkers do a good deal of "going out" to people, making many home visits to passive, blocked, harassed, and, in some cases, schizoid parents who "don't see anything wrong." Once again, one is fascinated with the whole process—how the caseworkers get a treatment relationship started, how they break through crippling defenses, or deal with such a need on the part of the parent to have his child remain neurotic that he has scarcely any understanding of the problem, much less any motivation to be helped. They are courageous and energetic caseworkers, and I believe they are making some discoveries as they go, not only about the clients, but also about the anxieties such a project stirs up in themselves.

As a major program for work on "getting started" Fritz Mayer, Leon Richman, and I are now undertaking an investigation at Bellefaire, a children's institution in Cleveland. We shall try to learn more about the determinants—in the child, in the casework process, and in the over-all atmosphere—of the child's readiness to communicate feelings.

Closely akin to our work, at least in spirit, is that of Henry Maas in California. Maas, too, is fascinated by the problem of "taking apart" the process of the casework interview, in an attempt to understand "what causes what" on a moment-to-moment basis as the interview proceeds. A necessary prelude to such work, of course, is to begin to identify the significant components of the

---

[20] See page 53 of this volume.
[21] James Mann, M.D., "Psychotherapy of Schizophrenia in an Outpatient Setting," *American Journal of Psychiatry*, Vol. 110, No. 6 (1953), pp. 448–453.

interview. We need to decide just what casework consists of if we want to study *what causes what* in the course of it. Workers do not typically record all their own activity in the course of an interview. More important, it is often unclear just what they thought a given move or maneuver on the part of the worker would lead to next in the client, and so forth. Casework, or at least interviewing, consists, however, of a complex and more or less deliberate blend of such actions, rationally directed in a pattern. Consequently, Maas is now engaged in interviewing interviewers. He offers them a series of situations that could arise in an interview, asks them what they would do, and, even more significantly, *why* they would do it.

Conclusion

I shall conclude by summarizing three major points:

1. The aim of research in general is to find out something; it is not simply to demonstrate competence in methodology. One can accelerate the process with good methods, but there is no *one* road to knowledge.

2. Caseworkers themselves have important opportunities to do a kind of research which is most sorely lacking in our field. This is thoughtful but courageous, systematic but imaginative research into new techniques for doing casework. Such research should come naturally to caseworkers. They have to do it for themselves. It will not be provided by those with an interest in general theory; it cannot take place merely by abstracting, in the university, from what is now going on.

3. A beginning in rigorous research related to practice problems has finally been made. It should offer guidelines and support to caseworkers willing to participate, too, in pushing forward the frontiers of knowledge. We who do the more theoretically-oriented studies shall want all the company we can find.

Index

A

Abbott, Edith, 14
Abbott, Grace, 14
Abraham, Karl, 140
Acknowledgments, 7
"Acting-out" behavior, 19, 49, 100–102, 105–106, 131–132, 136, 139, 170
Addams, Jane, 14
Adolescence, 147–148
Agency, responsibility in student research, 216
Aggression, 106–109, 138–139, 160, 249
Aggressive casework, 39, 274
Aichhorn, August, 19
American Social Science Association, 226
Anthropology, 227, 230, 234, 237, 239
Anxiety hysteria: 137–158, 164–173; case example, 174–182; diagnosis of, 164–168; genesis of, 159–160
Anxiety state: 140, 142, 143, 145; defenses against, 108; types of, 48–49
Atkinson, S. E., 272
Attitude therapy, 15, 27, 28
AUSTIN, Lucille N., Dynamics and Treatment of the Client with Anxiety Hysteria, 137, 16, 258

B

Balanced Expression of Oedipal Remnants, The (Gardner), 159
BARRY, Elizabeth, Some Problems in Protective Casework Technique: A Case Presentation, 126
Bartelme, Phyllis F., 270
Basic Concepts in Diagnosis and Treatment of Borderline States (Weinberger), 111
Bergman, Paul, 268

BIDDLE, Cornelia T., Casework Intervention in a School, 183
Blenkner, Margaret, 271
Borderline Personality: Structure, Therapeutic Considerations of the, 99; concepts of diagnosis and treatment, 49, 111–116, 137; types of, 99–100
Breuer, Joseph, 11

C

Cabot, Richard, 29
CAMBRIA, Sophie T., Responsibility of School and Agency in Student Research, The, 216
Cambridge-Somerville Youth Study, 268
Cannon, Mary Antoinette, 29
Case Presentation, 117–125, 126–136, 174–182
Casework: Modern, The Contribution of Ego Psychology to, 38; Personality Diagnosis in, 83; aggressive techniques, 39, 274; analysis of interview, 275; as an art, 229, 262; collaboration with other professions, 93, 233, 249, 254; group observation in, 190; protective techniques, 126–136; in school setting, 183–199; understanding of culture, 17; use of case study, 250; see also Diagnosis, Relationship, Treatment
Casework Intervention in a School, (Biddle), 183
Casework theory: establishment of, 263–264; testing of, 257–258
Caseworker: Reactions, The Impact of the Client's Unconscious on, 73
Chance, Erika, 271
Character disorders, 94, 95, 137, 139
Charity Organization Society, New York, 13, 32

277

Child guidance clinic, 14–16, 20, 28, 241, 243–244
Child psychiatry, 241–253
Child-rearing practices, 242–243, 249
Children, treatment of, 16, 193–199, 241; see also Child guidance clinic, Child psychiatry, Relationship, School
Clinical Research in a Child Psychiatry Setting (Gardner), 241
Columbia University, 237, 256
Communication, 192, 233, 237, 275
Community, 234–235, 239, 245–247
Community Service Society of New York, 255, 269, 271
Conscious Use of Relationship with the Neurotic Client, The (Perry), 164
Coyle, Grace, 254

D

Day, Florence, 30
Defense mechanisms: 43, 44, 90, 95, 100, 108, 111, 114, 139, 155; handling of, 23–24; projection, 165; reaction formation, 26; resistance, 20; understanding of, 20
Delinquency, 19, 249, 268
Dependency needs, 21–22, 50–51, 139, 179
Depression, 104–106, 145
Deprivation, 168–169
Devine, Edward T., 14
Diagnosis: Personality, in Casework, 83–96; clinical aspects of, 92–93; contribution of social science to, 239; formulation of, 89–100; research in, 249; and treatment of borderline states, 111–116; use of exploration, 88, 96
Diagnostic school of thought, 20–21, 39
Dynamics and Treatment of the Client with Anxiety Hysteria (Austin), 137

E

Education, see Learning, School, Schools of Social Work
Ego: analysis of, 47–48; boundaries of, 108; concepts of, 50–51; development of, 243; disturbances of, 99, 109, 111; functions of, 43, 90, 100–101, 106, 112, 114, 153; frustration tolerance, 50–51, 106, 115; organization of, 101; primitive aspects of, 114–115, 120; self-esteem, 44; strengths, 26, 43–48, 50, 70–71, 94, 100, 101, 110, 113, 115,

135–136, 145, 151, 164, 184; unconscious aspects of, 43; see also Defense mechanisms
Ego Psychology: Contributions to Modern Casework, 38–52; concepts of, 1–6, 41–45; development in psychoanalysis, 22–23; effect on casework, 23; formulation of, 41–45; interest in, 40, 111; self-reliance, 50, 52; unconscious factors, 52
Einstein, Albert, 47
Empathy, 274
Erikson, Erik H., 30
Ethnic materials, use of, 239–240; see also Anthropology

F

Family relationships, 14–16, 91, 159–163, 233; see also Relationship, parent-child
Family Service Association of Cleveland, 32, 274
Family Society of Philadelphia, 32
Federn, Paul, 20
FELDMAN, Yonata: Learning Through Recorded Material, 203; 18, 258
Ferenczi, Sandor, 25
Festinger, Leon, 272
Financial assistance, request for, 55
Finlayson, Alan D., 26
Fraiberg, Selma, 258
French, David, 259
Freud, Anna, 23, 41, 45–46, 48, 250
Freud, Sigmund: 36, 46, 58, 111, 263; contribution to social work, 11–37; effect on theory of learning, 34–35; ego theory, 42; influence on professional education, 28–35; hypnosis, 47; hysterical neuroses, 152; libido theory, 42; theory of personality, 15; use of transference, 27
Fromm, Erich, 17
Functional school of thought, 20–21, 25

G

GARDNER, George E.: Balanced Expression of Oedipal Remnants, The, 159; Clinical Research in a Child Psychiatry Setting, 241
GARRETT, Annette: Modern Casework: The Contributions of Ego Psychology, 38; The Worker-Client Relationship, 53; 14, 23, 30, 258, 274
Gesell, Arnold, 16
Getting Down to Cases in Casework Research (Polansky), 254

Glover, Edward, 19
Gordon, William E., 219, 221, 222
Group work, 11, 233, 238–239

H

HAMILTON, Gordon: A Theory of Personality: Freud's Contribution to Social Work, 11; 82, 258
Hanchette, Helen, 32
Harrison, Ethel G., 271
HOLLIS, Florence: Personality Diagnosis in Casework, 83; 258
Horney, Karen, 17
HUNT, Flora M., Initial Treatment of a Client with Anxiety Hysteria: A Case Presentation, 174
Hunt, J. McV., 269–270
Hutte, Herman A., 272

I

Identification, 104, 116, 135, 155, 160
Impact of the Client's Unconscious on the Caseworker's Reactions, The (Littner), 73
Initial Treatment of a Client with Anxiety Hysteria: A Case Presentation (Hunt), 174
Institute for Juvenile Research, 32
Institute of Welfare Research, 255, 269
Introjection, 155, 162

J

James, William, 29
Jarrett, Mary, 29
Jewish Board of Guardians, 32, 268
Jewish Family and Community Service of Chicago, 271
Johns Hopkins University, 13
Joyce, James, 25
Judge Baker Guidance Center, 32, 241, 244, 252
Jung, Carl, 12

K

KAUFMAN, Irving: Therapeutic Considerations of the Borderline Personality Structure, 99; 40
Kempshall, Anna, 32
Kenworthy, Marion, 29–30
Klein, Philip, 222, 224–225
Kogan, Leonard S., 269–270
Kounin, Jacob, 272, 274
Kretschmer, Ernst, 264

L

Latency period, 160–161
Lathrop, Julia, 14
Learning: Through Recorded Material (Feldman), 203; 109, 149, 190–191, 249; effect of personality theory on, 28–35; see also Schools of social work
Lehrman, Louis, 268
Lewin, Kurt, 263
Levy, David, 15, 28, 266
Libbey, Betsey, 32
Libido, 17, 89, 106, 109–110, 145; use of in casework, 25
LITTNER, Ner, Impact of the Client's Unconscious on the Caseworker's Reactions, The, 73
Lowrey, Lawson, 29

M

Maas, Henry, 230, 274
MacIver, Robert M., 229
Maeder, LeRoy, 30
Mann, James, 274
Marcus, Grace, 21–22
Marital problems, 141, 174–182
Marquis, Donald G., 257
Maternal attitudes: 242, 249; "momism," 242
Mayer, Fritz, 275
Medical care, 236, 249
Menninger, Karl, 16, 29
Mental deficiency, 249
Merton, Robert, 238
Meyer, Adolf, 13, 32
Milford Conference, 41
Miller, Roger, 269, 270
Modern Casework: The Contributions of Ego Psychology (Garrett), 38
Moreno, J. L., 262
Movement Scale, 260, 269

N

New York School of Social Work, 29, 237, 269
NICHOLLS, Grace, Treatment of a Disturbed Mother-Child Relationship: A Case Presentation, 117

O

Oedipal conflict, 138–158, 159–163, 164–165, 180–182, 183–187
Oedipal Remnants, The Balanced Expression of, 159
Omnipotence, 102–104, 114, 121
Ophuijsen, J. H. W. van, 32
Oppenheimer, J. Robert, 262

P

PARAD, Howard J., Introduction, 1
Parsons, Talcott, 238
Perception, study of, 272
PERRY, Sylvia, Conscious Use of Relationship with the Neurotic Client, The, 164
Personality Diagnosis in Casework, (Hollis), 83
Personality: classification of, 91–92, 96; see also Borderline personality, Ego, Freud
Personnel, availability of, 241, 245–246, 251, 255
POLANSKY, Norman A., Getting Down to Cases in Casework Research, 254
Pollak, Otto, 259
Poor Laws, 14
Preconscious, diagnosis of, 85–86
Preoedipal period, 160
Preston, Malcolm G., 272
Professional associations, 216, 240, 255, 266
Protective Casework Technique, Some Problems in, 126
Psychoanalysis: 58–59, 237; contributions of, 217, 226, 231, 243; criteria for, 158; defenses against anxiety, 48–49; free association, 25–26, 47, 89; influence on casework, 11–37, 137; influence on education, 28–35; neo-Freudians, 17; work with psychotics, 49
Psychology: clinical, 246, 252; dynamic, 226, 258–259; social, 227, 230, 239, 259; see also Ego psychology
Psychosis, fear of, 147–148
Psychotherapy, 268; see also Treatment
Public relations, 237
Puerto Rico, 234, 239
Putnam Children's Center, 250
Putnam, James J., 29

R

Rank, Otto, 25, 27
Records: use of, 203–215; use of tape recorder, 204
Redl, Fritz, 256
Reference groups, 238, 239, 249
Referrals, 188, 191
Relationship: Conscious Use of, with the Neurotic Client, 164; developing use of, 24–25, 52, 53; mother-child, 117–125; parent-child, 165, 185, 188, 207–214, 266, 274; reality aspects of,

94, 101–102, 104, 109–110, 115–116, 172; student-client, 205–215; teacher-child, 185, 190; unconscious aspects of, 75–81; worker-child, 193–199; worker-client, 13, 53–72, 110, 116, 152–154, 164–173, 273–274; worker-teacher, 185–193
Repetition compulsion, 101, 126
Research: Clinical, in a Child Psychiatry Setting, 241; Getting Down to Cases in Casework, 254; Responsibility of School and Agency in Student, 216; applied, 244; bias in, 223–224, 263; condition of, 254–257; curriculum, 216, 218–220, 221, 225; demonstration project, 261–262; ethical aspects of, 245, 246; federal grants, 245; goals of, 218–219; linked with service, 230–231; need for, 4–6, 241–242; requirements for, 216, 244, 251–252; as scientific method, 217–219; social science, 228–233; types of, 247–248; use of students in, 269–270
Resistance, 20, 47–48, 115, 142
Responsibility of School and Agency in Student Research, The (Cambria), 216
Reynolds, Bertha, 24, 30
Richman, Leon, 275
Richmond, Mary, 12, 13, 14, 24, 38, 39, 40, 52
Ripple, Lilian, 271
Robinson, Virginia, 24
Rogers, Carl, 268
Role, 162, 235, 236
Royce, Josiah, 29

S

School: Casework Intervention in a, 183; phobia, 244–245, 248; role of principal, 186–188; special project in Cleveland, 274; see also Students
Schools of social work, 225, 237, 238–240, 256, 258, 259; curriculum, 27, 31, 238–240; doctoral programs, 232, 247, 255; field teaching, 33, 220–224; student research, 216–225
Scientific knowledge, need for, 227, 229, 243, 248, 258
Self-awareness: 33–34, 39, 51, 81–82, 84–85, 86, 94, 150–151, 152, 155; client, 84–85, 86, 94, 150–151, 155; student, 33–34, 39; worker, 34, 51, 81–82, 151, 152, 189; see also Transference
Sexuality: 16, 84, 138–140, 142, 145, 147, 149, 150, 151, 152; development

of, 160–163, 165–166; diagnosis of, 89; discussion of, 170–172, 179, 181; heterosexuality, 166, 167, 170; identification, 160, 167; masturbation, 147; menstruation, 147; pubescence, 147

Sibling relationships: 149, 185; case example, 195–198

Smith College School for Social Work, 1–8, 29, 30, 271

Social Diagnosis, see Mary Richmond

Social environment: 235, 264; modification of, 49; reality factors, 40, 46

Social Science: in Social Work Practice and Education (Stein), 226; collaboration with, 266; contributions from social work, 232–233; contributions to social work, 217, 227–228, 256; student training in, 239–240; see also Social stratification, Schools of social work

Social Science Research Council, 237

Social Security Act, 22

Social stratification, 227–228, 233, 237, 266

Social Work Research Group, 255

Sociocultural profile, 235

Sociology, 226, 227, 230, 233, 239, 265

Some Problems in Protective Casework Technique: A Case Presentation (Barry), 126

Southard, Ernest, 29, 30

STEIN, Herman D., Social Science in Social Work Practice and Education, 226

Students: foreign, 236; research, 216–225; training needs of, 203–215; see also Schools of social work

Sublimation, 160, 161, 206

Sullivan, Harry S., 17

Superego, 90, 91, 94, 104, 105, 137, 155, 160

Supervision: 82, 220–221, 223, 236; influence of Freudian theory, 33; learning from, 31, 32; principles of, 34; see also Learning

Symbiosis, 249, 250

Symptom formation, 143, 160, 161, 162, 245, 250

T

Taft, Jessie, 21

Techniques, treatment: 68–72, 100, 102, 126–136, 137, 151–158, 241, 250, 260–261; advice, 154; clarification, 155; emotional release, 154–155; insight, 65, 68, 84, 115–116; manipulation, 152; support, 51, 84–86, 94, 104, 105–106, 125, 136, 145, 151, 170, 179; "uncovering," 48, 85, 94–95; see also Casework, Treatment

Theory of Personality, A: Freud's Contribution to Social Work (Hamilton), 11

Therapeutic Considerations of the Borderline Personality Structure (Kaufman), 99

Thesis project, 219–221; see also Research curriculum

Toys, use of in casework, 195

Training, professional: child guidance, 253; needs of foreign students, 237; see also Students, Schools of social work

Transference: ambivalence in, 18; capacity for, 139, 151; control of, 61–63, 81–82, 153; countertransference, 51, 58–59, 63, 81–82, 151; as diagnostic aid, 67–72; early use of in casework, 18, 24, 27; identification aspects of, 70; interpretation of, 63–71; neurosis, 56–58, 143, 144, 152; positive response to, 152, 156; in psychoanalysis, 56, 62, 69; reality aspects of, 53, 56, 59–60, 71; recognition of, 60–61; resistance to, 65, 67–68, 70; unconscious aspects of, 54, 62, 65–66, 74–75

Treatment of a Disturbed Mother-Child Relationship: A Case Presentation (Nicholls), 117

Treatment: of the Client with Anxiety Hysteria, Dynamics and, 137; classification of, 84–86, 96; criteria for, 19–20, 87–88, 93–96, 151, 157–158, 173–174, 271, 275; evaluation of, 250, 259–261; goals of, 172–173; planning of, 83, 89, 96, 113, 239, 245; problems of, 244; in psychosis, 20, 49; research aspects of, 275; see also Casework; Techniques, treatment; Transference

U

Unconscious: of the Client, Impact on the Caseworker's Reactions, 73; casework implications of, 17, 23, 89, 151; influence of, 213, 250; understanding of, 85–87; see also Freud, Transference

UNESCO, 237

United Charities of Chicago, 271
Universities, role of, 258
University of Chicago, School of Social
Service Administration, 256, 271

W

Waiting list, 244
Wayne State University, School of Social Work, 271, 272
WEINBERGER, Jerome L., Basic Concepts in Diagnosis and Treatment
of Borderline States, 111

Western Reserve University, School of
Applied Social Science, 269
White, William, 32
Whitehead, Alfred N., 217
Wisdom research, 257–258
Witmer, Helen, 261, 266
Work problems, 142, 149–150
Worker-Client Relationship, The (Gar-
rett), 53

Y

Yale University, 227